Other Titles in the Jossey-Bass Nonprofit and Public Management Series:

MEASURING PERFORMANCE IN PUBLIC AND NONPROFIT ORGANIZATIONS

MEASURING PERFORMANCE IN PUBLIC AND NONPROFIT ORGANIZATIONS

Theodore H. Poister

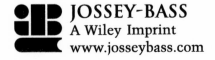

JOSSEY-BASS
A Wiley Imprint
www.josseybass.com

Published by Jossey-Bass
A Wiley Imprint
989 Market Street, San Francisco, CA 94103-1741   www.josseybass.com

Jossey-Bass books and products are available through most bookstores. To contact Jossey-Bass directly call
our Customer Care Department within the U.S. at 800-956-7739, outside the U.S. at 317-572-3986 or
fax 317-572-4002.

Jossey-Bass also publishes its books in a variety of electronic formats. Some content that appears in print
may not be available in electronic books.

In Chapter Ten, material describing the Fairfax County Economic Development Authority's documents,
including its mission statement, is used with the permission of Fairfax County Economic Development
Authority, Fairfax County, Virginia.

In Chapter Twelve, the summary of customer survey results from the *2002 Outcomes Study Report* of the
Girl Scout Council of Northwest Georgia is excerpted with the permission of Girl Scout Council of
Northwest Georgia, Inc.

Library of Congress Cataloging-in-Publication Data

Poister, Theodore H.
   Measuring performance in public and nonprofit organizations/Theodore
H. Poister.—1st ed.
      p. cm.—(The Jossey-Bass nonprofit and public management
series)
   ISBN 978-0-7879-4999-0 (acid-free)
   1. Organizational effectiveness—Measurement. 2. Nonprofit
organizations. 3. Public administration. 4. Performance—Measurement.
I. Title. II. Series.
   HD58.9.P65 2003

                                    2003005632

Printed in the United States of America
FIRST EDITION
HB Printing   10 9 8 7

THE JOSSEY-BASS
NONPROFIT AND PUBLIC MANAGEMENT SERIES

CONTENTS

TABLES, FIGURES, AND EXHIBITS

Tables

Figures

Exhibits

To my son,
Robert C. Poister,
a great guy whose performance
always more than measures up!

PREFACE

Performance measurement has really taken hold in government over the past several years, and over the past few years in the nonprofit sector as well. Although the idea has been around for some time, interest in performance measurement has been reinvigorated in public and nonprofit agencies in recent years as a result of the convergence of two forces: (1) increased demands for accountability on the part of governing bodies, the media, and the public in general, and (2) a growing commitment on the part of managers and agencies to focus on results and to work deliberately to strengthen performance. This shared commitment to both increased accountability and improved performance is embodied in the Government Performance and Results Act of 1993 at the federal level and similar results-oriented legislation in most state governments and some local jurisdictions as well.

Thus, in government, many stakeholders have an interest in the use of performance measures, including legislative bodies, other elected officials, chief executive officers or chief administrative officers, higher-level governmental units, managers and employees, customers and constituents, and relevant professional organizations. In the nonprofit sector, boards of directors, managers and employees, volunteers, consumers and clients, advocacy groups, and funding organizations all have a stake in the effective use of performance measures to improve management and decision making, performance, and accountability. As a result, there has been a great proliferation of performance measurement systems in government and the nonprofit sector over the past several years, ranging from those that are developed by agencies for internal use only to those that are maintained on websites and readily accessible to the public.

Benefits

Whereas many management approaches seem to come and go in government, sometimes resembling "flavor of the month" fads, from all appearances the interest in performance measurement is here to stay. This is because the use of measurement has a commonsense logic that is irrefutable, namely that agencies have a greater probability of achieving their goals and objectives if they use performance measures to monitor their progress along these lines and then take follow-up actions as necessary to ensure success. Conversely, managing programs or agencies without performance measures has been likened to flying blind, with no instruments to indicate where the enterprise is heading.

When performance measurement systems are designed and implemented effectively, they provide a tool for managers to maintain control over their organizations, and a mechanism for governing bodies and funding agencies to hold organizations accountable for producing the desired kinds of results. Performance measures are critical elements of many kinds of results-oriented management approaches, including strategic management, results-based budgeting, performance management systems, process improvement efforts, performance contracting, and employee incentive systems. In addition, they produce data that can contribute to more informed decision making. Measures of output, productivity, efficiency, effectiveness, service quality, and customer satisfaction provide information that can be used by public and nonprofit organizations to manage their programs and operations more effectively. They can also help managers reward success and take corrective action to avoid replicating failure.

Performance measures focus attention throughout the organization on the priorities set by governing bodies or top management and can act as catalysts that actually bring about performance improvements. That is, everything else being equal, managers and employees will tend to perform toward the measures because they would rather "look good" than not look so good on established measures. Thus, appropriately configured performance measures motivate managers and employees to work harder and smarter to accomplish organizational goals and objectives. Finally, measurement systems can be used to communicate the results produced by the organization to an array of external as well as internal audiences, and at times they can help the organization make its case, for example in supporting budget requests to governing bodies or grant applications to funding agencies.

Challenges

These benefits do not materialize automatically, however. Designing and implementing effective performance measurement systems is a very challenging business, in terms of both addressing a number of methodological issues and managing organizational and institutional change. Although many public and nonprofit agencies have workable systems in place, others see their measurement systems fall apart before being completed, and still others end up installing systems that are not particularly helpful or are simply not used effectively. This often happens because the measurement systems were not designed appropriately to serve a particular purpose or because they were not implemented effectively in ways that build commitment and lead to their effective use.

Although a substantial literature on performance measurement has accumulated in the field of public administration, and to a lesser degree in the field of nonprofit management, there are still few sources that explain how to develop measurement systems in a thorough and detailed, yet accessible, manner. This book is written to help public and nonprofit managers design and implement effective performance measurement systems. Although it is concerned with providing accountability to governing bodies and higher-level authorities, the book focuses primarily on performance measurement at the agency level and on helping public and nonprofit agencies use performance measures to manage their programs and operations more effectively.

Overview of the Contents

This book approaches performance measurement holistically, focusing on the methodological challenges of defining useful indicators but also emphasizing the organizational and managerial context of performance measurement and the need to clarify the purpose of a measurement system and then design it specifically to serve that purpose. Indeed, a unique feature of this approach is its recognition of the fact that most effective measurement systems are designed and implemented not as stand-alone systems but rather in conjunction with other management and decision-making processes, such as planning, budgeting, and providing direction and control over the work of managers and employees. A measurement system that supports a strategic planning process, for example, will be very different from a system designed to analyze operating problems and track the progress of quality improvement efforts in the same agency, and although the same generic process for developing performance measures can be used to develop both these systems, failure to clarify the purpose at the outset and tailor the system to meet the information needs of that purpose can severely damage the chances of success.

Thus, I have organized this book into four major parts. Part One focuses on the management framework of performance measurement in public and non-profit organizations. Chapter One is a broad introduction to performance measurement within this context, looking at the evolution of the use of measures to operationalize results-oriented approaches to management and at the variety of purposes that measurement systems can support. Chapter Two presents a comprehensive process for designing and implementing effective measurement systems in public and nonprofit agencies.

Part Two is in many ways the heart of the book. It includes a number of chapters that address in detail the many methodological challenges inherent in developing measurement systems: identifying outcomes and other performance criteria to be measured, tying measures to goals and objectives, defining and evaluating the worth of desired performance measures, analyzing and reporting performance data, and processing the data so as to maintain the system.

Part Three consists of five chapters that focus on the development of performance measurement systems to support particular management and decision-making processes—namely, strategic planning and management, budgeting, performance management, process improvement, and comparative benchmarking—emphasizing the more particular challenges and unique features of each.

Finally, Part Four, and the last chapter of the book, returns to the overall process of designing and implementing measurement systems, identifies common problems that often confront managers in developing such systems, and presents a number of specific strategies for successfully implementing measurement systems in public and nonprofit organizations.

Audience

This book is intended for two principal audiences. First, managers and professional staff in public agencies at all levels of government, as well as in nonprofit organizations and foundations, are frequently involved in developing performance measurement systems and often seek guidance in these efforts. This book is designed to help them in determining what kinds of systems to develop and in designing and implementing such systems effectively. Internal and external program evaluators, as well as other professional consultants, will also find this book to be very useful along these lines.

Second, many university degree programs offering graduate professional education emphasize public management and performance measurement in their curricula. These include programs in planning, public policy, and program evaluation in addition to public administration and nonprofit management. Whether they use this book as a text or as supplemental reading, students and teachers in a variety of courses in these fields will find it to be a valuable source of understanding of the problems and prospects regarding the use of performance measures in the public and nonprofit sectors. This book will also be useful as supplemental reading in management or evaluation-oriented courses in graduate programs in particular substantive areas, such as health policy or education administration, where performance measurement is a crucial issue.

Acknowledgments

This book was a while in the making, and before embarking on this project I had been involved with performance measurement in a number of venues over the years. Thus, several individuals have contributed directly or indirectly to this volume by providing opportunities to develop measurement systems, allowing access to existing measurement systems, or serving as mentors by sharing with me their knowledge and experiences regarding the design, implementation, and use of performance measures.

These individuals, many of them long-time friends, include Thomas D. Larson, former secretary of transportation in Pennsylvania and former administrator of the Federal Highway Administration; Richard H. Harris Jr., director of the Center for Performance Excellence in the Pennsylvania Department of Transportation (PennDOT); Joe Robinson Jr., director of PennDOT's Performance Improvement and Metrics Division; David Margolis, director of the Bureau of Fiscal Management at PennDOT; William E. Nichols Jr., general manager of the Williamsport Bureau of Transportation (WBT) in Williamsport, Pennsylvania; Kevin Kilpatrick, planning and grants administrator at WBT; James Lyle, former director of business process improvement at the Georgia Department of Administrative Services and currently executive director of Georgia Public Television; Gerald Gillette, former principal operations analyst in the Office of Child Support Enforcement of the Georgia Department of Human Resources; Terry Lathrop, former deputy director of the City of Charlotte, North Carolina, Department of Transportation; the late Patrick Manion, former deputy city manager of Phoenix, Arizona; Dr. Stuart Berman, chief of the Epidemiology and Surveillance Branch, Division of STD Prevention of the U.S. Centers for Disease Control; Bernie Benson, officer for chapter information management of the American Red Cross; Meg Plantz, vice president for outcomes assessment at United Way of America; and Sal Alaimo, outcomes measurement manager of the Girl Scout Council of Northwest Georgia,

Inc. In addition, numerous students in the master's program in public administration at Georgia State University over the years, as well as participants in several professional development programs conducted for the Evaluators' Institute in San Francisco and Washington, D.C., as well as for individual government agencies, have provided further insight regarding problems, challenges, and strategies for success in working with performance measures.

I would also like to express my appreciation to Martha Martin, a recently retired senior secretary in the Department of Public Administration and Urban Studies at Georgia State University, for her uncomplaining, dedicated, and very professional help in processing many iterations of the chapters that make up this book. In addition, I would like to express my deep gratitude to my wife, Molly Poister, caterer extraordinaire with an everlasting sunny and cheerful disposition, for maintaining equilibrium around the household as deadlines approached.

Special Thanks

Most important, I wish to acknowledge the special assistance provided by Julia Melkers, a friend and former colleague at Georgia State University, who is currently serving on the public administration faculty at the University of Illinois at Chicago. In addition to graciously agreeing to contribute chapters on budgeting and data processing to this volume, coauthor the chapter on analyzing performance data, and provide feedback on several other draft chapters, Julia helped conceive of the plan for this book and has been instrumental in bringing it to reality. Her ready collaboration has been invaluable in broadening the scope of this book and addressing important topics that are often treated superficially at best, and I deeply appreciate her interest, her personal support, and her many contributions to this work.

As always, however, responsibility for any inaccuracies, omissions, or inappropriate interpretations rests solely with the author.

Roswell, Georgia   Theodore H. Poister
March 2003

THE AUTHOR

Theodore H. Poister is professor of public administration in The Andrew Young School of Policy Studies at Georgia State University, where he specializes in public management and applied research methods. He has published widely in these areas in earlier books and in public administration journals, and he has conducted applied research along these lines in such diverse policy areas as housing, criminal justice, community health, mental disabilities, and child support enforcement, as well as transportation. Poister has a long-standing interest in both the methodological and managerial challenges of performance measurement, and he has been involved in performance measurement projects with a number of state agencies in Pennsylvania and Georgia, various local governments and nonprofit organizations, the U.S. Centers for Disease Control, and the Transportation Research Board. He also conducts professional development programs on performance measurement in government and the nonprofit sector for the Evaluators' Institute and has conducted similar programs for several government agencies.

MEASURING PERFORMANCE IN PUBLIC AND NONPROFIT ORGANIZATIONS

PART ONE

THE MANAGEMENT FRAMEWORK FOR PERFORMANCE MEASUREMENT

Performance measurement—the process of defining, monitoring, and using objective indicators of the performance of organizations and programs on a regular basis—is of vital concern to managers in government and the nonprofit sector. The chapters in Part One discuss the evolution of performance measurement in these fields and locate it in the context of results-oriented approaches to management. They also convey the variety of purposes that can be served by measurement systems and a sense of why performance measurement is so important. A crucial point made in Part One is that performance measurement systems are often not stand-alone systems, but rather are essential to support or operationalize other management and decision-making processes, such as planning, budgeting, performance management, process improvement, and comparative benchmarking. Thus it is imperative for system designers to clarify a system's intended uses at the outset and to tailor the system to serve those needs. These chapters also discuss the limitations of performance measurement systems, as well as the challenges and difficulties that are inherent in developing them, and they present a holistic process for designing and implementing effective performance measurement systems.

CHAPTER ONE

INTRODUCTION TO PERFORMANCE MEASUREMENT

What are performance measures, and how are they used in government and nonprofit organizations? What are performance measurement systems, and for what purposes are they designed and implemented? Why has this subject generated such great interest and excitement in the field of public administration? What is the status of performance measurement in the field today?

The question of how to measure agency and program performance effectively in ways that help improve performance is clearly one of the big issues in public management (Behn, 1995) and in the nonprofit sector as well (Young, 1997). This chapter introduces some basic concepts and principles regarding performance measures and provides some background on how they have developed over time. More important, it discusses a variety of uses of performance measures and explains why measurement systems have become so essential to results-oriented public and nonprofit managers.

The Scope of Performance Measurement

Performance measures are objective, quantitative indicators of various aspects of the performance of public programs or agencies. As will be clear throughout this book, different kinds of performance measures are defined to track particular dimensions of performance, such as effectiveness, operating efficiency, productivity, service quality, customer satisfaction, and cost-effectiveness. Performance measurement, then, refers to the process of defining, observing, and using such measures. As is often the case in the field of public management, there is not uniform usage of key terms here. Although some use the term *performance measurement* to refer to defining and collecting data on performance and reserve the term *performance monitoring* to refer to the utilization of the data in management and decision-making systems, there is by no means universal agreement on this in practice. Thus, the terms performance measurement and performance monitoring are used interchangeably in this volume.

Why Measure Performance?

Performance measurement is intended to produce objective, relevant information on program or organizational performance that can be used to strengthen management and inform decision making, achieve results and improve overall performance, and increase accountability. Osborne and Gaebler point out in the book *Reinventing Government*, "What gets measured gets done" (1992, p. 146). In other words, performance measurement tends to have an impact on—indeed, should be designed to have an impact on—behavior and decisions. Performance measurement tends to focus attention on what is being measured and on performance itself, and to motivate people and organizations to work to improve performance, at least on those dimensions that are being monitored.

Harry Hatry, a longtime proponent of performance measurement at the Urban Institute, has for some time used a sports analogy to point out the need for performance measurement: "Unless you are keeping score, it is difficult to know whether you are winning or losing" (1978, p. 1). Performance measures help managers and others assess the status of their agencies' performance and gauge their progress in delivering effective programs. Or, as Osborne and Gaebler state, "If you don't measure results, you can't tell success from failure" (p. 147). Furthermore, "if you can't see success, you can't reward it" (p. 198), and "if you can't recognize failure, you can't correct it" (p. 152). Thus, performance measures are essential for letting managers know "how things stand" along the way so that they can act accordingly to maintain or improve performance.

Background: Early Development

Performance measurement is not a new idea. Rather, it is an established concept that has taken on greatly renewed importance in the current context of public and nonprofit management. Measuring workload and worker efficiency was clearly part of the scientific management approach that influenced government reformers in the early twentieth century, and the International City Management Association produced a publication on measuring municipal activities as early as 1943 (Ridley and Simon, 1943). In the federal government, interest in performance measures ignited when systems analysis processes were brought into the Department of Defense during the Kennedy administration, and it spread to other agencies when the Johnson administration implemented a planning-programming-budgeting (PPB) system (DeWoolfson, 1975; Lyden and Miller, 1978). Although program budgeting was dropped by subsequent administrations, many federal agencies retained a residual interest in its analytical component and the use of performance measures. In addition, some state governments began experimenting with program-oriented budgeting systems and the use of performance measures in conjunction with the budgeting process (Mowitz, 1970; Schick, 1971; Howard, 1973).

Along the way, various state, county, and municipal governments began to experiment with performance measurement in conjunction with efforts to strengthen their management and budgeting systems. In addition, interest in program evaluation became widespread in the 1970s as governmental agencies at all levels recognized the need to assess the effectiveness of newer social programs (Suchman, 1967; Weiss, 1972; Rossi and Williams, 1972; Rossi, Freeman, and Wright, 1979). This movement encouraged agencies to track measures at regular intervals and monitor program performance over time; performance measures were also required in conducting one-time discrete program evaluations (Wholey, 1979).

Thus, Harry Hatry and colleagues at the Urban Institute began publishing materials that promoted the use of performance measures and provided instruction on how to develop and use them (Hatry and Fisk, 1971; Waller and others, 1976; Hatry and others, 1977). Others applied this kind of work in greater depth in particular program areas (Poister, 1983). In addition to this primarily methodologically oriented work, other authors talked more about how to incorporate performance measures in larger management processes (Grant, 1978; Altman, 1979; Steiss and Daneke, 1980; Wholey, 1983; Epstein, 1984). A related but separate stream of articles focused on performance measures as they play into the budgeting process (Grizzle, 1985; Brown and Pyers, 1988). Many public agencies experimented with performance measurement for different purposes throughout this period. At the local level, for example, Phoenix, Arizona, Charlotte, North Carolina, and Dayton, Ohio, have been using systematic performance measures in their budgeting and performance management processes for decades. Aside from such "stellar" cities, a large number of surveys and other studies have suggested substantial usage of performance measures among local jurisdictions. (Fukuhara, 1977; Usher and Cornia, 1981; Poister and McGowan, 1984; Cope, 1987; O'Toole and Stipak, 1988; Poister and Streib, 1989, 1994; Ammons, 1995b).

Despite all this activity and enthusiasm, however, a sense began to pervade some quarters, at least, that the promise and potential of performance measurement greatly exceeded its actual usefulness in practice. In part this was a matter of methodological sophistication, or the lack of it, as measuring the outcomes produced by many public programs was found to be a very difficult undertaking. Indeed, one of the underlying premises of a book on *The Search for Government Efficiency* (Downs and Larkey, 1986) was that for a variety of reasons most governmental jurisdictions were incapable of measuring the performance of their programs.

More important, interest in performance measurement seemed to wane somewhat in the mid-1980s because measures were increasingly perceived as not making meaningful contributions to decision making. Many public agencies had succumbed to the "DRIP" syndrome—data rich but information poor—and concluded that the time and effort invested in measurement systems were not justified by the results. Promoted as a tool for improving effectiveness, performance measurement itself was now seen by some as a case of performance not living up to promise. In part this was a result of managers' failures to forge clear linkages between measurement systems and management and decision-making processes, but at a higher level it also reflected a lack of political will in institutionalizing commitments to monitor and utilize performance data.

The "New" Performance Measurement in Government

However, a number of forces in the field of public administration reinvigorated interest in performance measurement in the 1990s. Taxpayer revolts, pressure for privatization of public services, legislative initiatives aimed at controlling "runaway" spending, and the devolution of many responsibilities to lower levels of government generated increased demands to hold governmental agencies accountable to legislatures and the public in terms of what they spend and the results they produce. Responding in part to these external pressures and motivated in part by their own imperative to produce cost-effective services, public managers began using a number of approaches to strengthen the management capacity of their organizations. Most notably, these included strategic planning (Nutt and Backoff, 1992; Bryson, 1995; Berry and Wechsler, 1995), more encompassing strategic management processes (Steiss, 1985; Eadie, 1989; Koteen, 1989; Vinzant and Vinzant, 1996; Poister and Streib, 1999b), quality improvement programs and reengineering processes (Cohen and Brand, 1993; Davenport, 1994; Hyde, 1995; Kravchuck and Leighton, 1993), and benchmarking practices (Bruder, 1994; Walters, 1994; Keehley and others, 1997), as well as reformed budgeting processes (Joyce, 1993; Lee, 1997). These and other results-oriented management tools required sharply focused performance measurement systems to provide baseline data and evaluate effectiveness.

The convergence of these externally and internally driven forces has led to the current resurgence of interest in performance measurement, signaled by such articles as "The Case for Performance Monitoring" (Wholey and Hatry, 1992) and "Get Ready: The Time for Performance Measurement Is Finally Coming!" (Epstein, 1992). Indeed, the "how-to" issue of performance measurement has been identified as one of the three big questions in contemporary public management (Behn, 1995). Many proponents have been addressing this issue in articles that identify barriers to meaningful performance measures and discuss strategies for developing and implementing measurement systems that can be used effectively (Glaser, 1991; Bouckaert, 1993; Ammons, 1995a; Kravchuck and Schack, 1996).

The renewed emphasis on performance measurement was stimulated in part by resolutions of the Governmental Accounting Standards Board (1989), the National Academy of Public Administration (1991), the American Society for Public Administration (1992), and the National Governors' Association (1994). All these resolutions urged governments to institute systems for goal setting and performance measurement. At the national level, this thrust toward results-oriented public management is embodied by the Government Performance and Results Act of 1993, which requires agencies throughout the federal government to engage in strategic planning, goal setting, and performance measurement on a very systematic basis (National Academy of Public Administration, 1997; Newcomer and Wright, 1996; Wholey and Newcomer, 1997).

Many state governments have implemented macro-level processes for statewide strategic planning, budgeting, and performance measurement, such as the Oregon Benchmarks program, Minnesota Milestones, and similar programs in Florida, Virginia, Texas, and Minnesota, with some well ahead of the federal government in this regard (Broom, 1995; Aristiqueta, 1999). In fact, recent research has found that, either through legislation or administrative mandates, forty-seven of the fifty state governments use some form of performance-based budgeting and require agencies to report associated performance measures (Melkers and Willoughby, 1998), although "problems in defining performance" and "difficulties in establishing appropriate performance measures" are the most frequently cited problems in implementing these systems (Melkers and Willoughby, 2001). Thus, as in the federal government, most state agencies have been working, at a surface level at least, to develop macro performance measures, and they may be defining more detailed programmatic performance indicators within their strategic frameworks in the future.

As mentioned earlier, local governments have been experimenting with performance measurement for some time, and measures—some fairly conventional and others more innovative—have been identified for a wide variety of service areas (Ammons, 2001). Two fairly recent surveys have estimated that from 35 to 40 percent of municipal jurisdictions have performance measurement systems in place, at least in selected departments or program areas (Governmental Accounting Standards Board, 1997; Poister and Streib, 1999a); another recent study found that one-third of U.S. county governments use some form of performance measurement (Berman and Wang, 2000). In addition, a few comparative measurement projects have been initiated at the local level, in which groups of cities have worked together to define uniform performance measures to benchmark their performance against each other in selected program areas (Coe, 1999; Kopczynski and Lombardo, 1999).

Performance Measurement in the Nonprofit Sector

Performance measurement is increasingly viewed as important by managers of nonprofit organizations as well (Schuster, 1997; Berman and West, 1998). By the early 1990s, nonprofit health and human service agencies were commonly tracking measures regarding financial accountability, program products or outputs, quality standards in service delivery, demographics and other participant characteristics, efficiency, and client satisfaction (Taylor and Sumariwalla, 1993). Over the past decade the emphasis has shifted to developing measures of outcomes (United Way of America, 1998). Similar to the convergence of forces that has brought about a heightened commitment to performance measurement in government, this has come about in the nonprofit sector because funding sources (including government agencies, private corporations, and foundations), accrediting bodies, managed-care entities, the general public, and nonprofit leaders themselves all share a concern with producing results (Hendricks, 2002).

Under the umbrella of the United Way of America, many national nonprofit organizations in the field of health and human services, such as the American Cancer Society, the American Foundation for the Blind, Big Brothers Big Sisters of America, Girls Incorporated, Girl Scouts of the USA, Boy Scouts of America, Goodwill Industries International, the American Red Cross, and the YMCA of the USA, have become heavily involved in outcome measurement. They have promoted the use of performance measures by conducting research in this area, designing processes for the development and utilization of measurement systems, and providing resources and assistance to help their local chapters or affiliates measure their own performance (Plantz, Greenway, and Hendricks, 1997). Other national nonprofit organizations, such as Easter Seals and the National Multiple

Sclerosis Society, are also showing great interest in outcomes-oriented performance measurement systems, as are many local nonprofit agencies.

Given that many nonprofit agencies are engaged in providing services to clients or the public at large in pursuing social betterment goals, as is the case with many governmental organizations, and given that they are concerned with the same kinds of performance criteria, such as program effectiveness, operating efficiency, service quality, and client satisfaction, the process of performance measurement is very similar in the nonprofit sector and the public sector, especially in terms of technical issues. In terms of managing the process, however, nonprofit organizations face some different challenges in developing and implementing measurement systems (Hendricks, 2002). For example, local chapters of some national nonprofit organizations have much greater autonomy than do the decentralized field offices of many government agencies, so uniform performance measurement requirements and processes cannot be mandated the same way. In addition, resources for providing information, training, and technical assistance regarding measurement systems are not as readily available in the nonprofit sector as in government.

Thus, in both the public and nonprofit sectors, this stepped-up commitment to performance measurement is supporting efforts to provide a clearer focus on mission and strategy, improve management and decision making, improve performance itself, and increase accountability to governing bodies and external stakeholders, including funding agencies and the public. In contrast to earlier attempts at developing performance measurement systems—which often appeared to be less purposeful, less focused, and less well aligned with other evaluative and decision-making processes—the current generation of measurement systems are more mission driven and results oriented. More often, the "new" performance measurement is tied to a strategic framework, emphasizes the customer perspective, measures performance against goals and targets, and incorporates measurement systems in other management processes in meaningful ways (Poister, 1997). Most important, rather than rely on general-purpose tracking systems, public and nonprofit managers are learning to articulate specific needs and uses of performance measures and then tailor the design and implementation of measurement systems to serve those purposes effectively.

Uses of Performance Measures

A principal theme of this book concerns managing for results and the use of performance measures as tools to support results-oriented approaches in public and nonprofit administration. The test of useful performance measures is that over time they facilitate actual improvement in organization or program performance. In order to be useful, therefore, a measurement system must be designed to serve the needs of the particular management process it is intended to support. Performance measurement systems are used to support a variety of management functions, including the following:

- Monitoring and reporting
- Strategic planning
- Budgeting and financial management
- Program management
- Program evaluation
- Performance management
- Quality improvement, process improvement
- Contract management
- External benchmarking
- Communication with the public

Each of these functions can be carried out in ways that facilitate results-oriented management, and in each case performance measures are critical to provide the feedback that allows it to focus on results. Yet these are very different, though often complementary, management functions that serve different purposes. Each of these functions represents a distinct use of and a specific set of requirements for performance measures. Thus, any given measurement system needs to be tailored to its purpose and developed very deliberately to support its intended use.

Monitoring and Reporting

Probably the most traditional use of performance measures in government and nonprofit organizations is for monitoring and reporting on program activities and agency operations. Such systems often focus on resources consumed, transactions completed, and products or services provided, but they may also include measures of efficiency, productivity, service quality, or even results achieved. In some cases, such measures are used to report on "service efforts and accomplishments" in conjunction with accounting processes (Harris, 1995; Halachmi and Bouckaert, 1996) When these measures are reported to top management, elected officials, legislatures, or governing boards, they are providing for accountability of agency operations to these stakeholders. Although decisions and actions may well be prompted by these data, such reporting systems are relatively passive in nature because they are usually not embedded in formalized decision making or management processes.

Strategic Planning

At the other end of the spectrum, a more proactive use of performance measures is in conjunction with strategic planning efforts. Emphasizing an organization's "fit" with its external environment, strategic planning approaches are designed to identify the most fundamental issues facing an organization in the long run and to develop strategies to resolve those issues effectively (Bryson, 1995). A critical part of this process often entails a so-called SWOT analysis to assess organizational strengths and weaknesses as they relate to external opportunities and threats, and existing performance measurement systems are often important sources of information about these strengths and weaknesses. The resulting strategic plans usually define strategic goals and objectives, and it is essential, then, to define and monitor performance measures in order to track progress in implementing strategic initiatives and accomplishing strategic goals and objectives. In some cases, desirable measures are actually defined first and then used to specify objectives and target levels to be achieved on these indicators of success. For the most part, it is performance measurement in conjunction with this kind of strategic management that is called for by the Government Performance and Results Act and similar state legislation.

Budgeting and Financial Management

The principle of allocating resources according to the results that are achieved by public or nonprofit programs, rather than basing allocations primarily on the analysis of inputs, has been at the core of efforts to reform budgeting processes over many decades. It is also the basis of the move toward results-based budgeting or performance-based budgeting, which is sweeping through the United States currently. Such budgeting systems require performance measures of outputs and outcomes, efficiency, and cost-effectiveness, in order to assess the relationships between resources and results and to compare alternative spending proposals in terms of the results they would produce. Although a good deal of caution is warranted concerning the feasibility of implementing and actually using such systems, due to both political and methodological factors (Joyce, 1997), attempts to inject performance measures into budgeting processes, or at least make them available to decision makers, are likely to continue at a deliberate pace. But performance measures may be used at several different stages of the budget process, and although elected officials may have difficulty in committing wholeheartedly to performance-based budgeting principles, agencies may still find the performance data to be useful in managing their programs (Joyce and Tompkins, 2002).

Program Management

Measurement systems focusing on program rather than agency performance are often used, not surprisingly, to strengthen program management. Measures that track resources consumed, activities conducted, transactions completed, clients served, outputs produced, services rendered, and—one hopes—results and impacts achieved should obviously be of great interest to program managers. The kind of information that can be provided by a balanced set of such indicators, particularly if they are tracked on a regular basis, can help managers stay abreast of overall program performance; identify problems; and sometimes make changes in design, implementation, or service delivery systems in order to strengthen program performance.

Program Evaluation

Performance measures are a very basic element of program evaluations; quantitative evaluations cannot be undertaken without defining at least some measures of program performance and collecting data on those measures. Moreover, performance measurement systems support the program evaluation function. First, existing measurement systems can provide a descriptive "read" on program performance that can indicate whether programs are ready to be evaluated as well as help target evaluation resources cost-effectively (Wholey, 1979). Second, ongoing performance measurement systems in which key indicators are observed repeatedly at regular intervals automatically accumulate time-series databases. These databases lend themselves very directly to interrupted time-series designs and multiple time-series research designs that are often appropriate for more analytical program evaluations. In addition, they also facilitate comparison group designs and other nonexperimental and quasiexperimental designs for evaluations (Henry and McMillan, 1993; Harkreader and Henry, 2000).

Performance Management

As used here, the term *performance management* refers to the process of directing and controlling employees and work units in an organization and motivating them to perform at higher levels. Providing feedback to employees on their performance is a central element of effective approaches to performance management, and this feedback is frequently provided by performance measures. In particular, management by objectives (MBO) systems have a long history in government and have proven to be quite effective due to their emphasis on goal setting, participative decision making, and objective feedback (Rodgers and Hunter, 1992). Although the feedback on performance used in MBO-type systems may come from a variety of sources, existing performance measurement systems sometimes fill this purpose (Epstein, 1984; Poister and Streib, 1995). In addition, the term *performance monitoring system* is sometimes used to refer to less individualized management systems that set targets for programs or organizational units to achieve, using performance measures that are monitored in order to evaluate performance (Swiss, 1991).

Quality Improvement

The quality movement, which has surged through the public sector over the past two decades, is basically a fact-based, data-based approach to improving operations and service delivery. At its core, what has become a fairly conventional quality improvement process consists of groups of employees or cross-functional teams working to identify problems in their work processes, analyze the causes of those problems, and develop solutions in order to improve both quality and productivity. Performance measures are an integral part of this process, even though they may not be routinized in ongoing, permanent measurement systems. In contrast to the macro-level measures often tracked with annual data for purposes of strategic planning or results-based budgeting, for example, the measures used most frequently in quality improvement processes tend to be more detailed, or more micro-level, and shorter-term indicators. Most often, these measures focus on such items as resource quality, equipment downtime, cycle times, waiting time, accuracy versus error rates, overall service quality, employee productivity, and, sometimes, outcomes. Furthermore, because the quality improvement approach places strong emphasis on customer service and customer satisfaction, this kind of analysis often uses customer feedback measures.

Contract Management

Because of the rapidly growing interest in privatization and in contracting out service delivery to third-party providers, contract management is a hot topic in public administration. Furthermore, the thrust toward increased accountability and results-oriented management has led to even greater interest in performance contracting, which refers to focusing such contracts more on what service providers will accomplish than on the front end of the process—that is, the resources providers will use and the specific activities they will carry out (Behn and Kant, 1999). For government agencies that are contracting out responsibilities for program implementation or service delivery, this requires setting clear outcome-oriented objectives and defining appropriate performance measures to track success in attaining those objectives (Kettner and Martin, 1995). For many nonprofit agencies that are contracting with government agencies to deliver public services, performance contracting entails tracking key results indicators and reporting them to the funding agency.

External Benchmarking

As mentioned earlier, interest is also developing in the public and nonprofit sectors in the practice of external benchmarking, that is, comparing an agency's performance against that of other similar agencies or programs. Whereas corporate-style benchmarking emphasizes more intensive communication and often site visits with "star performers" to learn about successful strategies and tactics that might be adapted to other companies, in the public and nonprofit sectors the first step usually involves statistical benchmarking—analyzing comparative performance measures across a set of similar jurisdictions, such as city governments (Urban Institute and International City/County Management Association, 1997) or organizations, such as state transportation departments (Hartgen and Presutti, 1998). Such peer-group comparisons can be useful for a particular agency in seeing how its performance stacks up within its public service industry, identifying top performers, and searching for leading-edge practices that might be helpful in boosting performance.

Communication with the Public

In part as an extension of their use in traditional monitoring and reporting, performance measures are also beginning to be used to communicate with the public about agency or program performance. In keeping with the trend of increasing accountability, many public agencies produce "report cards" on a regular basis to report on their performance to the public at large via printed materials, press conferences, and the Internet. Good examples include the following:

> State-by-state performance measures and outcome measures reported for the Title V Block Grant Program by the Maternal and Child Health Bureau, Health Resources and Services Administration, U.S. Department of Health and Human Services (accessed at www.mchdata.net)

> A report card produced by the Pennsylvania Department of Transportation, published monthly, presenting performance data for a different program area each month (accessed at www.dot.state.pa.us)

> A report card produced by the District of Columbia, which reports on the status of numerous district- and agency-level strategic goals and objectives (accessed at www.dc.gov/mayor/scorecards/index.shtm)

A progress report produced by the United Way of Metropolitan Atlanta, which presents goals in each major program area and reports progress in accomplishing the goals (accessed at www.unitedwayatl.org/VirtualCommunity/)

Performance Measurement Systems

Performance measures are monitored and used most effectively through performance measurement systems, management systems that track selected performance measures at regular time intervals so as to assess performance and enhance programmatic or organizational decision making, performance, and accountability. Measurement systems are the principal vehicle for observing, reporting, and using performance measures, and most people who are directly involved in performance measurement are engaged in designing, implementing, managing, maintaining, or using performance measurement systems.

As shown in Figure 1.1, in addition to the general management function, performance measurement systems consist of three components, which pertain to data collection and processing, analysis, and consequent action or decision making. First, management is responsible for clarifying and communicating the strategic framework within which the performance measurement system will be used—including the agency's mission, strategies, goals, and objectives, and the targets to be attained—and ensuring that the system is appropriately oriented to that framework. Second, management is responsible for the design, implementation, and maintenance of the agency's programs, services, and operations, as well as standards, and for using measurement systems to improve overall performance.

With respect to the measurement system itself, management needs to clarify its purpose and make sure that it is designed to serve the intended uses. As indicated earlier, a measurement system designed to support strategic planning, for example, will look very different from one that is developed to facilitate quality improvement, performance contracting, or external benchmarking processes. (The special emphases and features of some of these different applications are discussed in Chapters Nine through Thirteen.) Finally, for the system to be successful, management must not only define or approve the measures and system design but also be committed to using the data to improve performance.

Data Component

Data collection and processing are often the most time consuming and costly aspect of performance measurement. The data are often input by decentralized organizational units in dispersed locations, and they must be aggregated and

FIGURE 1.1. PERFORMANCE MEASUREMENT SYSTEMS.

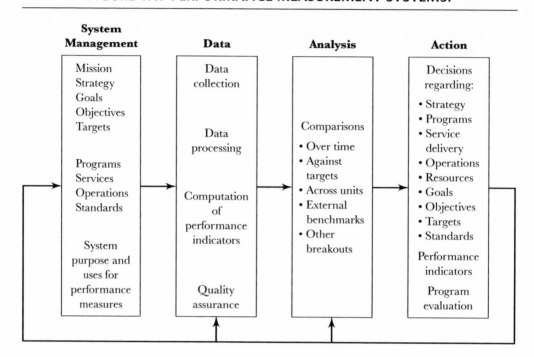

integrated in common databases, as discussed in Chapter Eight. Because the raw data themselves usually do not constitute the actual performance indicators, the indicators must be computed from the raw data elements, often in the form of averages, percentages, rates and ratios, and rates of change. In addition, the system must produce reports, displayed in formats that are useful given the purpose, and disseminate them to the targeted users on a specified schedule. Also as discussed in Chapter Eight, there needs to be a system for ensuring the integrity of the data through a process for verifying the reliability of both data input and processing.

Analysis Component

As will be made clear in Chapter Six, the performance measures by themselves are often not particularly useful because they are largely devoid of context. In order to convert the indicators into *information* and to facilitate any meaningful interpretation, they need to be compared with something.. Usually, the most important comparisons show performance measures over time—has performance been improving, deteriorating, or simply static?—or against predetermined objectives or targets—is performance where we want it to be? As shown in Figure 1.1, other useful comparisons break performance data down across units such as programs or operating units, decentralized field offices, projects, or grantee agencies. In addition, benchmarking performance measures against other comparable agencies or programs is sometimes useful, as can be other breakouts of the data, for instance across various clientele groups.

Action Component

If the principal test of an effective measurement system is the extent to which it leads to improved performance, then the results must be used to inform decision making. Managers should pay attention to the performance data and consider the results in making decisions regarding overall strategy, program design and implementation, service delivery systems, ongoing operations, resource acquisition and use, and a variety of support systems. Obviously, in complex environments the performance measures should not be expected to be the sole drivers of such complex decisions, but they should influence the courses of action that managers choose in trying to improve performance. The performance data can also be used to refine goals and objectives, targets, and standards as the agency gets more experience with the system, possibly "raising the bar" for expectations as actual performance improves over time. Finally, performance trends can be used to decide if and when comprehensive evaluations should be undertaken for particular programs.

Problems and Prospects for Performance Measurement

Used appropriately, effective performance measurement systems can help public and nonprofit managers make better decisions, improve performance, and both require and provide general accountability. When they are designed and implemented effectively, performance measures focus attention on goals and objectives, provide feedback on important aspects of agency or program performance, and motivate managers and employees to work harder and smarter to improve performance. They can also help redirect resources more effectively, evaluate the efficacy of alternative approaches, and gain greater control over operations, even while allowing increased flexibility at the operating level. As has been seen, measurement systems can be very important tools in the quest for results-oriented management, and studies show that the data they produce are used in planning, resource allocation, program management, and reporting on performance to elected officials, citizens, and the media (De Lancer Julnes and Holzer, 2001).

But are performance measures themselves effective in terms of strengthening the "bottom line" of performance? Do they lead to improved performance in the form of more effective programs, improved service quality, greater customer satisfaction, and more efficient operations? Tightly structured evaluations of the effectiveness of measurement systems implemented in the "action setting" of public and nonprofit management are simply not available. However, fragmentary data from surveys and case studies suggest that the answer to this question is clearly yes. For example, a set of comparative case studies on the use of results-oriented management strategies in several states, such as Minnesota, Oregon, Texas, Florida, and Virginia, found numerous instances of agencies or managers reporting that the performance data obtained from their measurement systems had in fact helped improve internal operations, address performance problems, and improve program performance (Aristiqueta, 1999).

Similarly, in a survey of municipal managers conducted a few years ago, 38 percent of responding cities indicated that they had performance measurement systems in place, either on a citywide basis or in selected departments (Poister and Streib, 1999a). Of the jurisdictions with measurement systems, 57 percent rated their systems as at least somewhat effective in strengthening management and decision making, with 37 percent saying they were very effective. More important, more than 70 percent of those respondents with comprehensive measurement systems reported that the measures have led to moderate or substantial improvement in service quality, and 46 percent indicated that they have contributed to moderate or substantial reductions in the cost of city operations.

There is also a variety of individual case study and anecdotal evidence indicating that measurement systems have led to real service improvements and other tangible impacts. Reports by a number of public managers do in fact provide examples of successful cases in which performance measurement systems have served as a catalyst for improved service quality, greater program effectiveness, enhanced responsiveness to customers, or more efficient operations (Syfert, 1993; Ammons, 2000; Epstein and Campbell, 2000; Mallory, 2002). Indeed, a review of best practices in government drawn from the Exemplary State and Local Awards Program sponsored by the National Center for Public Productivity identified performance measurement systems as a critical element of leading-edge results-oriented management (Holzer and Callahan, 1998). Citing a number of cases, ranging from housing and economic development, health care, and youth services to value engineering, insurance and risk management, and growth management, this study concluded that measurement-based management systems are becoming models for the entire public sector.

Limitations of Performance Measurement

Performance measurement is not, however, a panacea for all the problems and challenges that confront effective organizations and programs. Many of the problems that public and nonprofit organizations seek to address are at least somewhat intractable, with no easy solutions in sight, and the available resources are often inadequate to address them effectively. In addition, decisions regarding strategies, priorities, goals, and objectives are often made in heavily politicized contexts characterized by competing interests at different levels, forceful personalities, and the abandonment of principle in favor of compromise. Thus, although the purpose of measurement systems is to help improve performance through influencing decisions, they cannot be expected to control or dictate what those decisions will be. Performance measurement systems are intended to inject objective, results-oriented information into decision-making processes, but even at lower management levels they can be ignored and will not automatically be used.

Another difficulty is that not all agencies and programs lend themselves equally well to performance measurement. Whereas developing performance measures for production-oriented agencies with more tangible service delivery systems is often relatively straightforward, the process is likely to be much more difficult (or tenuous at best) in agencies whose activities admittedly have only very indirect connections to the desired results. For example, the U.S. Environmental Protection Agency has a program that is intended to work with eastern European countries to encourage them to adopt stricter policies in order to improve air and water quality. Not only are the results very much long term, but intangible factors may be of paramount importance, and the causal linkages within a complex web of influencing factors are less clear, making it more challenging to develop useful performance measures than is the case with more production-oriented programs.

Policy-oriented units, such as planning agencies, research programs, or policy analysis and evaluation offices, can be difficult to incorporate in performance measurement systems because their influence on tangible results is often difficult to sort out and because those results often are not expected to materialize for years, or even decades. Therefore, annual measures of "outcomes," for instance, may seem meaningless or like simply going through the motions, without any real value. Similarly, it is often difficult if not impossible to measure the impact of support functions—such as fleet maintenance, printing shops, mail and courier services, office supply, property management, purchasing, personnel, budgeting and finance, and information management—in terms of improving the effectiveness of the service delivery units they serve, and thus outcome measures for these functions are usually not available. In addition, for prevention programs—for instance, those aimed at limiting the spread of a disease or minimizing the injuries, fatalities, property damage, and other hardship due to natural disasters—the results in terms of negative impacts that do not occur can be very difficult to capture with performance measures.

Nevertheless, results-oriented managers in all public and nonprofit organizations should be vitally concerned with tracking the performance of their programs, and where it may not be feasible or worthwhile to measure actual results on a regular basis, it can still be helpful to monitor more immediate measures relating to such issues as the amount of work conducted, the timeliness and quality of that work, the efficiency with which it is conducted, the degree to which it is seen as being responsive to customers and clients, and the extent to which it is completed within budget. No matter how limited or comprehensive the indicators are, however, it is important to recognize at the outset that performance measurement systems provide data that are *descriptive* but not rigorously evaluative. That is, performance measures by themselves do not provide a clear indication of cause and effect or of the extent to which a program or agency might be responsible for producing the results observed. Although measurement systems do generate data that can often be used in more rigorous program evaluations, care must be taken not to overinterpret the performance measures themselves.

Performance measures can also encourage undesirable responses. Although the logic of performance measurement holds that providing objective information on program or agency performance will lead to decisions and actions designed to strengthen performance, that will not automatically follow. As will be seen in Chapter Five, inappropriate measures or unbalanced sets of indicators can actually lead to goal displacement and behavior that detracts from rather than enhances performance. Worse, performance measures can be abused. When the primary management response to negative performance data is to place blame on certain individuals or units, for example, or to penalize managers in some way for problems over which they have no control, the impact of the measurement system is counterproductive and tends to result, at least in the long run, in deteriorating performance levels.

In addition, performance measurement systems may simply require too much time and effort. Public and nonprofit agencies need to develop measurement systems that serve their needs while maintaining a reasonable balance between usefulness and cost. When such systems are particularly onerous in terms of data collection and processing, for instance, yet yield little information that is actually of interest to management, the systems are not cost-effective.

Finally, performance measurement systems run the risk of being ignored. Some agencies invest resources in maintaining measurement systems but rarely look at the accumulating data in a serious way. For the system to contribute to improved performance, it must be utilized. As advocates like to point out, equipping an automobile with a speedometer does nothing by itself to ensure the safe driving of that vehicle. By the same token, performance measures by themselves have no chance of improving performance unless they are used very deliberately to manage agencies and programs more effectively.

The Outlook for Performance Measurement

Despite these limitations, the outlook for performance measurement is very positive. Yes, defining useful measures can be a challenge, implementing measurement systems effectively can be difficult, and incorporating them in management and decision-making processes in meaningful ways requires deliberate effort and sustained commitment. But these things can be done—and should be done in most public and nonprofit organizations—and experience shows that performance measures can be designed and implemented successfully and used effectively to improve decision making, enhance performance, and increase accountability.

It is clear that performance measurement is here to stay. Although there are still detractors and skeptics in abundance, a consensus has evolved among results-oriented public and nonprofit managers that good measurement systems are effective management tools. And the need for measurement systems has been reinforced by numerous legislative bodies and governing boards. Thus, the question at this point is not *whether* to measure performance but rather *how* to design and implement measurement systems most effectively: how to design overall systems to serve different purposes; how to identify the aspects of performance that should be tracked; how to tie performance measures to goals and objectives; how to manage data collection and processing; how to analyze and present performance data to their intended audiences; how to ensure that performance measures will be used effectively to inform decisions and enhance performance.

Public and nonprofit managers need to learn more about how to do performance measurement. Thus, the purpose of this book is to clear up the mystique surrounding performance measures and address these kinds of issues in order to help managers implement and use measurement systems more effectively.

CHAPTER TWO

DEVELOPING EFFECTIVE PERFORMANCE MEASUREMENT SYSTEMS

How do you go about creating and installing a performance measurement system in a public or nonprofit organization? How can you ensure that such a system is designed to meet the needs it is intended to serve? What are the essential steps in the design and implementation process? Those who have responsibility for developing performance measurement systems must proceed very deliberately and systematically if they are to develop systems that are used effectively for their intended purposes. This chapter presents a step-by-step process for developing measurement systems that really can help manage agencies and programs more effectively.

The Design and Implementation Process

Performance measurement systems come in all shapes and sizes, from those that monitor detailed indicators of a production process or service delivery operation within one particular agency every week, to others that track a few global measures for an entire state or the nation as a whole on an annual basis. Some systems are intended to focus primarily on efficiency and productivity within work units, whereas others are designed to monitor the outcomes produced by major public programs. Still others serve to track the quality of the services provided by an agency and the extent to which clients are satisfied with these services.

Yet all these different kinds of measurement systems can be developed with a common design and implementation process. The key is to tailor the process both to the specific purpose for which a particular system is being designed and to the program or agency whose performance is being measured. Exhibit 2.1 outlines a process for designing and implementing effective performance measurement systems. It begins with securing management commitment and proceeds through a sequence of essential steps to full-scale implementation and evaluation.

Step One: Securing Management Commitment

The first step in the process is to secure management commitment to the design, implementation, and utilization of the performance measurement system. If those who have responsibility for managing the agency, organizational units, or particular programs do not intend to use the measurement system or are not committed to sponsoring its development and providing support for its design and implementation, the effort will have little chance of success. Thus, it is critical at the outset to make sure that the managers of the department, agency, division, or program in question—those whose support for a measurement system will be essential for it to

EXHIBIT 2.1. PROCESS FOR DESIGNING AND IMPLEMENTING PERFORMANCE MEASUREMENT SYSTEMS.

1. Secure management commitment.
2. Organize the system development process.
3. Clarify purpose and system parameters.
4. Identify outcomes and other performance criteria.
5. Define, evaluate, and select indicators.
6. Develop data collection procedures.
   - Provide for quality assurance.
7. Specify the system design.
   - Identify reporting frequencies and channels.
   - Determine analytical and reporting formats.
   - Develop software applications.
   - Assign responsibilities for maintaining the system.
8. Conduct a pilot and revise if necessary (optional).
9. Implement full-scale system.
10. Use, evaluate, and modify the system as appropriate.

be used effectively—are on board with the effort and committed to supporting its development and use in the organization. It is important to have the commitment of those at various levels in the organization, including those who are expected to be users of the system and those who will need to provide the resources and ensure the organizational arrangements needed to maintain the system.

It may be helpful to have commitments from external stakeholders—for example, customer groups, advocacy groups, and professional groups. If agreement can be developed among the key players regarding the usefulness and importance of a system, with support for it ensured along the way, the effort is ultimately much more likely to produce an effective measurement system. If such commitments are not forthcoming at the outset, it is probably not a workable situation for developing a useful system.

Step Two: Organizing the System Development Process

Along with a commitment from higher levels of management, the individual or group of people who will take the lead in developing the measurement system must also organize the process for doing so. Typically, this means formally recognizing the individual or team that will have overall responsibility for developing the system, adopting a design and implementation process to use (like the one shown in Exhibit 2.1), and identifying individuals or work units that may be involved in specific parts of that process. This step includes decisions about all those individuals who will be involved in various steps in the process—managers, employees, staff, analysts, consultants, clients, and others. It also includes developing a schedule for undertaking and completing various steps in the process. Beyond timetables and delivery dates, the individual or team taking the lead responsibility might find it helpful to manage the overall effort as a project. We will return to issues concerning the management of the design and implementation process in Chapter Fourteen.

Step Three: Clarifying System Purpose and Parameters

The third step in the process is to clarify the purpose of the measurement system and the parameters within which it is to be designed. Purpose is best thought of in terms of utilization. Who are the intended users of this system, and what kinds of information do they need from it? Will this system be used simply for reporting and informational purposes, or is it intended to generate data that will assist in making better decisions or managing more effectively? Is it being designed to monitor progress in implementing an agency's strategic initiatives, inform the budgeting process, manage people and work units more effectively, support quality improvement efforts, or compare your agency's performance against other similar organizations? What kinds of performance data can best support these processes, and how frequently do they need to be observed?

Chapters Nine through Thirteen discuss the design and use of performance measures for these various purposes, and it becomes clear that systems developed to support different management processes will themselves be very different in terms of focus, the kinds of measures that are used, the level of detail involved, the frequency of reporting performance data, and the way in which the system is used. Thus, it is essential to be clear about the purpose of a performance measurement system at the outset so that it can be designed to maximum advantage.

Beyond the question of purpose and connections between the performance measurement system and other management and decision-making processes, system parameters are often thought of in terms of both scope and constraints. Thus, system designers must address the following kinds of questions early on in the process:

- What is the scope of the new system? Will it focus on organizational units or on programs? Will it cover a particular operating unit, a division, or the entire organization? Do we need data for individual field offices, for example, or can the data simply be "rolled up" and tracked for a single, larger entity? Should the measures comprehend this entire, multifaceted program or just this one particular service delivery system?

- Who are the most important decision makers regarding these agencies or programs, and what kinds of performance data do they need to have? Are there multiple audiences for the performance data to be generated by this system, possibly including both internal and external stakeholders? Are reports produced by this system likely to be going to more than one level of management?

- What are the resource constraints within which this measurement system will be expected to function? What level of effort can be invested in support of this system, and to what extent will resources be available to support new data collection efforts that might have to be designed specifically for this system?

- Are any particular barriers to the development of a workable performance measurement system apparent at the outset? Are some data that would obviously be desirable to support this system simply not available? Would the cost of some preferred data elements clearly exceed available resources? If so, are there likely to be acceptable alternatives? Is there likely to be resistance to this system on the part of managers, employees, or other stakeholders whose support and cooperation are essential for success? Can we find ways to overcome this problem?

The answers to these kinds of questions will have great influence on the system's design, so you need to address them very carefully. Sometimes these parameters are clear from external mandates for performance measurement systems, such as legislation of reporting requirements for jurisdiction-wide performance and accountability or monitoring requirements of grants programs managed by higher levels of government. In other cases, establishing the focus may be a matter of working closely with the managers who are commissioning a performance measurement system in order to clarify purpose and parameters before proceeding to the design stage.

Step Four: Identifying Outcomes and Other Performance Criteria

The fourth step in the design process is to identify the intended outcomes and other performance criteria to be monitored by the measurement system. What are the key dimensions of performance of the agency or program that you should be tracking? What services are being provided, and who are the customers? What kind of results are you looking for here? How do effectiveness, efficiency, quality, productivity, customer satisfaction, and cost-effectiveness criteria translate into this particular program area?

Chapter Three is devoted to the subject of identifying program outcomes and other performance criteria. It introduces the concept of logic models that outline programmatic activity, immediate products, intermediate outcomes, and ultimate results and the presumed cause-and-effect relationships among these elements. Analysts, consultants, and other system designers can review program plans and prior research and can work with managers and program delivery staff, as well as with clients and sometimes other external stakeholders, to clarify what these elements really are. Once a program logic model has been developed and validated with these groups, the relevant performance criteria can be derived directly from the model. Chapter Four further elaborates on the all-important linkage of performance measures to goals and objectives.

Step Five: Defining, Evaluating, and Selecting Indicators

When you have developed a consensus about *what* aspects of performance should be incorporated in a particular monitoring system, you can then address the question of *how* to measure these criteria. As discussed in Chapter Five, this involves defining, evaluating, and then selecting preferred performance indicators. This is really the heart of the performance measurement process. How should certain measures be specified? What about the reliability and validity of proposed indicators? How can you "capture" certain data elements, and to what extent will this entail collecting "original data" from new data sources? Is the value of these indicators worth the investment of time, money, and effort that will be required to collect the data? Will these measures set up appropriate incentives that will serve to help improve performance, or could they actually be counterproductive?

This is usually the most methodologically involved step in the process of designing performance measurement systems. It cuts to the heart of the issue: How will you measure the performance of this agency or program on an ongoing basis? The ideas come from prior research and other measurement systems as well as from goals, objectives, and standards and from the logical extension of the definition of what constitutes strong performance for a particular program. Sometimes it is possible to identify alternative indicators for particular measures, and in fact the use of multiple measures is sometimes well advised. In addition, there are often trade-offs between the quality of a particular indicator and the practical issues involved in trying to operationalize it. Thus, as discussed in Chapter Five, it is important to identify potential measures and then *evaluate* each one on a series of criteria in order to decide which ones to include in the monitoring system.

Step Six: Developing Data Collection Procedures

Given a set of indicators to be incorporated in a measurement system, the next step in the design process is to develop procedures for collecting and processing the data on a regular basis. The data for performance monitoring systems come from a wide variety of sources, including agency records, program operating data, existing management information systems, direct observation, tests, clinical examinations, various types of surveys, and other special measurement tools. As discussed in Chapter Eight, in circumstances where the raw data already reside in established data files maintained for other purposes, the data collection procedures involve "extracting" the required data elements from these existing databases. Within a given agency, this is usually accomplished by programming computer software to export and import specific data elements from one database to another. Sometimes, particularly with respect to grant programs, for example, procedures must be developed for collecting data from a number of other agencies and aggregating them in a common database. Increasingly, this is accomplished through interactive computer software over the Internet.

In other instances, however, operationalizing performance indicators requires collecting original data specifically for the purposes of performance measurement. With respect to tests, which may be needed to rate client or even employee proficiency in any number of skill areas or tasks as well as in educational programs, there are often a number of standard instruments to choose from or adapt; in other cases new instruments will have to be developed. This is also the case with respect to the kinds of medical, psychiatric, or psychological examinations that are often needed to gauge the outcomes of health care or other kinds of individual or community-based programs. Similarly, instruments may need to be developed for direct observation surveys in which trained observers rate particular kinds of physical conditions or behavioral patterns.

Some performance measures rely on surveys of clients or other stakeholders, and these require decisions about the survey mode—personal interview, telephone, mail-out, individual or group administered, or computer based—as well as the adaptation or design of specific survey instruments. In addition to instrument design, these kinds of performance measures require the development of protocols for administering tests, clinical examinations, and surveys so as to ensure the validity of the indicators as well as their reliability through uniform data collection procedures. Furthermore, the development of procedures for collecting original data, especially through surveys and other kinds of client follow-up, often require decisions about sampling strategies.

With regard both to existing data and to procedures for collecting original data specifically for performance measurement systems, we need to be concerned with quality assurance. As mentioned in Chapter One, performance measurement systems are worthwhile only if they are actually used by managers and decision makers, and this will happen only if the intended users have faith in the reliability of the data. If data collection procedures are sloppy, the data will be less than reliable and managers will not have confidence in them. Worse, if the data are biased somehow because, for example, records are falsified or people responsible for data entry in the field tend to include some cases but systematically exclude others, the resulting performance data will be distorted and misleading. Thus, as discussed in Chapter Eight, there needs to be provision for some kind of spot checking or systematic data audit to ensure the integrity of the data being collected.

Step Seven: Specifying the System Design

At some point in the design process, you must make decisions about how the performance measurement system will actually operate. One of these decisions concerns reporting frequencies and channels—that is, how often particular indicators will be reported to different intended users. As will become clear in Chapters Nine through Thirteen, how you make this decision will depend primarily on the specific purpose of a monitoring system. For example, performance measures developed to gauge the outcomes of an agency's strategic initiatives might be reported annually, whereas indicators used to track the outputs and labor productivity of a service delivery system in order to optimize workload management might well be tracked on a weekly basis. In addition to reporting frequency, there is the issue of which data elements go to which users. In some cases, for instance, detailed data broken down by work units might be reported to operating-level managers, while data on the same indicators might be rolled up and reported in the aggregate to senior-level executives.

System design also entails determining what kinds of analysis the performance data should facilitate and what kinds of reporting formats should be emphasized. As discussed in Chapter Six, performance measures do not convey information unless the data are reported in some kind of context through comparisons over time, against targets or standards, among organizational or programmatic units, or against external benchmarks. What kind of breakouts and comparisons should you employ? In deciding which analytical frameworks to emphasize, you should use the criterion of maximizing the usefulness of the performance data in terms of the overall purpose of the monitoring system. As illustrated in Chapter Seven, a great variety of reporting formats are available for presenting performance data, ranging from spreadsheet tables, graphs, and symbols to pictorial and "dashboard" displays; the objective should be to employ elements of any or all of these to present the data in the most intelligible and meaningful manner.

Furthermore, computer software applications have to be developed to support the performance measurement system from data entry and data processing through to the generation and distribution of reports, which increasingly can be done electronically. As discussed in Chapter Eight, a variety of software packages may be useful along these lines, including spreadsheet, database management, and graphical programs, as well as special software packages available commercially that have been designed specifically to support performance monitoring systems. Often some combination of these packages can be used most effectively. Thus, system designers will have to determine whether their particular performance monitoring system would function more effectively with existing software adapted to support the system or with original software developed expressly for that system.

A final element of system specification is to assign personnel responsibilities for maintaining the performance measurement system when it is put into use. As discussed in Chapter Fourteen, this includes assigning responsibilities for data entry, which might well be dispersed among various operating units or field offices (or both), as well as for data processing, quality assurance, and reporting. Usually, primary responsibility for supporting the system is assigned to a staff unit concerned with planning and evaluation, management information systems, budget and finance, management analysis, quality improvement, or customer service, depending on the principal use for which the system is designed. In addition, you must clarify who is responsible for reviewing and using the performance data, and you need to establish deadlines within reporting cycles for data entry, processing, distribution of reports, and review.

Step Eight: Conducting a Pilot

Very often it is possible to move directly from design to implementation of performance measurement systems, particularly in small agencies where responsibilities for inputting data and maintaining the system will not be fragmented or with simple, straightforward systems in which there are no unanswered questions about feasibility. In some cases, however, it can be a good idea to pilot the system, or elements of it at least, before committing to full-scale implementation. Most often, pilots are conducted when there is a need to test the feasibility of collecting certain kinds of data, demonstrate the workability of the administrative arrangements for more complex systems, get a clearer idea of the level of effort involved in implementing a new system, testing the software platform, or simply validating newly designed surveys or other data collection instruments. When there are real concerns about these kinds of issues, it often makes sense to conduct a pilot, perhaps on a smaller scale or sample basis, to get a better understanding of how well a system works and of particular problems that need to be addressed before implementing the system across the board. You can then make appropriate adjustments to the mix of indicators, data collection efforts, and software applications in order to increase the probability that the system will work effectively.

Step Nine: Implementing the Full-Scale System

With or without benefit of a pilot, implementing any new management system presents challenges. Implementation of a performance measurement system means collecting and processing all the required data within deadlines, "running the data" and disseminating performance reports to the designated users on a timely basis, and reviewing the data to track performance and use this information as an additional input into decision making. It also includes initiating quality assurance procedures and instituting checks in data collection procedures where practical to identify "stray values" and otherwise erroneous data.

With larger or more complex systems, especially those involving data input from numerous people in the field, some training may well be essential for reliable data. As discussed in Chapter Fourteen, however, the single most important factor for guaranteeing the successful implementation of a new monitoring system is a clear commitment from top management, or the highest management level that has commissioned a particular system, to providing reliable data and using the system effectively as a management tool.

Step Ten: Using, Evaluating, and Modifying the System

No matter how carefully a system may have been implemented, problems are likely to emerge in terms of data completeness, quality control, software applications, or the generation of reports. The level of effort required to support the system, particularly in terms of data collection and data entry, may also be a real concern as well as an unknown at the outset. Thus, over the first few cycles—most typically months, quarters, or years—it is important to monitor closely the operation of the system itself and evaluate how well it is working. And when said implementation and maintenance problems are identified, obviously they need to be resolved quickly and effectively.

Most important, managers must begin to assess the usefulness of the measurement system as a tool for managing more effectively and improving decisions, performance, and accountability. If a monitoring system is not providing worthwhile information and helping gain a good reading on performance and improve substantive results, managers should look for ways to strengthen the measures and the data or even the overall system. This is often a matter of fine-tuning particular indicators or data collection procedures, adding or eliminating certain measures, or making adjustments in reporting frequencies or presentation formats to provide more useful information, but it could also involve more basic changes in how the data are reported and used in management and decision-making processes. Finally, depending on what the performance data show, experience in using the system might suggest the need to modify targets or performance standards or even to make changes in the programmatic goals and objectives that the measurement system is built around.

A Flexible Process

Developing performance measurement systems is both an art and a science. It is a science because it must flow systematically from the purpose of the system and the parameters within which it must be designed and because the particulars of the system must be based on an objective logic underlying the operation of the agency, program, or service delivery system to be monitored. However, it is also an art because it is a creative process in terms of defining measures, reporting formats, and software applications and because it must be carried out in a way that is sensitive to the needs of people who will be using it and that will build credibility and support for the system along the way.

There is perhaps no precise "one right way" to develop a performance measurement system, and success will stem in part from tailoring the design and implementation process to the particular needs of the organization or program in question. Even though the steps outlined in this chapter are presented in a logical sequence, this should not be viewed as a rigid process. Indeed, as is true of any creative effort, designing and implementing performance measurement systems may at times be more iterative than sequential. Although the steps presented in Exhibit 2.1 are all essential, integrating them is much more important than performing them in a particular sequence.

Utilization is the primary test of the worth of any performance measurement system. Thus, performing all the steps in the design and implementation process with a clear focus on the purpose of a particular monitoring system and an eye on the needs of its intended users is critical to ensuring that the performance measures "add value" to the agency or the program. To this end, soliciting input along the way from people who will be working with the system—field personnel, systems specialists, analysts, and managers—as well as others who might have a stake in the system, such as clients or governing boards, can be invaluable in building credibility and ownership of the system once it is in place.

PART TWO

METHODOLOGICAL ELEMENTS OF PERFORMANCE MEASUREMENT

Performance measurement can be very challenging from a methodological perspective, and the chapters in Part Two address the key methodological concerns in some detail. First is the question of what to measure. Chapter Three discusses the use of program logic models to identify outcomes and other performance criteria and then presents various classes of measures, including measures of output, efficiency, productivity, effectiveness, service quality, customer satisfaction, and cost-effectiveness. Chapter Four focuses on tying performance measures to programmatic or organizational goals and objectives.

Second is the question of how to measure these dimensions of performance, and Chapter Five discusses the definition of operational indicators and their evaluation in terms of validity and reliability, timeliness, usefulness, and a number of other criteria.

Third is the question of what to do with the performance data once they have been collected. Chapter Six discusses the analysis of performance data, emphasizing the importance of comparisons—of current performance levels against past or recent trends, of actual performance against targets, across organizational or programmatic units, or against other agencies or programs, for example—in order to provide real information in an appropriate context. Chapter Seven illustrates a number of different kinds of tabular, graphical, and pictorial formats for displaying performance data as interesting and useful information. Finally, Chapter Eight discusses data processing requirements and approaches for supporting ongoing measurement systems.

CHAPTER THREE

IDENTIFYING REAL OUTCOMES AND OTHER PERFORMANCE MEASURES

How do you measure the effectiveness of a public program or the quality of the services it provides? How can you best gauge clients' satisfaction with these services on a systematic basis? What does efficiency mean with respect to a particular program? How do you gauge the productivity of employees working in a service delivery system? Obviously, in order for a measurement system to be useful, it must focus on the most appropriate aspects of performance. This chapter addresses the *what* of performance measurement: What are the important dimensions of program performance to address, and what are the principal kinds of measures to track performance?

Program Logic

Developing useful measures of program performance requires a clear understanding of what a program does and the results it is intended to accomplish (Poister, 1978; Wholey, 1979; Anthony and Young, 1999; Broom, Harris, Jackson, and Marshall, 1998). Program logic models represent the logic underlying a program's design, indicating how various components are expected to interact, the goods or services they produce, and *how* they generate the desired results—in other words, showing the logic by which program activities are expected to lead to targeted outcomes (Poister, 1978; Poister, McDavid, and Magoun, 1979; Hatry, Van Houten,

Plantz, and Greenway, 1996). Once you have clarified the program logic, you can identify the relevant performance measures systematically and confidently.

Program Logic Models

Public and nonprofit programs should be planned and managed with an eye toward specifying and achieving desirable results. They should be viewed as interventions involving service delivery or enforcement activity that is designed to address some problem, meet some need, or impact favorably on some unsatisfactory condition in a way that has been defined as serving the public interest. The positive impacts so generated constitute the program's intended results, which would justify support for the program in the first place. A program's intended results, or its outcomes, occur "out there" in the community, within a targeted area or target population, or across the nation or state or local jurisdiction generally, but not inside the program itself or the agency or organizational unit that operates it. Obviously, the intended results should be clearly understood and monitored on a regular basis. If a programmatic entity cannot articulate worthwhile results and provide evidence that programmatic activity is indeed producing them, continued support should be questioned at the very least.

Thus, any sound program design must be based on a set of assumptions regarding the services the program provides, the clients it serves or the cases it treats, its intended results, and the logic of how the use of resources in particular programmatic activities is expected to produce these results. Figure 3.1 shows a generic program logic that can help clarify these assumptions for any given public or nonprofit program. You can use such a model as an organizing tool for identifying the critical variables involved in program design, the role played by each in the underlying logic, and the presumed relationships among them.

Briefly, resources are used to carry on program activities and provide services that produce immediate products, or outputs. These outputs are intended to lead to outcomes, which are the substantive changes, improvements, or benefits that are supposed to result from the program. Frequently, these outcomes themselves occur in sequence, running from initial outcomes to intermediate and longer-term outcomes. Usually, the logic underlying a program design is also predicated on a flow of customers who are served by a program or a set of cases the program deals with. In addition, it is important to recognize the external factors in a program's environment or operating context that may influence its performance.

The sets of activities that make up the work of most public and nonprofit programs involve the provision of services or the enforcement of laws or regulations (or both). For example, the principal activities in a neighborhood health clinic might include conducting physical examinations and well baby checks, giving inoculations, and prescribing treatments and medications for illnesses and chronic

FIGURE 3.1. GENERIC PROGRAM LOGIC MODEL.

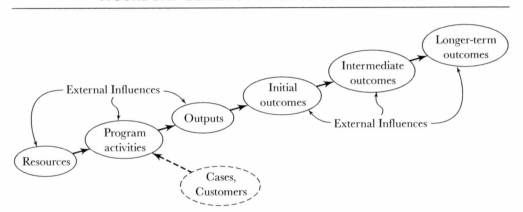

conditions; in the criminal investigations unit of a local police department, the principal activities would include conducting examinations of crime scenes, interviewing witnesses, examining physical evidence, checking out leads, and gathering additional information. These programmatic activities and the outputs they produce need to be identified clearly, whether they are carried on by public sector employees working in the program or by private firms or nonprofit organizations that are contracted to carry out service delivery.

The principal resources used by most public and nonprofit programs include personnel, physical facilities, equipment, materials, and contract services. Personnel may include volunteers as well as employees, and sometimes it is helpful to break personnel resources down into occupational categories; for example, to gauge labor productivity in a local police department, one might track the numbers of uniformed patrol officers, detectives, crime lab personnel, and support staff.

In many public and nonprofit programs, especially those carried on by production-type agencies, the work performed and the results obtained apply to cases or groups of cases that come into the program or are treated by the program in some fashion. Frequently, the cases are the program's primary customers (or consumers or clients). This is almost always true for human service and educational programs—patients treated in public hospitals, children served by a foster care program, clients aided in a counseling program, or students enrolled in a community college, for example—but customers are also often the principal cases in other types of programs, for instance disabled persons utilizing demand-responsive transportation services, or families living in dwelling units provided by a public housing authority.

In some programs, however, the most likely definition of cases may be something other than customers. For example, the customers of a state highway maintenance program are individual motorists, but it makes more sense to think of the cases to be processed as consisting of miles of road or road segments to be maintained. Similarly, the implicit customer of the Keep Nebraska Beautiful program is the public at large, but the "cases" treated by this program consist of small targeted geographical areas. Whereas the cases processed by a state's driver's license permitting program are individual applicants (the customers), the cases processed by a state's vehicle registration program are probably best defined as the vehicles rather than the customers who are registering them. Often a public or nonprofit program may define its cases in more than one way. For example, the Internal Revenue Service may consider the individual customer as the case with respect to its tax preparation assistance function but focus on the tax return as the case in terms of its collections and auditing functions.

It is important to identify external influences in thinking about a program's logic, because they may be critical in either facilitating or impeding success. Many of these external influences concern client characteristics or the magnitude or severity of need for the program, but they are by no means limited to that. Any factor or condition—be it physical, social, economic, financial, psychological, or cultural—that is likely to influence program performance and is largely beyond the control of the program or agency may be relevant to track as an external influence. For example, winter weather conditions may explain differences in the performance of a highway maintenance program from year to year; differences in labor market conditions may explain differences in the effectiveness of similar job training programs in different localities; variation in local industrial base, land use patterns, and commuting behavior are likely to influence the Environmental Protection Agency's success in enforcing clean air standards in different parts of the country. Such external factors are important to take into account in clarifying a program's underlying logic, because they can be extremely helpful in interpreting the meaning of performance data.

Outputs Versus Outcomes

The most important distinction to be made in identifying program logic is that between outputs and outcomes. Outputs represent what a program actually does, whereas outcomes are the results it produces. Operations managers appropriately focus on the production of high-quality outputs in an efficient manner, but managers who are concerned with overall performance must look beyond outputs to outcomes because they represent program effectiveness. In terms of program logic, outputs have little inherent value because they do not constitute direct benefits, but they are essential because they lead directly to these benefits or trigger the causal sequences of changes that lead to the desired results.

Outputs are best thought of as necessary but insufficient conditions for success. They are the immediate products or services produced by a program, and without an appropriate mix and quality of outputs, a program will not be able to generate its intended results. However, if the underlying program logic is flawed—if the assumptions of causal connections between outputs and results don't hold up in reality—then the desired outcomes will not materialize, at least not as a result of the program. Usually, the production of outputs is largely, although not exclusively, under the control of program managers, but outcomes tend to be influenced more strongly by a wider array of external factors that are beyond the program's control. Thus, the production of outputs is no guarantee that outcomes will result, and it is important therefore to measure outcomes directly in order to monitor program performance.

The list that follows shows typical outputs and outcomes for a few selected public services.

Outputs and Outcomes

Program	*Outputs*	*Outcomes*
Crime control	Hours of patrol Responses to calls for service Crimes investigated Arrests made Crimes solved	Reduction in crimes committed Reduction in deaths and injuries resulting from crimes Less property damaged or lost due to crime
Highway construction	Project designs Highway miles constructed Highway miles reconstructed	Capacity increases Improved traffic flow Reduced travel times
AIDS Prevention	Responses to hotline calls Seminars conducted AIDS antibody tests given AIDS patients treated Patients counseled or referred (or both)	Increased knowledge and treatment regarding AIDS Decrease in risky behavior Reduction in persons with HIV Decreased incidence and prevalence of AIDS Reduction in deaths due to AIDS Fewer babies testing positive for HIV

Juvenile justice boot camps	Physical training units completed	More youths achieving higher grade levels
	Educational units completed	More youths attending school
	Vocational training units completed	More youths engaged in gainful employment
	Behavioral shaping units completed	Fewer youths engaged in further criminal activity
	Youths discharged	
	Aftercare activity hours	

Outputs often represent the amount of work performed or the volume of activity completed, such as hours patrolled by the police, miles of highway constructed, AIDS education seminars conducted, or the number of vocational training classes conducted in a juvenile justice boot camp. Sometimes outputs are measured in terms of the number of clients or cases that have been treated—for example, the number of crimes investigated by the police, the number of AIDS patients given treatment or counseling, or the number of youths discharged from juvenile boot camps.

Outcomes, in contrast, are the substantive impacts that result from producing these outputs. Criminal investigations and arrests don't really count for much, for instance, if the police are not able to solve the crimes they are working on, and reconstructed highway segments don't serve any particular public interest if they don't result in improved flow of traffic and reduced travel times for the motorists using them. Similarly, AIDS awareness seminars are not particularly worthwhile if they don't lead to decreases in the kinds of risky behavior—unprotected sex and use of contaminated needles, for example—that spread HIV. Training units and hours spent in aftercare activity are not effective in attaining their rehabilitative purposes if the youths discharged from boot camps are not productively engaged in school or work and refraining from further criminal activity. Outcomes are the ultimate criteria for gauging program effectiveness, but as direct products of program activity, outputs are critical for achieving intended outcomes.

Given this careful distinction, however, it must be noted that the connections between outputs and outcomes are often more fluid than a simple dichotomy. It could be argued, for example, that arrests made by the police as the result of criminal investigations are really outcomes rather than outputs, although certainly not the ultimate outcome of their work. Similarly, it might make sense to think of services provided as outputs but services consumed as outcomes. For example, the number of training programs offered might be considered as a program's principal output, and the number of participants completing these programs could be thought of as an outcome. However, the number of participants trained is probably a better reflection of the amount of activity completed, or an output. Rather than making a very strict, dichotomous distinction between outputs and outcomes, what is important is to identify the real results targeted by a program and the sequence of accomplishments that must occur in order to achieve them. This might be thought of as a "results chain," a sequence from outputs to impacts, or the logic of program activities, outputs, initial outcomes, intermediate outcomes, and longer-term outcomes, the format used in this book.

Diverse Logic Models

Outputs, outcomes, and other elements can be identified in logic models that may be as general or detailed, or as simple or complex, as needed. Although it is always a mistake to "bend" reality to fit a preconceived model, the kind of program logic models presented here are quite flexible and can be adjusted to represent any public or nonprofit program. For example, the set of program components to be included can range from only one to numerous activities, and the connections between outputs and desired outcomes may be very direct, or they can occur through numerous initial and intermediate results. Similarly, the strands of logic that connect outputs to various outcomes can converge at different points and in different sequences along the way.

It should also be noted that although these models show the logic generally moving from left to right, they are not necessarily designed to reflect the chronological order in which treatments are provided; these are logic models, as opposed to flowcharts that show the sequence in which cases move through a system.

Air Traffic Control Program

Figure 3.2 shows a simplified logic model for the air traffic control program operated nationwide by the Federal Aviation Administration. The program's primary mission is to prevent collisions between airplanes in the air or on the ground through the enforcement of safety standards during takeoff, landing, and in-flight operations. The program's principal resources are professional air traffic controllers and support staff, the facilities or "towers" they work in, and the sophisticated computer and communications systems they use. The direct customers of this program are pilots flying airplanes, but the cases that air traffic controllers deal with are the commercial airline, general aviation, and military flight segments that come under their jurisdiction. Programmatic activity includes observing airplane positions, communicating with pilots about flight plans, and giving them instructions in order to maintain safety standards.

FIGURE 3.2. AIR TRAFFIC CONTROL PROGRAM LOGIC MODEL.

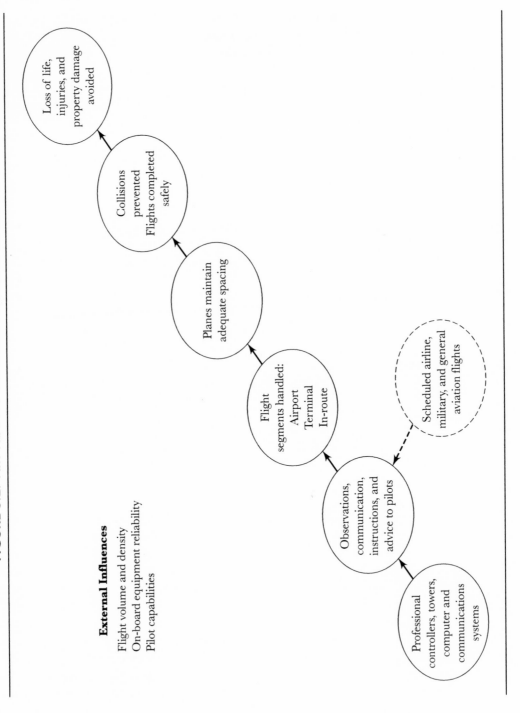

The immediate output of the air traffic control program is the number of flight segments handled at airports, in the "terminal" air space surrounding airports, and during in-flight operations. Indeed, the number of flight segments is the most direct measure of the volume of work performed by this program. The initial outcome produced by this work is that airplanes maintain adequate spacing among themselves and thus minimize the likelihood of collisions. This in turn leads to the intermediate outcome, the real desired result in this case: that collisions are prevented and that flight segments are completed safely. The longer-term outcome, or the broader impact, of this result is the avoidance of loss of life, injuries, and property damage caused by airplane collisions.

Although simple and straightforward, this example reflects the mission-driven orientation of program logic models as well as the critical distinction between outputs and outcomes. The purpose of having air traffic controllers do their work obviously is not to handle flight segments but rather to prevent airplane collisions and the injuries, fatalities, and property damage that result from them. Therefore, a meaningful set of performance measures would need to incorporate these outcomes. It should be noted that this example as presented in Figure 3.2 portrays only a single strand of program logic, which pertains to the air traffic control program's primary mission of preventing collisions. In fact, the program also has secondary responsibilities regarding weather and terrain avoidance and providing assistance in emergency situations. The logic model could easily be elaborated to represent a more complete program logic.

Crisis Stabilization Unit

Figure 3.3 shows a logic model for a very different kind of program, a bicounty crisis stabilization unit in suburban Atlanta, Georgia. The mission of this program is to provide effective and safe stabilization to persons experiencing symptoms of decompensation due to psychiatric illnesses or substance abuse or dependence. The consumers treated by the program are persons with subacute psychiatric diagnoses or a history of continuous substance abuse such that abrupt stoppage would cause physiological withdrawal. The principal resources of the unit are the facilities and supplies along with medical, professional, and support staff. The services they provide include medical assessment and treatment, psychiatric assessment, medication management, crisis intervention, case management, and individual and group therapy.

The crisis stabilization unit produces a variety of outputs that reflect the work actually performed in providing services, such as medical assessments and nursing assessments conducted, physical examinations conducted, medical detoxifications completed, psychiatric assessments, education program modules, therapy

FIGURE 3.3. CRISIS STABILIZATION UNIT PROGRAM LOGIC MODEL.

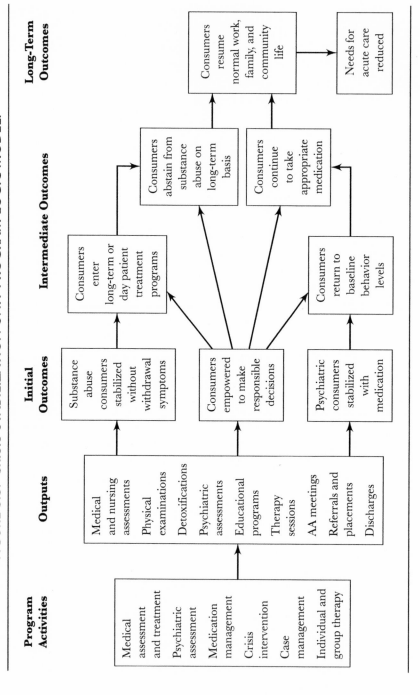

sessions, Alcoholics Anonymous meetings, and referrals or placements. The initial outcomes produced by these service outputs are substance abuse consumers who have been stabilized through detoxification without physiological withdrawal symptoms and psychiatric consumers who have been stabilized with medication. A complementary initial outcome relates to consumers being empowered through counseling, educational programs, and support groups to make more responsible decisions regarding their own behavior. For the substance abusers, the intermediate outcomes are that they enter appropriate long-term or day patient treatment programs and continue to abstain from drugs and alcohol over the long run. For the psychiatric consumers, the intermediate outcomes are that after being discharged from the unit they return to baseline or desired behavior levels and continue to take their appropriate medications. For both clientele groups, the intended longer-term outcomes are that they resume normal patterns of work, family, and community life and that all of this results in reduced need for acute care for these individuals.

Vocational Rehabilitation Program

Figure 3.4 represents the logic underlying a vocational rehabilitation program provided by a state human services department. The clients of this program are individuals whose disabilities caused by birth defects, injuries, or progressive long-term illnesses present them with special challenges in finding work and holding a job. The mission of the program is to help these clients prepare for resuming their occupations or learning new ones, securing suitable jobs, and remaining employed. To pursue this mission, the vocational rehabilitation agency provides a number of interdependent services, including counseling and guidance, occupational and related training, the provision of specialized equipment, employer development and job development, placement assistance, and on-the-job evaluations of clients' ability to do the required work.

The initial outcomes of all this activity are that clients have developed the knowledge and skills needed to engage in occupations that are viable for them and that they actually apply for suitable jobs in the competitive marketplace or, in some cases, in sheltered workshops. This leads to the intermediate outcome of clients actually being placed in suitable jobs. Once clients have secured suitable jobs, the program may provide on-the-job evaluations with recommendations to assist them in adjusting to new jobs. This is all aimed at helping clients continue working in suitable jobs and being successfully employed over the long run. To the extent that this longer-term outcome is achieved, the program's mission is being met effectively.

FIGURE 3.4. VOCATIONAL REHABILITATION PROGRAM LOGIC MODEL.

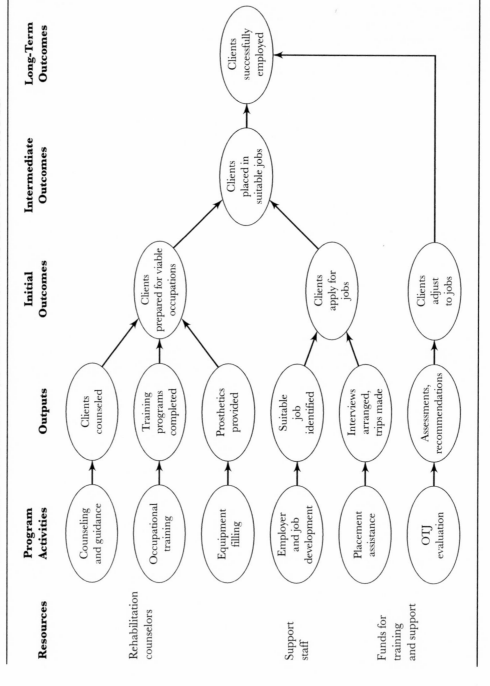

Teen Mother Parenting Education Program

As a fourth illustration, Figure 3.5 presents a logic model for a teen mother parenting education program operated by a nonprofit organization in a particular local area. The goals of the program are to help ensure that pregnant teenagers deliver healthy babies and that they are equipped to care for their babies. Service delivery consists of conducting classes on prenatal care and infant parenting, and the program's outputs could be measured in terms of the number of classes conducted or, more meaningfully, the number of pregnant teenagers completing the program.

The outcomes that the classes are intended to produce occur in two strands of logic. First, teens who complete the program will be knowledgeable about prenatal nutrition and health habits. This will lead to their following proper guidelines regarding nutrition and health, and this in turn will lead to a higher probability of the desired outcome, delivering healthy babies. Second, as an initial outcome of the classes, these teens will also be more knowledgeable about the proper care and feeding of and interaction with their infants, which will lead to the intermediate outcome of their actually providing the same to their babies once they are born. Then, the delivery of healthy babies and their receiving proper care should contribute to these babies' achieving appropriate twelve-month milestones regarding physical, verbal, and social development.

Performance Measures

The purpose of developing a logic model is to clarify what goes into a program, who its customers are, what services it provides, what immediate products or outputs it produces, and what outcomes it is supposed to generate. Once this logic has been articulated in a narrative, a schematic, or both, you can identify the most relevant measures of program performance on a very systematic basis. Although they are often combined into different categories, for the most part the relevant types of performance measures include measures of *output, efficiency, productivity, service quality, effectiveness, cost-effectiveness*, and *customer satisfaction*. Depending on the purpose of a given performance measurement system and the level of detail on which the monitoring may focus, various of these will be of paramount importance, but it usually makes sense to consider all of these types of measures in designing a performance measurement system. For any given program, all of these types of performance measures can generally be derived directly from the logic model.

FIGURE 3.5. TEEN MOTHER PARENTING EDUCATION PROGRAM LOGIC MODEL.

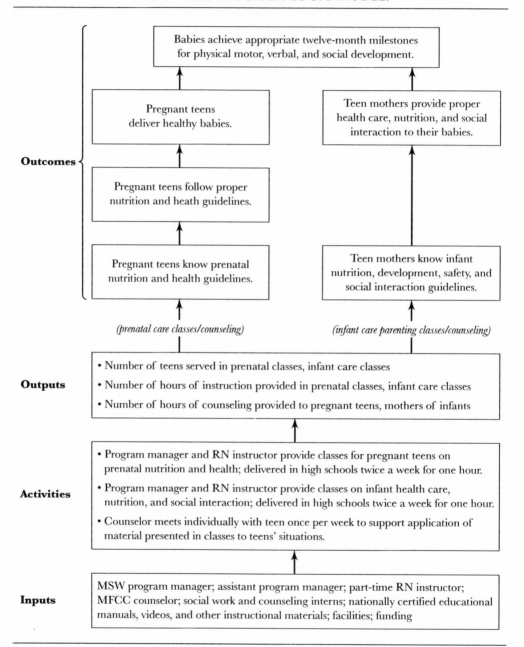

Source: United Way of America, 2002. Used by permission.

Resource Measures

Two other types of indicators, namely resource and workload measures, are usually not thought of as performance measures in their own right, but they are often used in computing other performance measures and are sometimes used in conjunction with other performance measures. All the various types of resources supporting a program can be measured in their own natural measurement units—for example, number of teachers, number of school buildings or classrooms, number of computer work stations in a local school system—or they can be measured and aggregated in their common measurement unit, which is dollar cost. Although resource measures constitute investment at the front end rather than something produced by the program, when managerial objectives focus on improving the mix or quality of resources—maintaining a full complement of teachers, for instance, or increasing the percentage of teachers with master's degrees—then it may be appropriate to track resource measures as indicators of performance. However, the principal use of resource measures in tracking program performance is as a basis for computing efficiency measures, such as the cost per hour of classroom instruction, or cost-effectiveness measures, such as the cost per student graduated.

Workload Measures

Workload measures are often of great concern to managers because they represent the flow of cases into a system or numbers of customers who need to be served. When work standards are in place or average productivity rates have been established, workload measures can be defined to represent resource requirements or the backlog of work in a production system—for example, the number of production hours needed to complete all jobs in the queue in a government printing office or the number of crew days required to complete all the resurfacing projects that would be needed to bring a city's streets up to serviceable standards. In some cases, when managerial objectives focus on keeping workloads within reasonable limits—not exceeding two work days pending in a central office supply operation, for example, or keeping the work weeks pending within two weeks in a disability determination program, or reducing the number of cases pending in a large county's risk management program by closing more cases than are opened in each of the next six months— then workload measures may appropriately be viewed as performance measures.

Output Measures

Output measures are important because they represent the direct products of public or nonprofit programs. They often measure volumes of programmed activity, such as the number of training programs conducted by a job training program, the number of seminars presented by an AIDS prevention program, the miles of new four-lane highways constructed by a state transportation department, or the hours of routine patrol logged in by a local police department. Outputs are often measured in terms of the amount of work that is performed—for example, the number of detoxification procedures completed by a crisis stabilization unit, the number of job interviews arranged for clients of a vocational rehabilitation program, or the gallons of patching material that are placed in the road by highway maintenance crews. Finally, output measures sometimes represent the number of cases that are dealt with by a program, such as the number of flight segments handled by the air traffic control program, the number of AIDS clients who receive counseling, or the number of crimes investigated by the police.

Outputs are sometimes measured at different stages of the service delivery process, and we can think of output chains occurring in some programs. For instance, the outputs of crime investigation are usually specified as the number of initial responses to crimes reported, the number of crimes investigated, and the number of arrests made. Juvenile justice boot camps will often measure the numbers of juveniles under their charge who complete various training modules and receive other services and the number of juveniles who are discharged from the camps as well as the number of aftercare visits or activities reported. All these stages of outputs are relevant to track because they all provide some indication of the amount of activity or work completed or the numbers cases being treated in some way.

Productivity Measures

Productivity indicators most often measure the rate of production per some specific unit of resource, usually staff or employees. To be meaningful they also must be defined in terms of some particular unit of time. For example, the number of flight segments handled per air traffic controller per hour and the number of lane-miles of highway resurfaced per maintenance crew per day are typical measures of labor productivity. Sometimes the specific resource used as the basis for a productivity indicator may measure equipment rather than personnel—for example, the number of standard "images" printed per large press per hour in a government printing office.

In some cases, productivity ratios use the unit of measurement in both the numerator and denominator, for example, the number of task-hours completed per production hour worked on a highway maintenance activity or the number of billable hours of work completed per production hour worked in a state government printing plant.

Staff-client ratios are sometimes loosely interpreted as productivity measures, but this may be misleading. For example, the number of in-house consumers per full-time staff member of a crisis stabilization unit may represent productivity because those consumers are all receiving treatment. However, the number of cases per adjuster in a state workers' compensation program doesn't really provide much information about the productivity of those employees, because some or many of those clients or cases may generate very little if any activity. The number of clients per employee in a vocational rehabilitation program may not be particularly useful either, again because the services actually being provided vary so widely from one client to the next; the number of clients counseled per vocational rehabilitation counselor would be more meaningful because it represents the amount of work performed per staff member.

Efficiency Measures

Like productivity indicators, measures of operating efficiency relate outputs to the resources utilized in producing them, but efficiency indicators look at the ratio of outputs to the dollar cost of the collective resources consumed in producing them. Thus, the cost per crime investigated, the cost per highway project design completed, the cost per AIDS seminar conducted, the cost per ton of residential refuse collected, and the cost per training program completed are all standard efficiency measures. In the case of air traffic control, productivity could be measured in terms of the number of flight segments handled per controller hour, and operating efficiency could be measured by the cost per flight segment handled.

It may be appropriate to track a variety of efficiency measures for a given program. For example, the cost per psychiatric assessment completed, the cost per detoxification procedure conducted, the cost per therapy session conducted, and the cost per support group meeting might all be relevant for a crisis stabilization unit, *if* it has an activity-based accounting system that can track the actual costs for these separate activities. Often more general measures are employed, such as the cost per highway lane-mile maintained or the cost per case in a child support enforcement program, but they are really based more on workload than outputs. One particular efficiency measure that is often used along these lines is the per diem, the cost per client per day in such "residential" programs as hospitals, crisis stabilization units, juvenile detention centers, and group homes for mentally disabled persons.

Service Quality Measures

The concept of quality pertains most directly to service delivery processes and outputs, because they define the service that is being provided. When we think about measuring outputs we tend to think first of quantity, *how much* service is being provided, but it is equally important to examine the *quality* of outputs as well. However, this is not primarily a distinction between "hard" and "soft" measures. Although service quality is usually assessed subjectively at an individual level, performance measurement systems track quality using more objective, quantitative data in the aggregate.

The most common dimensions of the quality of public and nonprofit services include turnaround time, accuracy, thoroughness, accessibility, convenience, courtesy, and safety. For example, people who are trying to renew their driver's licenses tend to be most concerned about the accessibility of the location where they do this, the convenience afforded in completing the process, the total time including waiting time that it takes to complete the transaction, and, of course, the accuracy of the paperwork that is processed (so that they won't have to return or to repeat part of the process). In the FAA's air traffic control program, the most important indicator of service quality is the number of "controller errors" per million flight segments handled, instances in which controllers allow pilots to breach minimum distances to be maintained between airplanes.

Frequently measures of service quality are based on standard operating procedures that are prescribed for service delivery processes. Quality ratings of highway maintenance crews, for instance, are usually defined by the extent to which the establishment of the work site, handling of traffic through or around the work site, and the actual work of patching potholes or resurfacing pavement comply with prescribed operating procedures for such jobs. Juvenile justice detention centers have operating procedures regarding such processes as safety inspections, fire prevention, key control, perimeter checks, the security of eating utensils, supervision, and the progressive use of physical force or chemical agents in order to ensure the security of the facility and the safety of the juveniles in their custody. Quality assurance ratings are really compliance measures, defined as the extent to which such processes are performed in compliance with prescribed procedures. Yet other quality indicators, such as the number of escapes or reported instances of child abuse, probably more meaningful in terms of overall program performance, are defined more directly in terms of a desired output, which in this example is juveniles detained safely and securely.

Effectiveness Measures

It is probably fair to say that effectiveness measures constitute the single most important category of performance measures because they represent the degree to which a program is producing its intended outcomes and achieving the desired results. These may relate to initial, intermediate, or longer-term outcomes. Effectiveness measures for the air traffic control program, for example, might include the number of "near misses" reported by pilots, the number of midair collisions, and the number of fatalities per one hundred million revenue passenger-miles flown.

The most important effectiveness measures tie back to the basic purpose of a given program. For example, the crisis stabilization unit exists to stabilize persons with psychiatric or drug-induced mental crises and help them modify behaviors in order to avoid falling into these same circumstances again. Thus, a key effectiveness measure might be the percentage of all initial admissions that constitute readmissions within thirty days. Similarly, the most important indicator of the effectiveness of a vocational rehabilitation program is probably the number or percentage of clients who have been successfully employed in the same job for six months. Along these same lines, the most relevant effectiveness measures for a juvenile detention center are probably the percentage of discharged youth who are attending school or engaged in gainful employment and the percentage who have not recidivated back into the criminal justice system within one year of having been discharged. Effectiveness measures for an AIDS prevention program would be likely to include morbidity and mortality rates for AIDS, along with the percentage of newborn babies who test positive for HIV.

Cost-Effectiveness Measures

Whereas indicators of operating efficiency are unit costs of producing outputs, cost-effectiveness measures relate cost to outcome measures. Thus, for the crisis stabilization unit, cost-effectiveness would be measured as the cost per stabilized consumer. For the vocational rehabilitation program, the most relevant indicators of cost-effectiveness would be the cost per client placed in suitable employment and the cost per client successfully employed for six months or more. The cost-effectiveness of criminal investigation activity would probably be measured as the cost per crime solved. Effectiveness measures often become more esoteric and present more difficult methodological challenges in operationalizing indicators. For example, the cost-effectiveness of highway construction might well be conceptualized as the cost per person-hour of reduced travel time, and the most relevant cost-effectiveness indicator for an AIDS prevention program would probably be the cost per AIDS fatality avoided. Both of these make complete sense in terms of program logic, but they would be difficult to operationalize.

Customer Satisfaction Measures

Measures of customer satisfaction are often closely related to service quality indicators, but the two are not identical and should be considered as separate categories of performance measures. Similarly, customer satisfaction measures are often associated with effectiveness measures, but they provide a different perspective on overall program performance. For example, measures of customer satisfaction with a vocational rehabilitation program might be based on data from client evaluation forms asking how satisfied they were with training programs they participated in, counseling services they received, and assistance that was provided in finding a job. These all focus on program outputs. In addition, clients who have been placed in jobs might be surveyed after several months to assess their satisfaction with these jobs, focusing on real program effectiveness. These customer satisfaction ratings may or may not square with more tangible measures of program outputs and effectiveness, but they do provide a complementary perspective.

One way of gauging customer satisfaction is to track complaints. For example, a public library system might monitor the number of complaints received from patrons per week in each branch library. Some public and nonprofit agencies use customer response cards to solicit immediate feedback regarding specific instances of service delivery. A government printing office, for instance, might track the percentage of their customers who rate their products as good or excellent. Probably the most frequently used means of soliciting customer feedback is the customer survey; for example, crime victims might be asked to report whether or not they were satisfied with the initial police response to their case. Similarly, a crisis stabilization unit might track the percentage of consumers rating their services as good or excellent; a highway maintenance operation might estimate the percentage of motorists who are satisfied or very satisfied with the condition of the roads they use.

Integrated Sets of Measures

Indicators in each of the categories discussed in this chapter can potentially be identified to measure the performance of most programs provided by governmental and nonprofit organizations. For example, Exhibit 3.1 illustrates the kind of performance measures that might be appropriate for monitoring the performance of the teen mother parenting education program discussed earlier. These measures are derived directly from the program logic model presented in Figure 3.5. The program outputs are the number of courses conducted and the number of participants completing the program. Thus, operating efficiency would be measured by the cost per course conducted, the cost per institutional hour and per counseling hour, and the cost per participant completing the program. Labor productivity could be measured by the number of pregnant teens completing the program per staff hour invested in its delivery.

EXHIBIT 3.1. TEEN MOTHER
PARENTING EDUCATION PERFORMANCE MEASURES.

Outputs

Number of prenatal classes conducted

Hours of instruction in prenatal classes

Number of infant care classes conducted

Hours of instruction in infant care classes

Number of participants completing prenatal classes

Numbers of participants completing infant care classes

Hours of counseling provided to pregnant teens

Hours of counseling provided to mothers of infants

Operating Efficiency

Cost per course completed

Cost per instructional hour

Cost per pregnant teen completing the program

Cost per counseling hour

Labor Productivity

Number of pregnant teens completing program per staff hour invested

Service Quality

Course evaluation ratings by participants

Effectiveness

Test scores regarding prenatal care and the care and feeding of and interaction with babies

Percentage of participants who eat at least four calcium servings and one serving of each of the other nutritional food groups daily

Percentage of participants who do not smoke

Percentage of participants who take a prenatal vitamin daily

Percentage of participants within proper ranges for prenatal weight gain

Percentage of newborn babies weighing at least 5.5 pounds and scoring 7 or above on the Apgar scale

Percentage of attendees observed to provide proper care and feeding of and interaction with babies

Percentage of attendees' babies clinically evaluated as achieving appropriate twelve-month milestones

Cost-Effectiveness

Cost per healthy baby achieving appropriate twelve-month milestones

Customer Satisfaction

Percentage of program completers reporting satisfaction with program after babies are born

Service quality might be measured by some professional assessment of the quality of the materials used in the course, teaching techniques employed, and the actual delivery of the course, or, as suggested in the previous list, we might rely on course evaluations from program participants.

Numerous effectiveness measures are shown because the program logic model shows two strands of results with multiple outcome stages in each. So the effectiveness measures include scores on tests regarding the kind of knowledge the program is designed to impart, the percentage of participants delivering healthy babies, the percentage of participants reported to be providing proper care and feeding of and interaction with their babies, and the percentage of these babies achieving appropriate twelve-month developmental milestones. Cost-effectiveness measures might be defined by relating costs to any of these outcomes, but the most compelling ones might be the cost per healthy baby achieving appropriate twelve-month milestones and the cost per repeat premature pregnancy avoided. Finally, the most meaningful indicator of customer satisfaction might be the percentage of those teens completing the program who report overall satisfaction with it at some time well after their babies have been born.

Developing Logic Models

Obviously, a critical first step in developing performance measures for public and nonprofit programs is to identify *what* should be measured. The program logic models presented in this chapter encourage focusing on end results—the real outcomes that a program is supposed to generate—and the outputs or immediate products that must be produced in order to bring about those results. Developing such logic models helps you identify what is important to measure.

How does one actually go about developing a logic model for a particular public or nonprofit program? Looking at formal statements of goals and objectives is a good place to begin, because they should articulate the kinds of outcomes that are expected to be produced. Because results-oriented management systems require performance measures that are directly tied to goals and objectives, we will look at this linkage in greater detail in Chapter Four. Beyond goal statements, program plans and other descriptions can provide the kind of information needed to flesh out a logic model.

Developing the model is often most successful when approached as a collaborative process, one that engages not only program managers but also employees, service delivery staff, consumers, agency clients, program advocates, and other concerned parties. Developing a logic model in this way may thus be an iterative process with a few rounds of review and revision. However, by building consensus on the model among these various stakeholders through such a process, you have greatly increased the probability that the performance measures derived from the model will be broadly supported.

Whatever approach you use in a particular performance measurement effort, the cardinal rule should be never to "bend" reality to fit a preconceived model. The model should only be thought of as a tool for understanding how the program is really intended to operate. Fortunately, the program logic methodologies presented here are very flexible and should be adaptable to almost any programmatic or organizational setting. Once you have developed the model, you can define appropriate measures of outputs, quality, efficiency, productivity, effectiveness, cost-effectiveness, and customer satisfaction with confidence.

CHAPTER FOUR

CLARIFYING PROGRAM GOALS AND OBJECTIVES

What are goals, objectives, and service standards? How should agency or program goals and objectives be stated so as to facilitate results-oriented management and performance measurement? How are goals and objectives related to performance indicators? This chapter discusses the kinds of goals and objectives used in public and nonprofit organizations; it also explores how performance measures are often derived from statements of goals and objectives and how sometimes the measures themselves are used to further specify goals statements.

Mission, Goals, and Objectives

Usually the most meaningful performance measures are derived from the mission, goals, objectives, and, sometimes, service standards that have been established for a particular program. This is because goals and objectives, and to a lesser extent mission and service standards, define the desired results to be produced by an agency or program. Thus, there is usually a very direct connection between goals and objectives on the one hand and outcomes or effectiveness measures on the other. Although it is often very useful to develop logic models to fully understand all the performance dimensions of a public or nonprofit program, depending on the purpose of the measurement system it is sometimes sufficient to clarify goals and objectives and then define performance measures to track their accomplishment.

It should be understood that there are no universal distinctions among these terms in the public management literature, and there is often considerable overlap among them, but the definitions used herein are workable and not severely incompatible with the distinctions made by others. *Mission* refers to the basic purpose of an organization or program, its reason for being, and the general means through which it accomplishes that purpose. *Goals* are general statements about the results to be produced by the program; *objectives* are more specific milestones to be achieved in order to accomplish the goals. Whereas goals are often formulated as very general, often timeless, sometimes idealized outcomes, objectives should be specified in more concrete terms, as will be seen in this chapter.

Strategic Framework: U.S. Department of Health and Human Services

The U.S. Department of Health and Human Services (DHHS) is a good example of a large federal department that has gone through the process of clarifying its mission, goals, objectives, and performance measures in compliance with the Government Performance and Results Act of 1993. The DHHS, with some fifty-nine thousand employees and an annual budget approaching $400 billion, manages more than three hundred programs in a wide variety of areas, such as medical and social science research, food and drug safety, financial assistance and health care for low-income individuals, child support enforcement, maternal and infant health, substance abuse treatment and prevention, and services for older Americans.

The department's formal mission statement is "To enhance the health and well-being of Americans by providing for effective health and human services and by fostering strong, sustained advances in the sciences underlying medicine, public health, and social services."

To pursue this mission, the DHHS has identified the six following strategic goals, which are formulated in very broad statements:

1. Reduce the major threats to the health and productivity of all Americans
2. Improve the economic and social well-being of individuals, families, and communities in the United States
3. Improve access to health services and ensure the integrity of the nation's health entitlement and safety net programs
4. Improve the quality of health care and human services
5. Improve the nation's public health systems
6. Strengthen the nation's health sciences research enterprise and enhance its productivity

For each of these strategic goals, the DHHS has defined a number of supporting objectives that are somewhat more targeted and specific in terms of desired behaviors, conditions, or circumstances. With respect to goal 1, for example, to reduce the major threats to the health and productivity of all Americans, objectives have been set as follows:

Objective 1.1: Reduce tobacco abuse, especially among youth

Objective 1.2: Reduce the incidence and impact of injuries and violence in American society

Objective 1.3: Improve the diet and level of physical activity of Americans

Objective 1.4: Reduce alcohol abuse and prevent underage drinking

Objective 1.5: Reduce the abuse and illicit use of drugs

Objective 1.6: Reduce unsafe sexual behaviors

Objective 1.7: Reduce the incidence and impact of infectious diseases

Objective 1.8: Reduce the impact of environmental factors on human health

As will be seen in subsequent chapters, performance measurement is often a process of sequential specification from very general goals to specific indicators. The challenge is often to ensure that the operational indicators that measure particular kinds of results do in fact represent the kinds of outcomes intended by the general goals. The eight objectives supporting goal 1 are still quite general statements of intended accomplishments, but they are clearly more focused indications of intended results that are tied directly to the goals.

In the next step in the sequence, each objective is fleshed out with multiple performance indicators, as illustrated in Table 4.1 for objective 1.3, improving the diet and level of physical activity of Americans. Data sources are provided for each measure, along with the most current estimate of performance and the level targeted for the year 2010. For example, one indicator that might reflect the influence of both diet and physical exercise is the proportion of Americans defined as being obese; the data would be taken from the National Health and Nutrition Examination Survey conducted by the Centers for Disease Control. For persons over twenty years old, the current estimate is that 23 percent are obese, whereas the target for 2010 is to bring that figure down to 15 percent. Obviously, each of these five performance indicators represents one "slice" or dimension of this particular objective, one perspective on what the results should look like. All five indicators are clearly aligned with the objective of improving Americans' diets and physical activity levels, and collectively they are intended to provide a balanced perspective on whether and the extent to which progress is made in accomplishing this objective over time.

Primary and Intermediate Goals: Highway Safety Programming

The National Highway Traffic Safety Administration (NHTSA) is responsible for reducing deaths, injuries, and economic losses resulting from motor vehicle crashes on the nation's highways. To accomplish this mission, the NHTSA sets and enforces safety standards for motor vehicle equipment and provides grants to state and local governments to enable them to conduct effective highway safety programs. As summarized in the outline that follows (adapted from Faigin, Dion, and Tanham, n.d.), its strategic plan articulates what it calls primary goals and intermediate goals and establishes indicators for measuring effectiveness in attaining them.

TABLE 4.1. STRATEGIC OBJECTIVES AND PERFORMANCE MEASURES: U.S. DEPARTMENT OF HEALTH AND HUMAN SERVICES.

Goal 1:   Reduce the major threats to the health and productivity of all Americans
Objective 1.3:   Improve the diet and level of physical activity of Americans

Indicators	Data Sources	Current (%)	2010 Target (%)
Proportion of Americans age 18 and over reporting engaging in physical activity five times a week for at least 30 minutes per time	National Health Interview Survey (CDC) HP2010	23	30
Proportion of Americans defined as obese (by age group)	National Health and Nutrition Examination Survey (CDC) HP2010	23 ($\geq$20 yrs.) 11 (6–19 yrs.)	15 5
Percentage of persons consuming fruits/vegetables five times per day	Behavioral Risk Factor Surveillance System (CDC) HP2010	15.5	62.5
Proportion of adults who report changes in their decisions to buy or use a food product because they read the food label	Consumers Surveys and Reports (Food and Drug Administration) APP	DNA	
Number of home-delivered meals	State Data Report APP	DNA	

Note: CDC = Centers for Disease Control; APP = Annual Performance Plan; HP2010 = Healthy People 2010.
Source: U.S. Department of Health and Human Services, 2000.

Highway Safety Goals and Performance Measures

I. Primary Outcomes and Measures
  A. To save lives on the nation's highways
    • Fatalities per 100 million vehicle miles traveled (VMT)
    • Fatalities per 100,000 population
  B. To prevent injuries on the nation's highways
    • Number of injured persons per 100 million VMT
    • Number of injured persons per 100,000 population
II. Intermediate Outcomes and Measures
  A. To reduce the occurrence of crashes (crash avoidance)
    • Number of crashes per 100 million VMT
    • Number of crashes per 100,000 registered vehicles
    • Number of drivers involved in crashes per 100,000 licensed drivers
    • Number of crashes with alcohol involvement per 100,000 licensed drivers
  B. To reduce the consequences of crashes (crashworthiness)
    • Fatalities per 1,000 crashes
    • Injuries per 1,000 crashes
    • Percentage of serious and greater injuries in towaway crashes
  C. To improve safety in key traffic segments
    • Motorcyclist fatalities per 100 million VMT
    • Motorcyclist injuries per 100 million VMT
    • Bicyclist fatalities per 100,000 population
    • Bicyclist injuries per 100,000 population
    • Pedestrian fatalities per 100,000 population
    • Pedestrian injuries per 100,000 population

As the outline shows, the primary goals (or what we referred to as long-term goals in the program logic models presented in Chapter Three) are to save lives and to prevent injuries. Overall performance in achieving these two outcomes is measured by the number of fatalities per 100 million VMT and the number of fatalities per 100,000 population, and the number of injuries per 100 million vehicle miles and per 100,000 population, respectively.

The intermediate goals that have to be targeted in order to achieve the longer-term goals are reducing the occurrence of crashes, reducing the consequences of crashes, and improving safety in key traffic segments. Again, multiple performance indicators have been developed for each of these goals.

Similar performance measures regarding fatalities and injuries involving motorcyclists, bicyclists, and pedestrians are also incorporated in this measurement system. Working further "backwards" in the program logic, the NHTSA also tracks such initial outcomes as the percentage of drivers and occupants using seat belts, as well as such program output measures as DUI laws passed, seat belt laws legislated in the states, crash avoidance and crashworthiness investigations concluded, automobile manufacturer recall campaigns, and crash avoidance products resulting from research and development efforts.

SMART Objectives

Program objectives should specify milestones to be attained within certain time periods, but in practice, statements of objectives are often overly general, vague, and open-ended in terms of time. Such poorly written objectives fail to convey any management commitment to achieve particular results, and they provide little guidance for defining meaningful measures to assess performance. Truly useful program objectives can be developed using the SMART convention; such objectives are **s**pecific in terms of the results to be achieved, **m**easurable, **a**mbitious but **r**ealistic, and **t**ime-bound (Broom, Harris, Jackson, and Marshall, 1998).

With respect to highway traffic safety programming, for example, the objective of reducing the number of highway accident fatalities down to no more than 15 per 100,000 U.S. residents by the year 2001 would be a SMART objective. Similarly, a SMART objective for a metropolitan public transit system might be to increase revenue-generating passenger trips by 25 percent over the next five years; a SMART objective for a community crime prevention program might be to reduce the number of reported burglaries by 10 percent over the next year; a SMART objective of a Big Brothers/Big Sisters program might be to increase by 20 percent over the next two years the number of youth in mentoring relationships with adults who have completed the prescribed training.

Performance Targets: Aviation Safety

As we have seen, SMART objectives provide a clear definition of the tangible results to be accomplished and are often accompanied by an indication of the specific measures that will be used to evaluate success or failure in achieving them. They also set targets in terms of how much impact is to be achieved within a given time frame. For example, the Federal Aviation Administration has established four goals for aviation safety, as described in Table 4.2. In this particular framework, the performance measures are defined precisely, and the objectives are actually specified as fiscal year 1999 targets or goals. (This example illustrates the lack of consistency in the use of such terms as *goals, objectives, targets,* and *standards,* which exists throughout the field, but it nevertheless also represents the implicit use of SMART objectives.) The data also show actual 1999 performance on these four outcomes as compared with the targets, along with the summary assessment that in this case none of these goals were in fact achieved in 1999.

TABLE 4.2. GOALS AND
PERFORMANCE MEASURES FOR AVIATION SAFETY, 1999.

Performance Measure	Fiscal Year 1999 Goal	Fiscal Year 1999 Performance	Goal Achieved?
Number of fatal aviation accidents for U.S. commercial air carriers per 100,000 flight hours	0.034 accidents per 100,000 flight hours	0.04 accidents per 100,000 flight hours	No
Number of dangerous incidents on airport runways (runway incursions)	270 incidents	322 incidents	No
Number of errors in maintaining safe separation between aircraft per 100,000 activities*	0.496 errors per 100,000 activities	0.57 errors per 100,000 activities	No
Number of deviations—that is, when an aircraft enters airspace without prior coordination—per 100,000 activities	0.099 deviations per 100,000 activities	0.18 deviations per 100,000 activities	No

*"Activities" are total FAA facility activities, as defined in *Aviation System Indicators 1997 Annual Report.* An example of an activity is an air traffic controller's providing guidance to a pilot who needs to make an instrument landing.

Setting Targets: Arizona and New Mexico Transportation Departments

Although most performance measurement systems establish target levels to be achieved for each indicator, some systems purposefully do not do so. The decision as to whether or not to set targets depends on the purpose of the measurement system and the management philosophy in the organization. For example, the Arizona Department of Transportation monitors the performance on a variety of indicators at five levels in the organization, from the "enterprise" level, reporting data on a few key measures to the governor's office on a monthly basis, down to performance indicators that have been tailored for individual work units. Consistent with a traditional results-oriented management approach, targets are set for each measure, and performance is evaluated in terms of the extent to which they are achieved.

The New Mexico State Highway and Transportation Department (NMSH&TD) tracks eighty-three indicators of performance in terms of seventeen key results in its Compass system, which is really the driving force of management and decision making in the department. However, in keeping with the continuous improvement philosophy underlying the department's quality improvement program, from which the Compass evolved, the NMSH&TD, unlike the Arizona Department of Transportation, prefers not to establish targets on these measures. This policy is based on the belief that targets can have "ceiling effects" and actually inhibit improvement rather than provide incentives to strengthen performance. Thus, the implicit objective is to continuously improve performance on these measures over time.

Nevertheless, the dominant approach in public and nonprofit organizations is to set targets and then measure performance in accomplishing them. How, then, are such targets established? How do managers arrive at targets of a 25 percent increase in transit ridership, a 10 percent decrease in burglaries, or a 20 percent increase in mentoring relationships with at-risk youth? There are at least three ways of approaching the issue:

Past Trends Approach. The most common approach is to look at current performance levels on the indicators of interest, along with the past trends leading up to these current levels, and then set targets that represent some reasonable degree of improvement over current performance. Current performance levels often serve as an appropriate point of departure, but in a less than stellar agency they may underrepresent the possibilities, so the question to ask is, To what degree should we be able to improve above where we are now?

Production Function Approach. A second approach is to analyze the service delivery process, assess the production possibilities, and determine what level of performance can reasonably be expected, given constraints on the system. The analysis might be performed for subunits and then rolled up to the agency or program as a whole. This "production function" approach works particularly well for setting output targets to be achieved by a production process, but it may be less helpful in setting appropriate targets for real outcomes when precise relationships between outputs and outcomes are not clearly understood.

Benchmarking Approach. Setting appropriate targets may be informed by comparative performance data on other similar agencies or programs. Benchmarking performance against other entities, as discussed in Chapter Thirteen, can help identify norms for public service industries as well as "star performers" in the field, which can be helpful in setting targets for a particular program or agency. A major challenge in using the benchmarking approach is to find truly comparable programs or agencies in the first place, or to make adjustments for differences in operating conditions in interpreting the performance of other entities as the basis for setting targets for a particular program or agency.

◆ ◆ ◆

Whichever of these approaches you use, the targets that you establish may represent current performance levels or, more than likely, incremental or even dramatic improvement above current performance. As suggested by the SMART acronym, it is desirable to set targets that are relatively ambitious, or "stretch" objectives, but that are also realistically achievable. Very modest targets do not challenge people to work harder and smarter to improve performance significantly, and overly aggressive targets tend to preordain failure and set up disincentives for working toward improved performance in the long run. Thus, finding a happy medium in setting targets often requires a careful assessment and sound judgment.

Results and Targets: United Way of Metropolitan Atlanta

It is becoming increasingly common for public and nonprofit agencies to set target levels for desirable outcomes identified through their strategic planning processes. Particularly when an agency has a wide variety of programs to manage, summarizing expected results and associated targets helps provide a strategic view of its portfolio of activities. Table 4.3, for example, shows desired outcomes targeted by the United Way of Metropolitan Atlanta in the areas of nurturing children and youth, strengthening families, economic self-sufficiency, and citizen involvement. Whereas the outcomes in the left-hand column are extremely general, the target levels in the right-hand column are very specific in terms of the nature of the expected results, the magnitude of impact, and, in several cases, a target year.

TABLE 4.3. RESULTS AND TARGETS: UNITED WAY OF METROPOLITAN ATLANTA.

Results	Targets
Nurturing Children and Youth Outcomes	
1. Affordable, quality preschool and child care	A. Approximately 20,000 new licensed or registered child-care spaces for 0–4 year-olds in working-parent households by 2005 B. 300 new accredited child-care centers by 2005 C. 250 accredited family child-care providers by 2005
2. Safe, productive, structured group activities outside of school hours	A. *Number of safe, structured and productive out-of-school slots and activities*
3. Parents involved in their children's education	A. Move from 33.1% to 28% of middle school students missing ten or more days B. Move from 39.6% to 32% of high school students missing ten or more days
4. Positive aspirations for the future and a belief they can attain them	A. Percentage of youth who remain stable one year after transitioning out of foster care (twice the baseline but not less than 50%) B. Move from 5.5% to 4.5% of students dropping out in grades 9–12

TABLE 4.3. RESULTS AND TARGETS:
UNITED WAY OF METROPOLITAN ATLANTA, Cont'd.

Results	Targets
Strengthening Families Outcomes	
5. Parenting skills and knowledge	A. 3,000 parents will increase their parenting knowledge and/or skills through UW-facilitated partnerships and initiatives by 2003 B. Move from 4,659 to 4,300 the number of substantiated child abuse cases
6. Problem resolution and coping skills	A. *Reduction in the number of inpatient days spent for mental health reasons* B. *Reduction in the number of emergency room visits due to mental health reasons*
Economic Self-Sufficiency Outcomes	
7. Skills developed to meet job market demand (Results 7 and 8 are linked) 8. Jobs that are retained and pay a living wage	A. 90% of graduates from United Way partner programs that are not placed in jobs will receive a documented referral to next stage of workforce development B. 700 low-income participants will be trained and placed in living wage jobs by United Way partner programs by 2003 (at least 50% of graduates) C. 85% of United Way partner job training program graduates placed at a living wage will retain at least a living wage for 60 days and 80% for 180 days
9. Neighborhood-based micro-enterprise and small business ownership	A. 600 graduates of micro-enterprise programs by 2003 B. 360 micro-enterprise businesses operating after three months of start-up by 2003 (while maintaining a 78% success rate) C. *Number of program graduates who experience a positive increase in personal income between program entry and one year after graduation* D. *Number of graduates who experience a positive increase in sales between program entry and one year after graduation*
Citizen Involvement Outcomes	
10. Affordable home ownership	A. 220 participants buy homes B. 330 participants in IDA initiative C. *Proportion of single-family homes in targeted neighborhoods that are owner-occupied*
11. Residents feel safe	A. *Number of residents feeling very safe out alone during the day* B. *Number of residents feeling very safe out alone at night*
12. Residents involved in neighborhood and civic issues	A. *Number of individuals calling 211 and other civic involvement partners who are successful in becoming involved in neighborhood and civic issues*

Source: United Way of Metropolitan Atlanta Indicators and Targets Chart (approved by the UW Board 02/21/01). Used by permission of United Way of Metropolitan Atlanta.

It is apparent that at least some of these targets were established based on incremental improvements over current performance levels—for example, with respect to the indicators linked to the goal of getting parents more involved in their children's education, as well as the target regarding the number of substantiated cases of child abuse, which is identified as an indicator of the desired outcome regarding the development of parenting skills and knowledge. Other targets, such as the one for achieving six hundred graduates of micro-enterprise programs by 2003, may have been based on programming levels planned by the agency. Some of these targets may have been established on the basis of the results accomplished in other comparable metropolitan areas around the country; for other expected results shown in Table 4.3, specific indicators and associated target levels have not yet been resolved, although preliminary definitions of the measures (shown in italics) have been developed.

Performance Standards and Service Standards

Further complicating the lexicon surrounding goals, objectives, and targets is the term *standards*. It is often used interchangeably with targets, but to some people standards refer to more routine performance expectations that are fairly constant over time, whereas targets may be changed more frequently as actual and potential trends change over time.

Performance standards, then, tend to relate to programmatic or agency outcomes, whereas service standards refer more often to internal service delivery processes.

Performance Standards: Child Support Enforcement

Consider the child support enforcement program operated by a state's department of human resources or social services. The mission of this program is to help families rise or remain out of poverty and reduce their potential dependency on public assistance, through the systematic enforcement of noncustodial parents' responsibility to provide financial support for their children. Figure 4.1 presents the logic model for this program, working through three basic components designed to obligate support payments by absentee parents, collect payments that are obligated, and assist absentee parents, if necessary, to secure employment so that they are financially able to make support payments. The logic moves through locating absentee parents, establishing paternity when necessary, and obtaining court orders to obligate support payments, as well as helping absentee parents to earn wages, but the bottom line is collecting payments and disbursing them to custodial parents to ensure that children receive adequate financial support.

FIGURE 4.1. CHILD SUPPORT ENFORCEMENT PROGRAM LOGIC MODEL.

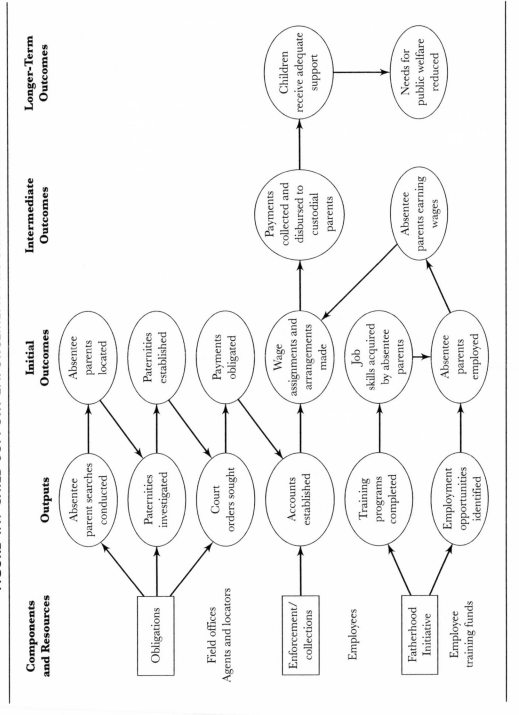

The following performance standards have been established for this program:

1. Establishing paternity for at least 80 percent of the children in the program's caseload who were born out of wedlock
2. Obligating support payments for at least 50 percent of the total number of cases
3. Keeping the cases that are in arrears in making payments to less than 50 percent
4. Collecting at least 40 percent of all the support that has been obligated

All four of these performance standards tie directly to initial, intermediate, or longer-term outcomes as specified in the program logic model. Although these standards might appear to be quite modest to the uninitiated, they are considered to be fairly ambitious by this particular agency, given current performance levels and the difficulties in tracking down some absentee parents, establishing paternity, securing court orders, and actually collecting payments.

In any case, these standards along with the program logic model suggest the kinds of performance measures shown in the following list:

Performance Measures for a Child Support Enforcement Program

- Productivity
  Noncustodial searches per locator
  Active cases maintained per agent
- Operating efficiency
  Cost per paternity investigation completed
  Cost per account established
  Cost per noncustodial parent completing training program
- Service quality/Customer service
  Percentage of custodial parents satisfied with assistance
- Effectiveness
  Percentage of children in caseload born out of wedlock with paternity established
  Percentage of total cases with support payments obligated
  Percentage of noncustodial parents earning wages
  Percentage of cases in arrears
  Percentage of obligated support collected
- Cost-effectiveness
  Total collections per $1 expenditure

The productivity measures shown include the number of noncustodial searches conducted per locator staff as well as the number of active cases maintained per child support enforcement agent, although the latter might well be considered to be more of a workload measure. The efficiency measures represent unit costs of such outputs as paternity investigations conducted, accounts established, and training programs completed. The one service quality indicator shown is actually a customer service indicator, the percentage of custodial parents who report being satisfied with the assistance they have received.

The most relevant effectiveness measures directly represent the performance standards shown earlier, including the percentage of caseload children born out of wedlock who have paternity established, the percentage with support payments obligated, the percentage of absentee parents earning wages, the percentage of cases in arrears on making payments, and the percentage of all obligated support that is collected. The percentage of noncustodial parents who are earning wages tracks the effectiveness of the fatherhood initiative. And, because the bottom line in terms of outcomes is measured by the dollar value of support payments collected, the most direct measure of cost-effectiveness is the value of total collections per $1 program expenditure.

Service Standards: A State Government's Office Supply Support Service

Service standards are specific performance criteria that are intended to be attained on an ongoing basis. They usually refer to characteristics of the service delivery process, service quality, or productivity in producing outputs. In some cases, service standards are distinct from a program's objectives, but probably more often service standards and objectives are synonymous or closely related. In any case, if there is not a clear sense about what a program's mission, goals, objectives, and perhaps service standards are, it is important to clarify them before attempting to identify meaningful measures of the program's performance.

The mission of a state government's office supply support service, for example, might be stated as follows: "To meet the needs of all state agencies, school districts, and local government jurisdictions for office supplies and other materials on a timely basis." At a particular point in time, its principal goals might be to improve service quality and maintain its market share in a competitive business environment. A supporting objective might be to increase the number of customer orders coming in to the central supply warehouse by 10 percent over the next year. The program might establish the following kinds of service standards:

- To deliver all shipments within three working days of receipt of orders
- To fill at least 95 percent of all orders completely in the first shipment (with no items on back order)
- To fill at least 99 percent of all orders correctly in the first shipment

A related productivity standard might be to ship twenty product lines per employee per hour.

These standards might be considered to be the objectives of the program, or there might be other objectives, such as increasing to 85 percent the percentage of customers indicating on response cards that they were satisfied with the service they received during the next year. Alternatively, if the program has only been achieving a "fill rate" of 80 percent, a key objective might be to raise it to 90 percent during the next year and achieve the standard of 95 percent by the following year. However mission, goals, objectives, and service or performance standards are configured, understanding what a program is supposed to accomplish can help tremendously in identifying critical performance measures.

Programmatic Versus Managerial Goals and Objectives

To be useful, performance measures should focus on whatever kinds of results managers want to accomplish. From a "purist" program evaluation perspective, appropriate measures are usually seen as focusing on programmatic goals and objectives, the real outcomes produced by programs and organizations "out in the field." However, from a practical managerial perspective, performance measures focusing on implementation goals and the production of outputs are often equally important. Thus, public and nonprofit organizations often combine programmatic or outcome-based goals and objectives along with more managerial or output-based goals and objectives in the same performance management systems.

Both programmatic and managerial objectives should be stated as SMART objectives and tracked with appropriate performance measures. For example, the programmatic objectives of a community crime prevention program might be to reduce person crimes by 20 percent and property crimes by 25 percent in one year along with the goal of having at least 90 percent of all residents feeling safe and secure in their own neighborhoods. These outcomes could be monitored with basic reported crime statistics and an annual neighborhood survey. More managerial objectives might include the initial implementation of community policing activities within the first six months and the start-up of at least twenty-five neighborhood watch groups within the first year. These outputs could be tracked through internal reporting systems.

An example of an organization's setting meaningful goals, service standards, and management objectives is a state workers' compensation program. All governmental jurisdictions maintain workers' compensation programs to ensure that employees who are injured in the course of their work are provided with appropriate medical treatment and, if necessary, rehabilitation services, time off from work, and other benefits as required by law. Figure 4.2 illustrates the underlying logic of a state government's workers' compensation program, which in addition to claims processing promotes safety in the workplace and emphasizes injured employees' returning to work as soon as practicable. From the state's point of view, the critical outcomes are that employees recover from their injuries and return to their work sites and regular jobs so that lost work days and operational disruptions are minimized. From the injured employees' perspective, the critical outcomes are not only that they recover from their injuries and return to work but also that financial support is provided if extended or even permanent absences from work are necessary.

The following list shows the goals, service standards, and management objectives that have been developed for this program:

Standards and Objectives for a Workers' Compensation Program

- Program goals
    - To promote safety programs in state government and assist state agencies in their efforts to prevent on-the-job employee injuries
    - To provide for proper and timely processing of workers' compensation claims in order to ensure that injured employees receive appropriate medical treatments, rehabilitation services, and other benefits as required by law
    - To implement a return-to-work program in order to facilitate the return of injured employees to productive work in their agencies as soon as practically possible
- Service standards
    - To file WC-1 reports (first reports of injuries) for all lost time claims to the State Workers' Compensation Board within twenty-one days of the date the employer becomes aware of injuries
    - To pay all workers' compensation lost time benefits that are approved within twenty-one working days of the date the employer becomes aware of injuries
    - To pay all medical bills associated with workers' compensation claims within sixty days of receipt of acceptable invoices
- Management objectives
    - To reduce the number of late WC-1 filings by 30 percent from last year
    - To maintain or improve on current caseloads by closing at least as many claims each month as the number of new cases created
    - To reduce the total cost of workers' compensation claims by 15 percent from last year through contracting with a managed care organization
    - To reduce lost time days by at least 15 percent annually through the implementation of an aggressive return-to-work program

FIGURE 4.2. STATE WORKERS' COMPENSATION PROGRAM LOGIC MODEL.

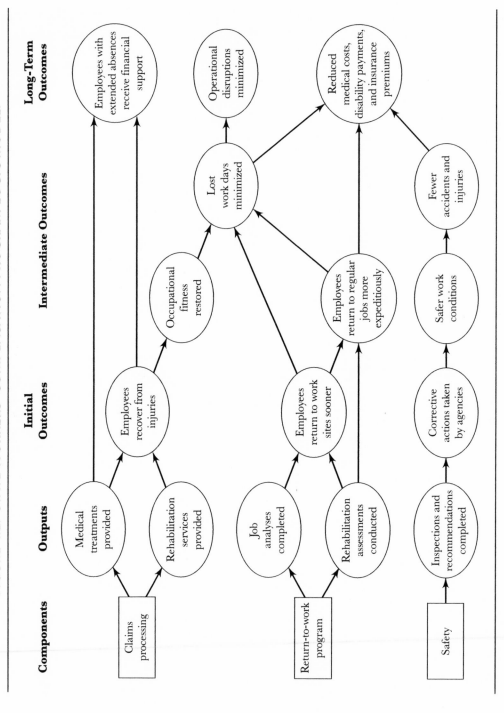

Of particular interest here are the objectives. Whereas the goals are appropriately more general, and the service standards are routine in a way, the objectives stated here call for specific changes in performance levels, for instance to reduce the number of late claim filings (a measure of output quality) by 30 percent from last year or to reduce the total cost of workers' compensation claims (a measure of operating efficiency) by 15 percent from last year. One objective focuses on managing workload by closing at least as many claims each month as the number of new cases opened; the last one focuses on a key measure of effectiveness: reducing the number of lost time days by at least 15 percent from last year through the implementation of an aggressive return-to-work program.

Given current performance levels in this particular agency, all four of these objectives are considered to be ambitious yet realistic, and they are all SMART objectives in terms of specifying the nature and magnitude of expected results within a particular time period. Straightforward performance indicators can be readily operationalized for each of these objectives, along with the service standards, and collectively they will provide management with a clear picture of the overall performance of this workers' compensation program.

Goals, Objectives, and Measures

In conclusion, managers need to forge close linkages between goals and objectives on one hand and performance measures on the other. It is critical to monitor measures of performance in terms of accomplishing outcome-oriented, programmatic objectives, but often it is important to track measures focused on the achievement of more managerially oriented objectives as well. In some instances, goals and objectives are stated in terms of the general kinds of results intended to be produced by programmatic activity; performance indicators must then be developed to track their achievement. In other cases, however, the objectives themselves are defined in terms of the measures that will be used to track results.

Sometimes performance standards or service standards are established and tracked independently; other times objectives or targets are set in terms of improving performance on those standards. Although there is not one right way to do it, the bottom line for results-oriented managers is to clearly define intended results through some mix of goals, objectives, standards, and targets and then track performance measures that are as closely aligned as possible with these results.

CHAPTER FIVE

DEFINING PERFORMANCE INDICATORS

O nce you have identified a program's intended outcomes and other performance criteria, how do you develop good measures of these things? What do useful performance indicators look like, and what are the characteristics of effective sets of performance measures? Where do you find the data to operationalize performance indicators? In order for monitoring systems to convey meaningful information about program performance, the measures used must be appropriate and meet the tests of sound measurement principles. This chapter begins to focus on the *how* of performance measurement: how to define measures of effectiveness, efficiency, productivity, quality, client satisfaction, and so forth that are valid, reliable, and truly useful.

Data Specification

Before we discuss the challenges of measurement issues per se, it may be helpful to picture the numerical or statistical forms in which performance indicators can be specified. The most common of these statistical formats—raw numbers, averages, percentages, ratios, rates, and indexes—provide options for defining indicators that best represent the performance dimensions to be measured.

Raw Numbers and Averages

Although some authorities on the subject might disagree, raw numbers often provide the most straightforward portrayal of certain performance measures. For example, program outputs are usually measured in raw numbers, and output targets are usually specified in raw numbers, such as the miles of shoulders to be regraded by a county highway maintenance program, the number of books circulated by a public library system, or the number of claims to be cleared each month by a state government's disability determination unit. Beyond outputs, effectiveness measures often track program outcomes in the form of raw numbers. For instance, a local economic development agency may track the number of new jobs created in the county or the net gain or loss in jobs at the end of a year; state environmental protection agencies monitor the number of ozone action alert days in their metropolitan areas.

Using raw numbers to measure outputs and outcomes has the advantage of portraying the actual scale of operations and impacts, and this is often what line managers are the most concerned with. In addition to programming and monitoring the number of vehicle-miles and vehicle-hours operated each month, for instance, a public transit system in a small urban area might set as a key marketing objective the attainment of a total ridership of more than two million passenger trips for the coming year. Although it might also be useful to measure the number of passenger trips per vehicle-mile or per vehicle-hour, the outcome measure of principal interest will be the raw number of passenger trips carried for the year. In fact, the transit manager might also examine the seasonal patterns over the past few years and then prorate the objective of two million passengers for the year into numerical ridership targets for each month. He or she would then track the number of passenger trips each month against those specific targets as the system's most direct outcome measure.

Sometimes, however, statistical averages can be used to summarize performance data and provide a clearer picture than raw numbers would. In an effort to improve customer service, for example, a state department of motor vehicles might monitor the mean average number of days required to process vehicle registration renewals by mail; a local public school system may track the average staff development hours engaged in by its teachers. Similarly, one measure of the effectiveness of an employment services program might be the median weekly wages earned by former clients who have entered the workforce; a public university system might track the effectiveness of its recruiting efforts by monitoring the median verbal and mathematics SAT scores of each year's freshman class. Such averages are more readily interpreted because they express the measure on a "typical case" basis rather than in the aggregate.

Percentages, Rates, and Ratios

Percentages, rates, and ratios are relational statistics that can often express performance measures in more meaningful context. *Percentages* can be especially useful in conveying the number of instances with desired outcomes, or "successes," as a share of a total number of cases—for example, the percentage of teen mothers in a parenting program who deliver healthy babies, the percentage of clients of a nonprofit agency working with persons with mental disabilities who are placed in competitive employment, and the percentage of those youths discharged from juvenile justice programs who don't recidivate back into the criminal justice system within six months.

Percentages can often be more definitive performance measures than averages, particularly when service standards or performance targets have been established. For instance, tracking the average number of days required to process vehicle registration renewals by mail can be a useful measure of service quality, but it doesn't provide an indication of the number of customers who do, or do not, receive satisfactory turnaround time. If a standard is set, however, say to process vehicle renewals within three working days, then the percentage of renewals actually processed within three working days is a much more informative measure of performance.

Expressing performance measures as *rates* helps put performance in perspective by relating it to some contextual measure representing exposure or potential. For instance, a neighborhood watch program created to reduce crime in inner-city neighborhoods might track the raw numbers of personal and property crimes reported from one year to the next. However, to interpret crime trends in the context of population size, the national Uniform Crime Reporting System tracks these statistics in terms of the number of homicides, assaults, robberies, burglaries, automobile thefts, and so on reported per 1,000 residents in a local jurisdiction. Similarly, the effectiveness of a birth control program in an overpopulated country with an underdeveloped economy might be monitored in terms of the number of births recorded per 1,000 females of childbearing age. Accident rates are usually measured in terms of exposure factors, such as the number of highway traffic accidents per 100 million vehicle-miles operated or the number of commercial airliner collisions per 100 million passenger miles flown. In monitoring the adequacy of health care resources in local communities, the Federal Health Care Financing Administration looks at such measures as the number of physicians per 1,000 population, the number of hospitals per 100,000 population, and the number of hospital beds per 1,000 population. Tracking such measures as rates helps interpret performance in a more meaningful context.

The use of *ratios* is very prevalent in performance measurement systems because they too express some performance dimension relative to some particular base. In particular, ratios lend themselves to efficiency, productivity, and cost-effectiveness measures because they are all defined in terms of input-output relationships. Operating efficiency is usually measured in terms of unit costs—for example, the cost per vehicle-mile in a transit system, the cost per detoxification procedure completed in a crisis stabilization unit, the cost per course conducted by a teen parenting program, and the cost per investigation completed by the U.S. Environmental Protection Agency. Similarly, productivity could be measured by such ratios as the tons of refuse collected per crew-day, the number of cases cleared per disability adjudicator, flight segments handled per air traffic controller, and the number of youths counseled per juvenile justice counselor. Cost-effectiveness measures are expressed in such ratios as the cost per client placed in competitive employment or the parenting program cost per healthy infant delivered.

Percentages, rates, and ratios are often preferred because they express some dimension of program performance within a relevant context. More important, however, they are useful because as relational measures they *standardize* the measure in terms of some basic factor, which in effect helps control for that factor in interpreting the results. As will be seen in Chapter Six, standardizing performance measures by expressing them as percentages, rates, and ratios also helps afford valid comparisons of performance over time, across subgroups, or between a particular agency and other similar agencies.

Indexes

An index is a scale variable that is computed by combining multiple measures or constituent variables into a single summary measure. For example, one way the Federal Reserve Board monitors the effectiveness of its monetary policies in preventing excessive inflation is the consumer price index (CPI), which is the calculated cost of purchasing a "standard" set of household consumer items in various markets around the country. Because indexes are derived by combining other indicators, scores, or repeated measures into a new scale, some of them seem quite abstract, but ranges or categories are often defined to help interpret the practical meaning of different scale values.

Indexes are used as performance measures in a variety of program areas. For instance the air quality index (AQI) is the standardized measure that state and local air pollution control programs use to monitor compliance with federal clean air standards and notify the public about levels of air pollution in their communities. State and local air monitoring stations and national air monitoring stations employ instruments called open path analyzers, which use ultraviolet, visible, or infrared light to measure concentrations of nitrogen dioxide, ozone, carbon monoxide, sulfur dioxide, and other gaseous pollutants in the air over a path of several meters up to several kilometers in length. In metropolitan areas, these measurements are taken daily and incorporated into formulas that are used to compute a value on the AQI, which ranges from 0 for pristine air, up to 500, which represents air pollution levels that would pose immediate danger to the public. For purposes of practical interpretation, the AQI is broken down into five categories: good, unhealthy for sensitive groups, unhealthy, very unhealthy, and hazardous.

The Adaptive Behavior Scale (ABS) is a standardized scale developed and updated by the American Association on Mental Retardation to assess the level of functioning of individuals with mental disabilities in two areas, personal independence and responsibility (Part 1) and social behaviors (Part 2). It is often used by public and nonprofit agencies working with people with mental impairments to assess their needs and to monitor the impact of various programs on clients' level of functioning. The overall scale consists of eighteen domains—for example, independent functioning, physical development, language development, self-direction, self-abusive behavior, and disturbing interpersonal behavior—which in turn have subdomains that are represented by a series of items. For example, one subdomain of the independent functioning domain concerns eating, and this is measured by four items focusing on the use of table utensils, eating in public, drinking, and table manners. The ABS is completed by a clinical examination or through a detailed interview with others who are familiar with the individual being assessed. Item points are summed for each domain and for the ABS as a whole, and the scores are converted to percentile ranks, standardized scores for persons with mental impairments (with a mean of 100), and age equivalency scores. Average ABS scores can also be used to track progress for groups of people, such as the clients of large residential facilities and programs that manage small community facilities for persons with developmental disabilities.

Indexes do not constitute a different type of statistical measure but rather are composite scales that represent the degree of some characteristic or condition. Thus, like other performance measures, they may be expressed as raw numbers, averages, or percentages. For example, a performance monitoring system might report the number of days with unhealthy air quality in Atlanta or the percentage of clients of a nonprofit agency in New Jersey whose adaptive behavior is in the "moderately independent" range.

◆ ◆ ◆

Many performance monitoring systems will include a mix of measures expressed in the various forms we've discussed here. For example, the following list, adapted from *Performance Measurement in State Departments of Transportation* (Poister, 1997), illustrates a sample of conventional measures used in tracking the performance of highway maintenance programs:

Illustrative Highway Maintenance Performance Measures

Performance Indicator	Performance Dimension	Statistical Form
Gallons of patching material applied	Resource	Raw number
Lane-miles resurfaced	Output	Raw number
Cost per lane-mile resurfaced	Operating efficiency	Ratio
Miles of shoulders graded per crew-day	Productivity	Ratio
Task hours completed per production hour	Productivity	Ratio
Mean quality assurance score	Quality	Average
Percentage of roads in compliance with AASHTO standards	Immediate outcome	Percentage
Average pavement quality index (PQI)	Immediate outcome	Median
Percentage of motorists rating ride quality as satisfactory	Customer satisfaction	Percentage
Customer Service Index (CSI)	Customer satisfaction	Raw number
Accidents per 100 million vehicle-miles with road condition as a contributing factor	Outcome	Rate

They include raw numbers of resource materials and outputs, ratios for efficiency and productivity indicators, mean average quality assurance scores, median PQI scores, percentages of satisfactory roads and satisfied customers, and accident rates related to road conditions.

Sources of Performance Data

The data used in performance measurement systems come from a wide variety of sources, and this has implications regarding the cost and effort of data collection and processing as well as quality and appropriateness. In some cases, appropriate data exist in files or systems that are used and maintained for other purposes, which then can be extracted or utilized for performance monitoring as well, whereas the data for other measures will have to be collected specifically for the purpose of performance measurement.

With regard to the highway maintenance measures shown in the preceding list, information on the gallons of patching material applied may be readily available from the highway department's inventory control system, and data on the number of lane-miles resurfaced, the miles of shoulders graded, and the actual task and production hours taken to complete these activities may be recorded in its maintenance management system. The cost of this work is tracked in the department's activity-based accounting system. The quality assurance scores are generated by teams of inspectors who "audit" a sample of completed maintenance jobs to assess compliance with prescribed procedures. The PQI and the percentage of roads in compliance with national American Association of State Highway and Transportation Officials (AASHTO) standards require a combination of mechanical measurements and physical inspection of highway condition and deficiencies. The percentage of motorists rating the roads as satisfactory may require a periodic mail-out survey of a sample of registered drivers. The accident rate data can probably be extracted from a data file on recorded traffic accidents maintained by the state police.

The categories of data shown in the following list are not intended to be exhaustive or mutually exclusive, but they do indicate major sources of performance data:

Sources of Performance Data

- Existing data compilations
- Clinical examinations
- Agency records
- Tests
- Administrative records
- Surveys
- Follow-up contacts
- Customer response cards
- Direct observation
- Specially designed instruments

Sometimes existing databases that are maintained by agencies for other purposes can meet selected performance measurement needs of particular programs. Many federal agencies maintain compilations of data on demographics, housing, crime, transportation, the economy, health, education, and the environment that may lend themselves to tracking the performance of a particular program. Many state government agencies and some nonprofit organizations maintain similar kinds of statistical databases, and a variety of ongoing social surveys and citizen polls also produce data that might be useful as performance measures.

Agency and Administrative Records

By far the most common source of performance data consists of agency records. Public and nonprofit agencies responsible for managing programs and delivering services tend to store transactional data that record the flow of cases through a program, the number of clients served, the number of projects completed, the number of services provided, treatment modules completed, staff-client interactions documented, referrals made, and so on. Much of this focuses on service delivery and outputs, but other transactional data maintained in agency records relate further down the output chain, regarding the disposition of cases, results achieved, or numbers of complaints received, for instance. In addition to residing in management information systems, these kinds of data are also found in service requests, activity logs, case logs, production records, records of permits issued and revoked, complaint files, incident reports, claims processing systems, and treatment and follow-up records, among other sources.

Beyond working with transactional data relating specifically to particular programs, you can also tap administrative data concerning personnel and expenditures, for example, to operationalize performance data. In some cases these administrative data may also be housed in the same programmatic agencies that are responsible for service delivery, but often they reside in central staff support units, such as personnel agencies, training divisions, budget offices, finance departments, accounting divisions, and planning and evaluation units. Sources of such administrative data might include time, attendance, and salary reports as well as budget and accounting systems and financial, performance, and compliance audits.

Follow-Up Contacts

In some program areas where the real outcomes are expected to materialize "outside the agency" and perhaps well after a program has been completed, it is necessary to make follow-up contacts with clients to track effectiveness. Often this can be accomplished through the context of follow-up services. For example, after juvenile offenders are released from boot camp programs operated by a state's Department of Juvenile Justice, the department may also provide aftercare services in which counselors work with these youths to help them readjust to their home or community settings; encourage them to engage seriously in school, work, or other wholesome activities; and try to help them stay away from further criminal activity. Through the follow-up contacts, the counselors are also able to keep track of the juveniles' status in terms of involvement in gainful activity versus recidivism. Many kinds of human service programs—vocational rehabilitation and teen parenting education programs, for instance—use similar kinds of follow-up contacts with clients as a source of data on program outcomes. In other cases where follow-up contact is not a part of normal programmatic activity, former clients can be contacted or surveyed via the mail, telephone, or personal visits expressly for the purpose of soliciting information for measures of service quality, customer satisfaction, and program effectiveness.

Direct Observation

Many times measuring outcomes requires some type of direct observation, by means of mechanical instruments or personal inspections, in contexts other than follow-up client contacts. For example, state transportation departments use various kinds of mechanical and electronic equipment to measure the condition and surface quality of the highways they maintain, and environmental agencies use sophisticated measuring devices to monitor air quality and water quality. In other cases, trained observers armed with rating forms make direct physical inspections to obtain performance data. For instance, local public works departments sometimes use trained observers to assess the condition of city streets, sanitation departments may use trained observers to monitor the cleanliness of streets and alleys, and transit authorities often use them to check the on-time performance of the buses.

Clinical Examinations

Some performance monitoring data come from a particular kind of direct observation: clinical examinations. Physicians, psychiatrists, psychologists, occupational therapists, speech therapists, and other professionals may all be involved in conducting clinical examinations of program clients or other individuals on an ongoing basis, generating streams of data that might feed into performance measurement systems. For example, data from medical diagnoses or evaluations may be useful not only in tracking the performance of health care programs but also in monitoring the effectiveness of crisis stabilization units, teen parenting programs, vocational rehabilitation programs, disability programs, and workers' compensation return-to-work programs, among others. Similarly, data from psychological evaluations might be useful as performance measures in correctional facilities, drug and alcohol abuse programs, behavioral shaping programs for persons with mental disabilities, and violence reduction programs in public schools.

Test Data

Tests are instruments designed to measure individuals' knowledge in a certain area or their skill level in performing certain tasks. Obviously these are most relevant for educational programs, as local public schools routinely use classroom tests to gauge students' learning or scholastic achievement. In addition, some states use uniform "Regents" type examinations, and there are a plethora of standardized exams that are used on a widespread basis, which facilitate tracking educational performance on a local, state, or national level and allow individual schools or school districts to benchmark themselves against others or vis-à-vis national trends. Beyond education programs, testing is used to obtain performance data in a wide variety of other kinds of training programs, generating measures ranging from the job skills of persons working in sheltered workshops to the flying skills of Air Force pilots and fitness ratings of police officers.

Surveys and Customer Response Cards

Public and nonprofit agencies also employ a wide range of personal interview, telephone, mail-out, and other self-administered surveys to generate performance data, most often focusing on service quality, program effectiveness, and customer satisfaction. In addition to surveys of clients and former clients are surveys of customers, service providers or contractors, other stakeholders, citizens or the public at large, and even agency employees. However, survey data are highly reactive, and you must take great care in the design and conduct of surveys to ensure high-quality, "objective" feedback.

One particular form of survey that is becoming more prevalent as a source of performance data is the customer response card. These are usually very brief survey cards containing only a handful of very straightforward questions that are given to customers at the point of service delivery, or shortly thereafter, to monitor customers' satisfaction with the service they received in that particular instance. Such response cards might be given out, for example, to persons who just finished renewing their driver's license, individuals just about to be discharged from a crisis stabilization unit, child support enforcement clients who have just made a visit to their local office, or corporate representatives who have just attended a seminar about how their firms can do business with state government. These response cards not only serve to identify and, one hopes, resolve immediate service delivery problems but also generate data that in the aggregate can be very useful in monitoring service quality and customer satisfaction with a program over time.

Specially Designed Measurement Tools

Although the vast majority of the measures used in performance monitoring systems come from the conventional sources we have already discussed, in some cases it is desirable or necessary to design special measurement instruments to gauge the effectiveness of a particular program. For example, the national Keep America Beautiful program and its state and local affiliates use a photometric index developed by the American Public Works Association to monitor volumes of litter in local communities. Briefly, the photometric index is operationalized by taking color slides of a sample of ninety-six-square-foot sites in areas that are representative of the community in terms of income and land use. The specific kinds of sites include street curb fronts, sidewalks, vacant lots, parking lots, dumpster sites, loading docks, commercial storage areas, and possibly rural roads, beaches, and parks. There may be on the order of 120 such sites in the sample for one local community, and the same exact sites are photographed each year.

After the pictures are taken, they are projected over a grid map, and the "littered" squares in each photograph are counted. The resulting photometric index value, which is computed as the number of littered squares per slide, is tracked each year as an indicator of the extent to which the program is having an impact in terms of reducing the accumulation of litter in each of these specific kinds of sites as well as in the community at large. This particular measurement instrument, specially designed to monitor a principal intended outcome of the Keep America Beautiful program, is probably best categorized as a form of indirect observation.

Validity and Reliability

As we have seen, for some performance measures good data may be readily at hand, whereas other measures may require follow-up observation, surveys, or other specially designed data collection procedures. Although available data sources can obviously be advantageous in terms of time, effort, and cost, readily available data are not always good data—but they aren't always poor quality either. From a methodological point of view, "good" data are data with a high degree of validity and reliability—that is, they are unbiased indicators that are appropriate measures of performance and provide a reasonable level of objective statistical reliability.

Reliability

Technically speaking, performance *indicators* are performance measures defined operationally in terms of how the measure is actually taken or how the data are collected. For example, the operational indicator for the number of students entering a state's university system each year might be the number of students recorded as having enrolled in three or more classes for the first time during the preceding academic year by the registrar's office at each of the institutions in the system. Similarly, the operational indicator for the number of passengers carried by an urban transit system might be the number counted by automatic registering fareboxes; the percentage of customers who are satisfied with the state patrol's process for renewing drivers' licenses might be measured by the percentage who check off "satisfied" or "very satisfied" on response cards that are handed out to people as they complete the process.

The reliability of such performance indicators is a matter of how objective, precise, and dependable they are. For instance, if repeated queries to a university registrar's office asking how many students are enrolled in classes during the current semester yield a different number every time, the measure lacks consistency or dependability and thus is not very reliable. The range of responses might provide an indication of roughly how many students are enrolled in classes, but it certainly is not a very precise indicator.

From a measurement perspective, the perfect performance indicator may never exist because there is always the possibility of some error in the measurement process. To the extent that the error in a measure is random and unbiased in direction, this is a reliability problem. Although quality assurance processes need to be built into data processing procedures, as discussed in Chapter Eight, there is always a chance of accidental errors in data reporting, coding, and tabulating, and this creates reliability problems. For example, state child support enforcement programs track the percentage of noncustodial parents who are delinquent in making obligated payments, and computing this percentage would seem to be a simple matter; at any given point in time the parent is either up-to-date or delinquent in making these payments. However, the information on the thousands of cases recorded in the centralized database for this program pertaining to numbers of children in households, establishment of paternity, obligation of payments, and current status comes from local offices and a variety of other sources in piecemeal fashion. Although up-to-date accuracy is critical in maintaining these records, errors are made and "slippage" in reporting does occur, so that at any one point in time, the actual accounts are likely to be off the mark a little (or maybe a lot) one way or the other. Thus, in a system that tracks this indicator on a monthly basis, the computed percentage of delinquent parents may overstate the rate of delinquency some months and understate it other months. Even though there is no systematic tendency to overrepresent or underrepresent the percentage of delinquent parents, this indicator is not highly dependable or reliable.

A lack of inter-rater reliability often presents problems in performance data. If a number of trained observers rating the condition of city streets look at the same section of street at the same time, using the same procedures, definitions, categories, and rating forms, yet the rating they come up with varies substantially from observer to observer, this measure of street condition clearly is not very reliable. Even though the observers have been trained to use this instrument the same way, the actual ratings that result appear to be based more on the *subjective* impressions of the individual raters than on the *objective* application of the standard criteria. Such problems with inter-rater reliability can occur whenever the indicator is operationalized by different individuals observing cases and making judgments, as might the case, for instance, when housing inspectors determine the percentage of dwelling units that meet code requirements, when workers' compensation examiners determine the percentage of employees injured on the job who require longer-term medical benefits, or when staff psychologists rate the ability of mildly and moderately retarded clients of an nonprofit agency to function at a higher level of independence.

Validity

Whereas reliability is a matter of objectivity and precision, the validity of a performance measure concerns its *appropriateness*, the extent to which an indicator is directly related to and representative of the performance dimension of interest. If a proposed indicator is largely irrelevant or only tangentially related to the desired outcome of a particular program, then it will not provide a valid indication of that program's effectiveness. For example, scores on the verbal portion of the SATs have sometimes been used as a surrogate indicator of the writing ability of twelfth graders in public schools, but the focus of these tests is really on vocabulary and reading comprehension, which are relevant but only partially indicative of writing capabilities. In contrast, the more recently developed National Assessment of Educational Progress test in writing provides a much more direct indicator of students' ability to articulate points in writing and to write effective, fully developed responses to questions designed specifically to test their writing competence.

As another example, the aim of a metropolitan transit authority's welfare-to-work initiative might be to facilitate moving employable individuals from dependence on welfare to regular employment by providing access to work sites through additional transportation services. As possible measures of effectiveness, however, the estimated number of homeless individuals in the area would be largely irrelevant, and the total number of employed persons and the average median income in the metropolitan area are subject to whole hosts of factors and would be only very marginally sensitive to the welfare-to-work initiative. More relevant measures might focus on the number of individuals reported by the welfare agency to have been moved off the welfare rolls, the number of "third shift" positions reported as filled by manufacturing plants and other employers, or the number of passenger trips made on those particular bus trips that have been instituted as part of the welfare-to-work initiative. However, each of these measures still falls short as an indicator of the number of individuals who were formerly without jobs and dependent on welfare who now have jobs by virtue of being able to get to and from work on the transit system.

Most proposed performance measures tend to be at least somewhat appropriate and relevant to the program being monitored, but the issue of validity often boils down to the extent to which they provide fair, unbiased indicators of the performance dimension of interest. Whereas reliability problems result from random error in the measurement process, validity problems arise when there is systematic bias in the measurement process, producing a systematic tendency either to overestimate or to underestimate program performance. For instance, crime prevention programs may utilize officially reported crime rates as the principal effectiveness measure, but as is well known, many crimes are not reported to police for a variety of reasons. Thus, these reported crime rates tend to underestimate the number of crimes committed in a given area during a particular time period. On the other hand, the percentage of total crimes reported as "solved" by a local police department would systematically overstate the effectiveness of the police if it includes cases that were initially recorded as crimes and subsequently determined not to constitute crimes but were still carried on the books labeled as "solved" crimes.

Developing valid indicators of program effectiveness is often particularly challenging because the desired outcomes are somewhat diffuse, only tenuously connected to the program, or impacted by numerous other factors beyond the program's control, or because they simply do not lend themselves to practical measurement. For example, a performance monitoring system for the U.S. Diplomatic Service might track the use of resources, numbers of strategy sessions, numbers of contacts with representatives from other countries, numbers of agreements signed, and so on, but much of the work occurs informally and behind closed doors, progress is open to very subjective interpretation, and the real impact in terms of maintaining the peace or gaining strategic advantage is difficult to determine. Alternatively, consider the U.S. Forest Service, for which the real impact of conservation measures and reforestation programs implemented now will not materialize until several decades into the future. In such cases, the most practical approach may be to rely primarily on output measures or to try to identify reasonable proximate measures, as discussed later in this chapter.

Even for public and nonprofit programs whose intended outcomes are a lot closer to being "in reach," defining valid outcome indicators may still be difficult. For instance, a crisis stabilization unit may monitor the percentage of its consumers who complete treatment and are discharged but who then turn up again as readmissions in the unit within thirty days. However, discharged consumers may move out of the area or turn up at some other facility with the same problems within thirty days, or they may become unstabilized with the same psychiatric or substance abuse problems they were experiencing before but simply not get needed help the next time around. Thus, the percentage of readmissions within thirty days would certainly be a relevant measure, but it is likely to be a biased indicator with a tendency to underestimate the percentage of discharged consumers who in fact do not remain stabilized for very long.

For many human service programs, it is difficult to follow clients after they leave the program, but that is often when the real outcomes occur. The crisis stabilization unit observes consumers only while they are actually short-term residents of the facility, and thus it cannot track whether they continue to take prescribed medications faithfully, begin to use drugs or alcohol again, or continue participating in long-term care programs. Appropriate measures of effectiveness are not difficult to define in this case, but operationalizing them through systematic client follow-up would require significant additional staff, time, and effort that is probably better invested in service delivery than in performance measurement.

As another example, a teen mother parenting program can track clients' participation in the training sessions, but it will have to stay in touch with all program completers in order to determine the percentage who deliver healthy babies, babies of normal birth weight, babies free from HIV, and so on. But what about the quality of parental care given during the first year of the infants' lives? Consider the options for tracking the extent to which the teen mothers provide the kind of care for their babies that is imparted by the training program. Periodic telephone or mailout surveys of the new mothers could be conducted, but in at least some cases their responses are likely to be biased in terms of presenting a more favorable picture of reality. Alternatively, trained professionals could make periodic follow-up visits to the clients' homes, primarily to help the mothers with any problems they are concerned about, and by talking with the mothers and observing the infants in their own households, they could also make assessments of the adequacy of care given. This would be feasible if the program design includes follow-up visits to provide further support, and it would probably provide a more satisfactory indicator even though some of the mothers might be on their best behavior during these short visits, possibly leading to more positive assessments that overstate the quality of care given to the infants on a regular basis.

Bases of Validity

Although validity is partly a matter of subjective judgment, there are four bases on which to "validate" performance measures. First, many indicators simply have *face validity;* that is, they are clearly valid measures "on the face of it." For instance, the number of fares paid as recorded by registering fareboxes on its buses during a given month is obviously a valid measure of a local transit system's ridership for that month. *Consensual validity* is conferred on a performance measure when a number of experts and others working in the field develop an apparent consensus that it is appropriate. For instance, there is a consensus among managers of local government fleet maintenance operations that the percentage of vehicles that are available for use, on the average, is a valid indicator of their programs' effectiveness. Note that in both of these examples there is clearly room for error. If some individuals board the buses and actually make transit trips without paying a fare, then that indicator systematically undercounts ridership; in the case of the fleet maintenance operations, some vehicles could be allowed to remain in service or go back into service when they have serious operating problems, in which case that indicator would overstate program effectiveness. However, it should be kept in mind that validity, like reliability, is still a matter of degree.

Correlational validity occurs when some indicator that is being tested correlates well statistically with another indicator that is already considered to be a proven measure. For instance, the international roughness index (IRI) directly measures the smoothness of a highway's surface, but transportation departments feel comfortable using it as an indicator of overall ride quality because in panel studies that have been conducted on a rigorous experimental basis, IRI values correlate highly with motorists' rating of ride quality based on their firsthand experience.

Predictive validity is conferred on an indicator when values on that measure at present can be used to reliably predict some outcome in the future. For example, consider military bases whose principal mission is to train and otherwise prepare forces for combat readiness. Monitoring resources, activities, and outputs is fairly straightforward for these operations, but measuring combat readiness directly will be possible only when the forces they have trained become engaged in actual combat. However, if it has been determined, based on past experience, that effectiveness ratings of troops' performance in simulated maneuvers have correlated strongly with their performance when they have subsequently been committed to combat, then these effectiveness ratings have predictive validity as an indicator of combat readiness.

Common Measurement Problems

In working through the challenge of defining useful operational indicators, system designers should always anticipate likely problems and try to avoid or circumvent them. Common problems that can jeopardize reliability, validity, or both include noncomparable data, tenuously related proximate measures, tendencies to under- or overreport data, poor instrument design, observer bias, instrument decay, reactive measurement, nonresponse bias, and cheating.

Noncomparability of Data

Whenever data are entered into the system in a decentralized process, noncomparability of data is a possibility. Even though uniform data collection procedures are prescribed, there is no automatic guarantee that they will be implemented exactly the same way from work station to work station or from site to site. This can be a real problem within a single agency or program, as people responsible for data input from parallel offices, branches, or work units find their own ways to expedite the process in the press of heavy workloads, and they may end up counting things differently from one another. Thus, in a large agency with multiple data entry sites, care must be taken to ensure uniform data entry.

In large agencies delivering programs through a decentralized structure, for example a state human services agency with 104 local offices, the central office may wish to track certain measures in order to compare the performance of local offices, or it may want to roll up the data to track performance on a statewide basis. Particularly if the local offices operate with a fair degree of autonomy, there may be significant inconsistencies in how the indicator is operationalized from one local office to the next. This could jeopardize the validity of comparisons among the local offices as well as the statewide data. The probability of noncomparable data is often greater in state and federal grant programs, when the data input is done by the individual grantees—local government agencies or nonprofit organizations—who, again, may set up somewhat different processes for doing so.

The problem of noncomparable data is often especially acute with respect to benchmarking efforts, in which a number of governmental jurisdictions or nonprofit agencies provide their own data to a central source (using uniform procedures, one hopes). There may be substantial discrepancies in the way they maintain their own data and enter them into the centralized system, thereby largely invalidating comparisons among them.

Tenuous Proximate Measures

When it is difficult to define direct indicators of program performance or is not practical to operationalize them, it is often possible to use *proximate measures* instead. Proximate measures are indicators that are thought to be approximately equivalent to more direct measures of performance. In effect, proximate measures are less direct indicators that are assumed to have some degree of correlational or predictive validity. For example, records of customer complaints are often used as an indicator of customer satisfaction with a particular program. Actually, customer complaints are an indicator of *dis*satisfaction, whereas customer satisfaction is usually thought of as a much broader concept. Nevertheless, in the absence of good customer feedback via surveys, response cards, or focus groups, data on complaints often fill in as proximate measures for customer satisfaction.

Similarly, the commonly stated purpose of local public transit systems is (1) to meet the mobility needs of individuals who don't have access to private means of transportation and (2) to reduce usage of private automobiles in cities by providing a competitive alternative. However, transit systems rarely track measures of these intended outcomes directly, but rather monitor overall passenger trips as a proximate measure that they believe to be correlated with these outcomes.

Sometimes when it is difficult to obtain real measures of program effectiveness, monitoring systems rely on indicators of outputs or initial outcomes as proximate measures of longer-term outcomes. For example, a state department of administrative services may provide a number of support services, such as vehicle rentals, office supply, and printing services to the other operating agencies of state government. The real impact of these services would be measured by the extent to which they enable these operating departments, their customers, to perform their functions more effectively and efficiently. However, the performance measures used by these other agencies are unlikely to be at all sensitive to the marginal contribution of the support services. Thus, the department of administrative services might well just monitor indicators of output and service quality on the assumption that if the line agencies are using these support services and are satisfied with them, then the services are in fact contributing to higher performance levels on the part of these other agencies.

Although proximate measures can often be useful, validity problems emerge when they are only tenuously related to the performance criteria of interest. Suppose, for example, that a state economic development agency sees its mission as helping stimulate additional business investment, economic activity, job creation, and exporting of goods and services to overseas markets. It would be difficult for the agency to measure its impact directly, and for some reason it settles on the dollar value of personal income taxes paid each year as a proximate measure of its effectiveness. Taxes paid will be linked to economic development activities to some degree, if only tenuously, but they may be more directly influenced by various other factors. If, for instance, more retired persons are moving into the state each year, personal income taxes are likely to increase, and this indicator would make the program look good even if it is not at all effective. Conversely, the state may be in a period of economic decline and experience an out-migration of population and businesses. Personal income taxes paid each year will therefore be declining, and this indicator would make the program's performance appear to be ineffective even if the program itself had some notable success in convincing some business firms not to pull up stakes and in helping attract new industry to replace some of the economic activity that has fled the state.

Under- or Overreporting

Whereas some measures are simply "sloppy" and overrepresent some cases while undercounting others, thereby eroding reliability, other performance indicators have a tendency to under- or overreport on a systematic basis, creating validity problems. As mentioned earlier, for instance, reported crime statistics tend to underestimate actual crimes committed because for various reasons many crimes go unreported to the police. Periodic victimization surveys may provide more valid estimates of actual crimes committed, but they require considerable time, effort, and resources. Thus the official reported crime statistics are often used as indicators of the effectiveness of crime prevention programs or police crime-solving activities even though they are known to underestimate actual crime rates. In part this is workable because the reported crime statistics may be valid for tracking trends over time, say on a monthly basis, as long as the tendency for crimes to be reported or not reported is constant from month to month.

One critical concern of juvenile detention facilities is to eliminate, or at least minimize, instances of physical or sexual abuse of children in their custody by other detainees or by staff members. Thus, one performance measure that is important to them is the number of child abuse incidents occurring per month. But what would be the operationalized indicator for this measure? One possibility would be the number of such incidents *reported* each month, but this really represents the number of *allegations* of child abuse. Considering that some of these allegations may well be unfounded, this indicator would systematically tend to overestimate the real number of such incidents. A preferred indicator would probably be the number of child abuse incidents that are recorded on the basis of full investigations when such allegations are made. However, as is true of reported crime rates in general, this measure would underestimate the actual number of child abuse incidents if some victims of child abuse in these facilities are afraid to report them.

Poor Instrument Design

Sound design of measuring instruments is essential for effective performance measurement. This is particularly important with surveys of customers or other stakeholders; items that are unclear or that incorporate biases can lead to serious measurement problems. Often such surveys include questions that are vague, double-barreled, or ambiguous, and because respondents are likely to interpret them in different ways, the resulting data include a considerable amount of "noise" and thus are not very reliable.

A more serious problem arises when surveys include biased items—leading questions that, intentionally or not, prompt respondents to answer in a certain way. For example, an agency's ongoing customer satisfaction survey could include questions and response choices that are worded in such a way as almost to force respondents to give programs artificially high ratings. This would obviously overestimate customer satisfaction with this program and invalidate the survey data. These kinds of problems can also apply to other modes of performance measurement, such as trained observer ratings and other specially designed measurement tools. The important point here is that care should always be taken to design measurement instruments that are clear, unambiguous, and unbiased.

Observer Bias

Biased observers are another source of severe validity problems. Even with a good survey instrument, for instance, an interviewer who has some definite bias, either in favor of a program or opposed to it for some reason, can obviously bias the responses in that direction by introducing the survey, setting the overall tone, and asking the questions in a certain way. In the extreme, the performance data generated by the survey may actually represent the interviewer's biases more than they serve as a valid reflection of the views of the respondents.

Clearly, the problem of observer bias is not limited to survey data. Many performance measures are operationalized through observer ratings, including inspection of physical conditions, observation of behavioral patterns, or quality assurance audits. In addition, performance data from clinical evaluations by physicians, psychologists, therapists, and other professionals can also be vulnerable to observer biases. To control for this possibility, careful training of interviewers and observers and emphasis on the need for fair, unbiased observation and assessment are essential.

Instrument Decay

In addition to sound instrument design, consistent application of the measure over time is critical to performance monitoring systems, precisely because they are intended to track key performance measures over time. If the instrument changes over time, it can be difficult to assess the extent to which trends in the data reflect real trends in performance versus changes in measurement procedures. For example, if a local police department begins to classify as crimes certain kinds of reported incidents that previously were not counted as crimes, then everything else being equal, reported crime rates will go up. These performance data could easily be interpreted as indicating that crime is on the rise in that area or that crime prevention programs are not working well there, when in reality the upward trend simply reflects a change in recording procedures.

Instrument decay refers to the erosion of integrity of a measure as a valid and reliable performance indicator over time. For instance, as part of a city sanitation department's quality control effort, it trains a few inspectors to conduct "spot checks" of neighborhoods where residential refuse collection crews have recently passed through, to observe the amount of trash and litter that might have been left behind. At first the inspectors adhere closely to a regular schedule of visiting randomly selected neighborhoods and are quite conscientious about rating cleanliness according to prescribed guidelines, but after several months they begin to slack off, stopping through neighborhoods on a hit-or-miss basis and making casual assessments that stray from the guidelines. Thus, the measure has decayed over this period and lost much of its reliability, and the data therefore are not really very meaningful.

Alternatively, a local transit system begins classifying certain kinds of transfers from one route to another as separate passenger trips, which was not done previously. Thus, its long-term trend lines show increasing numbers of passenger trips at this point, an invalid impression that is attributable only to a change in measurement procedures. Instrument decay is a persistent problem in performance measurement, and it must be dealt with in two ways. First, when measurement procedures are intentionally changed, usually in an attempt to improve validity, it is important to document the change and to note it in presentations of the data that incorporate periods before and after the change was instituted. Second, whether or not the definitions of measures are changed, it is important to maintain the integrity of the measures by ensuring close conformity with prescribed measurement procedures over time.

Reactive Measurement

Sometimes measurements can change because people involved in the process are affected by the program in some way or react somehow to the fact that the data are being monitored by someone else or used for some particular purpose. For instance, if a state government introduces a new scholarship program that ties awards to grades students earn in high school, teachers might begin, consciously or unconsciously, to be more lenient in their grading. In effect, their standards for grading, or how they actually rate students' academic performance, change in reaction to the new scholarship program, but the resulting data would suggest that students are performing better in high school now than before, which may not be true.

Or consider an inner-city neighborhood that forms a neighborhood watch program in cooperation with the local police department, aimed at increasing personal safety and security, deterring crime, and helping the police solve crimes that are committed. As this program becomes more and more established, residents' attitudes toward both crime and the police change, and their propensity to report crimes to the police increases. This actually provides a more valid indicator of the actual crime level than used to be the case, but the data are likely to show increases in reported crimes even though this is simply an artifact of reactive measurement.

As illustrated by these two examples, reactive measurement may or may not have adverse impact, but it can weaken the validity of performance measures and create misleading impressions of comparisons over time. Thus, it makes sense to try to anticipate situations in which the measurement process itself might react to program stimuli, and to try to discern what the effect on the resulting performance data might be. Sometimes an analysis of other key measures that would not be reactive—such as SAT scores in the grade inflation example—or a comparison of trends in other cases not affected by the program, such as an analysis of reported crime statistics versus victimization survey data in neighborhoods with and without neighborhood watch programs, can help assess the likelihood of reactive measurement and its potential impact on performance data.

Nonresponse Bias

The quality of performance monitoring data is often called into question by virtue of being incomplete. Even with routine record-keeping systems and transactional databases, agencies often are unable for a variety of reasons to maintain up-to-date information on all cases all the time. So, at any one point in time when the observations are being made or the data are being "run," say at the end of every month, there may be incomplete data in the records. If the missing data are purely a random phenomenon, this weakens the reliability of the data and can create problems of statistical instability. If, however, there is some systematic pattern of missing data, if for instance the database tends to have less complete information on the more problematic cases, this can inject a systematic bias into the data and erode the validity of the performance measure. Although the problem of nonresponse bias may technically be a sampling issue, its real impact is to introduce bias or distortion into performance measures.

Thus, in considering alternative performance indicators, it is a good idea to ascertain the basis on which the measure is drawn in order to assess whether missing data might create problems of validity or reliability. For example, almost all colleges and universities require applicants to submit SAT scores as part of the admissions process. Although the primary purpose of these test scores is help in the selection process, average SAT scores, or the midspread of SAT scores, can be used to compare the quality of applicants to that of different institutions or to track proficiency of a particular university's freshmen class over several years.

However, SAT scores are also sometimes used as a proximate measure of the academic achievement of the students in individual high schools or school systems, and here there may be problems due to missing cases. Not all high school students take the SATs, and those who do tend to be the better students; therefore, average SAT scores tend to overstate the academic proficiency of the student body as a whole. In fact, teachers and administrators can influence average SAT scores for their schools simply by encouraging some students to take the test and discouraging others. Thus, as a indicator of academic achievement for entire schools, SAT scores are much more questionable than, for example, standard exams mandated by the state for all students. When missing cases pose potential problems, it is important to interpret the data on the basis of the actual cases on which the data are drawn. Thus, average SAT scores can be taken as an indicator of the academic achievement of those students from a given high school who chose to take the exam.

When performance measures are derived from surveys, missing cases can result in flawed indicators due to possible nonresponse biases. Most surveys generate response rates well below 100 percent. If those individuals who do respond to a survey tend to be those who are most interested in a program, for instance, or more involved with it, more familiar with its staff and services, more supportive of it, or more concerned with the future of the program one way or another, then their responses may not be very representative of what the overall data would look like if everyone had responded. The problem of nonresponse bias is even more notorious with respect to customer response card systems, in which some customers return cards frequently while others never respond. If those customers who do turn in response cards tend to be a few active supporters, the resulting data will be artificially favorable, whereas if the only customers returning cards are those who have serious grievances with a program, the data will be skewed to highly negative ratings.

Nonresponse bias can be very problematic when performance measures, especially effectiveness measures, come from follow-up contacts with former clients, whether through surveys, follow-up visits, or other direct contact. Especially with respect to human service programs, it is often difficult to remain in contact with all those individuals who have been served by a program or who completed treatment some time ago. And it may be the case that certain kinds of clients are much less likely to remain in contact. As would probably be the case with vocational rehabilitation programs, teen mother parenting programs, and especially crisis stabilization units, for example, those former clients who are the most difficult to track down are often those with the least positive outcomes, those for whom the program may have been least effective. They may be the most likely ones to move from the area, drop out of sight, leave the "system," or fall through the cracks. Obviously, the nonresponse bias of data based on follow-up contacts that will necessarily exclude some of the most problematic clients could easily lead to overstating program performance. This is not to say that such indicators should not be included in performance monitoring systems—because often they are crucial indicators of long-term program effectiveness—but rather that care must be taken to interpret them within the confines of actual response rates.

Cheating

In addition to all the methodological issues that can compromise the quality of performance monitoring data, a common problem that can destroy validity and reliability is cheating. If performance measurement systems are indeed used effectively as a management tool, they carry consequences in terms of decisions regarding programs, people, resources, and strategies. Thus, managers at all levels of the organization want to "look good" in terms of the performance data. Suppose, for example, that air force bases whose function is training pilots to fly combat missions are evaluated in part by how close they come to hitting rather ambitious targets that have been set concerning the number of "sorties" flown by these pilots. The sorties are the principal output of these training operations, and there is a clear definition of what constitutes a completed sortie. If the base commanders are under heavy pressure to achieve these targets, however, and actual performance is lagging behind these objectives, they might begin to count all sorties as full sorties even though some of these have to be cut short for various reasons and are not really completed. This tampering with the definition of a performance measure may seem to be a rather subtle distinction—and an easy one for the commanders to rationalize given the pressure to maintain high ratings—but it would represent willful misreporting to make a program appear to be more effective than it really is.

Performance measurement systems provide incentives for organizations and programs to perform at higher levels, and this is the core of the logic underlying the use of monitoring systems as performance management tools. Human nature being what it is, then, it is not surprising that people in public and nonprofit organizations will sometimes be tempted to cheat—selectively reporting data, purposefully falsifying data, or otherwise "cooking the books" in order to present performance in a more favorable light. This kind of cheating is a real problem, and it must be dealt with directly and firmly. One strategy to ensure the quality of the data is to build sample audits into the overall design of the system, as will be discussed in Chapter Eight. Another approach is to use penalties or other sanctions as disincentives to discourage cheating, as will be discussed in Chapter Fourteen.

In terms of the performance measures themselves, sometimes it is possible to use complementary measures that will help identify instances in which the data don't seem to add up, thus providing a check on cheating. In a state highway maintenance program, for instance, foremen inputting production data from the field might be tempted to misrepresent the level of output produced by their crews by overstating such indicators as the miles of road resurfaced, the miles of shoulders graded, or the feet of guardrail replaced. If these data are only marginally overstated, they will appear to be reasonable and will probably not be caught as errors. If, however, a separate system is used to report on inventory control and the use of resources, and these data are input by different individuals in a different part of the organization, then it may be possible to track these different indicators in tandem. Numbers that don't seem to match up would trigger a data audit to determine the reason for the apparent discrepancy. Such a safeguard might be an effective deterrent against cheating.

Other Criteria for Performance Measures

From the standpoint of managerial effectiveness, the measures used in performance monitoring systems should meet various other criteria in addition to validity and reliability, as shown in the list that follows. Although some of these criteria apply in particular to each individual performance indicator, collectively they define the characteristics of effective *sets* of performance measures.

Criteria for Useful Performance Measures

- Valid and reliable
- Meaningful and understandable
- Balanced and comprehensive
- Clear regarding preferred direction of movement
- Timely and actionable
- Resistant to goal displacement
- Cost-sensitive (nonredundant)

Meaningful Measures

Performance measures should be *meaningful;* that is, they should be directly related to the mission, goals, and intended results of a program, and they should represent performance dimensions that have been identified as part of the program logic. To be meaningful, performance measures should be important to managers, policymakers, employees, customers, or other stakeholders. Managers may be more concerned with productivity and program impact, policymakers may care more about efficiency and cost-effectiveness, and clients may be more directly concerned with service quality, but for a performance indicator to be meaningful it must be important to at least one of these stakeholder groups. If no stakeholder is interested in a particular measure, then it cannot be particularly useful as part of a performance measurement system. Performance indicators must also be *understandable* to stakeholders. That is, the measures need to be presented in such a way as to explain clearly what they consist of and how they represent some aspect of performance.

Balanced and Comprehensive Measures

Within the scope and purpose of a given monitoring system, a set of performance measures should be balanced and comprehensive. A fully comprehensive measurement system should incorporate all the performance dimensions and types of measures discussed in Chapter Three, including both outputs and outcomes and, if relevant, service quality and customer satisfaction in addition to efficiency and productivity. Even with systems that are more narrowly defined—focusing solely on strategic outcomes, for example, or, at the other extreme, focusing solely on operations—the measurement system should attempt to include indicators of every relevant aspect of performance. Perhaps most important, the monitoring system for a program with multiple goals should include a balanced set of effectiveness measures rather than emphasize some intended outcomes while ignoring others that may be just as important.

For example, the list that follows (from Bugler and Henry, 1998) shows a balanced set of performance indicators that are tracked to monitor the effectiveness of the State of Georgia's HOPE Scholarship program, which was initiated in 1994. HOPE pays the cost of full tuition for any institution in the university system of Georgia, plus $100 per semester for books, for any student who graduates from a high school in the state with a B average or higher as long as that student maintains a B average or higher in college. It also reimburses Georgia students who attend private colleges in the state the equivalent of public school tuition as long as they meet the same requirements. The goals of the program, which is funded by revenue from the state lottery, are to motivate students to achieve better grades in high school, enable more high school graduates to go on to college, increase the number of minority students attending college, motivate more students from low-income families to attend college, encourage more Georgia high school graduates to attend colleges in Georgia rather than other states, and motivate college students in Georgia to perform better academically and remain in college through graduation. Collectively, the indicators shown here, which are tracked on an annual basis, provide a balanced portrait of the impact of the HOPE Scholarship program.

HOPE Scholarship Effectiveness Measures

- The number of HOPE Scholarship recipients
- The number of students entering Georgia institutions of higher education
- The percentage of high school students with a B or higher grade-point average
- The percentage of HOPE recipients still in college one, two, and three years after entering
- The average grade-point average and credit hours earned per year by HOPE recipients
- The percentage of initial recipients who retain the scholarship after one, two, and three years
- The number and percentage of entering freshmen who are African Americans
- The number of Pell grant applications from Georgia
- The number of Georgia college students funded by Pell grants
- The number of Georgia students attending selected colleges in other states

Measures with Clear Preferred Direction of Movement

In order for a performance indicator to be useful, there must be agreement on the preferred direction of movement on the scale. If an indicator of customer satisfaction, for example, is operationalized as the percentage of respondents to an annual survey who say they were satisfied or very satisfied with the service they have received from a particular agency, higher percentages are taken to represent stronger program performance, and managers will want to see this percentage increase from year to year.

Although it might seem that this should go without saying, the preferred direction of movement is not always so clear. On one hand, for instance, such indicators as the student-faculty ratio or the average class size are sometimes used as proximate measures of the quality of instructional programs at public universities, on the theory that smaller classes offer greater opportunity for participation in class discussions and increased attention to the needs of individual students both in and out of class. On that score, then, the preferred direction of movement would be to smaller class sizes. On the other hand, college deans often like to see classes filling up with more students in order to make more efficient use of faculty time and cover a higher percentage of operating costs. Thus, from a budgetary standpoint, larger class sizes might be preferred. Generally speaking, if agreement on targets and the preferred direction of movement cannot be reached in such ambiguous situations, then the proposed indicator should probably not be used.

Timely and Actionable Measures

To be useful, performance measures also should be timely and actionable. One of managers' most common complaints about performance measurement systems is that they do not report the data in a timely manner. When performance measures are designed to support a governmental unit's budgeting process, for instance, the performance data for the most recently completed fiscal year should be readily available when budget requests or proposals are being developed. In practice, however, sometimes the only available data pertain to two years earlier and are simply out-of-date as a basis for making decisions regarding the current allocation of resources. Performance data that are intended to be helpful to managers with responsibility for ongoing operations—such as highway maintenance work, central office supply, claims processing operations, or child support enforcement customer service—should probably be monitored more frequently, on a monthly or quarterly basis, in order to facilitate addressing operational problems more immediately. Although reporting frequency is really an issue of overall system design, as discussed in Chapter Two, it also needs to be taken into account in the definition of the measures themselves.

To be actionable, the indicator must be tied to something within a program's sphere of influence, some criterion that the program or management can have an impact on. As long as performance measures are tied to appropriate goals and objectives, they are usually actionable, even though the program rarely has anything approaching total control over desired outcomes. For example, it is often an uphill struggle, but transit authorities can be held accountable for maintaining ridership, and juvenile detention centers can be expected to reduce recidivism rates. Thus, ridership and recidivism rates are actionable measures for these organizations.

In contrast, some proposed performance indicators may be well beyond the control of the program and thus not actionable. For instance, one way in which public hospitals track their performance is through surveys of patients who have been recently discharged, because they can provide useful feedback on the quality and responsiveness of the services they received. Suppose, however, that one particular item on such a survey refers to the availability of some specific service or treatment option. The responses to this item are consistently and almost universally negative, but the reason for this is that none of the insurance companies involved will cover this option, something that is beyond the control of the hospital. Thus, because there is little or no chance of improving performance in this area, at least under the existing constraints, this measure cannot provide any new or useful feedback to hospital administrators.

Measures That Are Resistant to Goal Displacement

One of the most critical issues in the definition of performance measures concerns goal displacement, the tendency of managers and others to perform directly toward the indicators themselves to the detriment of the real goals of the program or organization. For instance, if a local school district focuses too sharply on students' performance on certain standardized tests as a measure of academic achievement, teachers who are familiar with that particular testing strategy and format may be inclined to "teach to the test" at the expense of real learning in their classes. Similarly, if managers in a state's disability determination unit are under pressure from the Social Security Administration to improve productivity, and the key performance measures are defined as the number of claims closed per full-time-equivalent employee per week and the percentage of cases closed within seventy days, the managers could focus single-mindedly on disposing of claims quickly and lose sight of the need to be fair and accurate in determining which claims are eligible for disability benefits.

Although performance measurement systems are intentionally designed to influence behavior in positive ways, when goal displacement occurs it affects performance adversely. For example, a state transportation department that is trying to revitalize the productivity of its highway maintenance program may emphasize the number of lane-miles that are resurfaced each month as a key output indicator. If maintenance supervisors and foremen know that top management is focusing on this particular measure and tying real rewards and penalties to it, they will naturally want to resurface as many lane-miles as possible, everything else being equal. This may produce the desired results, but if the maintenance crews are hard pressed to achieve these output targets or are overzealous in trying to "look good" on this measure, they may engage in quick "dump and run" operations resulting in poor-quality resurfacing jobs that fail to improve ride quality appreciably and will have to be repeated on shorter than average cycle times. Or the maintenance managers might concentrate the resurfacing jobs on roads with lower traffic volumes where the work can be completed more easily and quickly, but this would have little impact on improving ride quality on those roads that are used most heavily by motorists. Or they could program extraordinary amounts of resurfacing work to the exclusion of other kinds of maintenance work, such as drainage improvements, which would have a long-term negative impact on overall highway condition. Thus, working to perform well on the specific resurfacing indicator could actually be counterproductive in terms of the more important goals of improving ride quality, placing a high priority on those roads that are used the most heavily, and maintaining the overall condition of the roads in the long run.

Goal displacement most often arises from unbalanced performance measures, and it can usually be avoided by defining sets of indicators with balanced incentives that channel performance toward desired outcomes. For example, the desired outcome of a vocational rehabilitation program is to help clients prepare for and find satisfactory employment. A key performance measure here might be the percentage of clients exiting the program who are subsequently employed. This indicator certainly points in the right direction, but if it is the only measure of success, it could prompt staff to engage in practices that would maximize the percentage employed yet be counterproductive in the long run. They might push clients into the lowest-paying jobs or part-time jobs that are easy to get, at the expense of placing them in more satisfactory positions. They could also give top priority to placing those clients who are already more marketable to gain quick successes at the expense of helping clients with severe disabilities, for whom it tends to be much more difficult to find jobs. However, it is not difficult to define additional indicators that would control for this kind of behavior, such as the following:

- The percentage of all employed clients who work thirty-five hours or more per week
- The percentage of all employed clients who are employed in competitive, self-employed, or business enterprise type employment
- The percentage of severely disabled clients who have achieved competitive, self-employed, or business enterprise type employment
- The percentage of all employed clients with earnings equal to or greater than the minimum wage
- The percentage of employed clients earning wages above the poverty level of $645 per month for a family of one

Tracking performance on such a set of outcome measures would not only provide a more complete picture of program effectiveness but also reduce the likelihood of goal displacement by restoring balance to the incentive structure. Because it would be in the agency's interest to perform well across the board on this mix of indicators, the agency would be much less inclined to place its clientele in less competitive jobs and fail to emphasize the needs of severely disabled clients.

Cost-Effective Performance Measures

The principle that performance measures should be cost-effective should go without saying, but it cannot be emphasized too strongly. Implementing measurement systems can entail considerable cost, especially in data collection and processing, and the results should be worthwhile. Some types of measures are more costly than others. For example, special-purpose surveys, inspections, and clinical evaluations tend to be more expensive than routinely recorded transactional data, but collecting even the more routine agency data can be time consuming and require considerable extra effort, especially if they must be input by dispersed staff out "in the field" and then be confirmed on a sample basis by a quality control unit.

Thus, collecting and processing performance data should be viewed as a purposeful investment that will provide useful information to managers and policymakers. Although it is obviously desirable to develop a balanced set of indicators to monitor a program's performance, sometimes there are trade-offs between quality and cost when those measures that are the most meaningful, or those with the strongest validity and reliability, are also the most costly. Certainly care should be taken not to include overly redundant performance measures or fairly extraneous indicators that could be costly to obtain without adding much information about a program's performance. Ultimately, however, it usually comes down to making a judgment about the usefulness of proposed performance measures in relation to the cost, time, and effort expended in collecting them.

Guidelines for Defining Performance Measures

Clearly, defining useful performance measures can be challenging. For some organizations and programs it may be a very straightforward process, but in other cases the specification of good performance indicators may require substantial ingenuity and careful judgment in addition to sound logic. Summing up much of the discussion in this chapter, what follows are a few guidelines for defining useful performance indicators:

- Work directly from program logic models and clear statements of goals, objectives, and service standards to define performance indicators.
- Attempt to develop balanced sets of performance indicators, but avoid overly redundant or only tangentially related measures.
- Reject proposed indicators that will not be meaningful to managers, policymakers, and other relevant stakeholders.

- Wherever possible, define indicators that will have a high degree of face validity to intended users and external audiences.
- Examine the validity and reliability of proposed measures and, everything else being equal, select those that are the least problematic given their intended usage.
- Use proximate measures where necessary, but avoid those that are only tenuously related to the performance criteria of interest.
- Try to anticipate problems of goal displacement and incorporate other indicators to counteract it as appropriate.
- Make judicious assessments of trade-offs between the quality of performance indicators versus the cost of collecting the data.
- Define measures for which clear "data trails" will be available in order to allow for effective quality assurance procedures.
- Provide clear definitions of data sources and data collection procedures to facilitate uniform reporting from decentralized sites.

CHAPTER SIX

ANALYZING PERFORMANCE DATA

When a governmental or nonprofit agency has developed a set of performance indicators and implemented a system for tracking them on a regular basis, what kind of analysis can help make effective use of the performance data? What kinds of comparisons are most appropriate for converting data into *information* and interpreting the results in a meaningful way? Using two local public transit systems as illustrations, this chapter presents the four principal ways of analyzing the data generated by performance monitoring systems so as to assess how well or poorly a program is actually performing: over time, against targets, among subunits, and against external benchmarks.

Public Transit System Performance Model

Figure 6.1 presents a basic model of the logic underlying a conventional public transit system consisting of a primary service delivery component and two support components, (1) maintenance and (2) planning and marketing. Inputs into the system are such resources as employees, vehicles, facilities, equipment, and materials, which can be measured in their individual units or summarized as dollar costs. The program itself is a production process in which policy, design, and operational parameters such as marketing strategies, routes and schedules, fare structure, and preventive maintenance procedures determine exactly how these resources are converted into outputs.

FIGURE 6.1. LOCAL TRANSIT SYSTEM LOGIC MODEL.

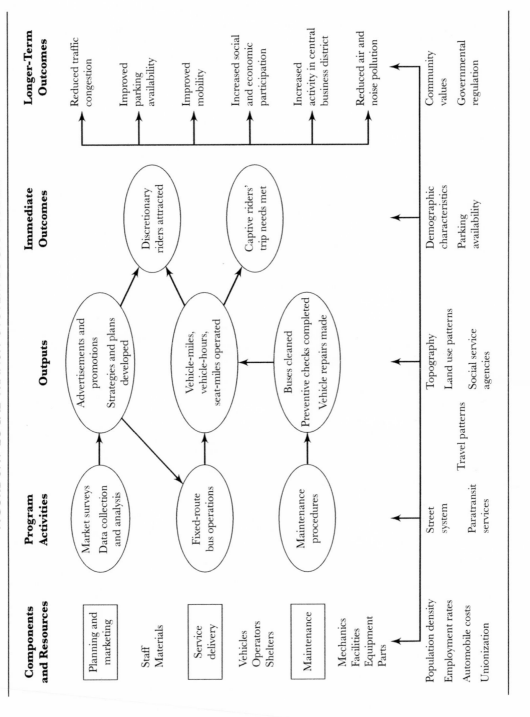

The principal outputs of a transit system—those produced directly by the service component—are vehicle-miles and vehicle-hours operated, measures of the amount of service provided to the community. Another output measure, seat-miles of service provided, represents the system's capacity. It is at the output stage of the transit system logic that interdependencies among the program components begin to appear. For example, the maintenance outputs—buses cleaned, preventive maintenance checks conducted, and repairs completed—contribute to both the ability to produce the service outputs—vehicle-hours and miles operated—as well as the quality of these outputs. Similarly, some of the planning and marketing outputs, such as strategies and plans, feed directly into the service components.

Although various policy objectives are often assigned to public transit, its overall objective may best be summarized as providing affordable mobility. Thus, the immediate outcomes are usually seen as meeting the travel needs of so-called captive riders, those who don't have alternative means of transportation available, and attracting discretionary riders to the system. Over the long run, increased mobility and transit ridership can also contribute to broader impacts relating to other community goals, such as more widespread participation in social and economic activities, increased activity in the central business district, reduced traffic congestion, improved parking availability, and even reduced air and noise pollution. The model also recognizes numerous environmental variables ranging from demographics and employment rates to topography, land use patterns, and travel patterns that can facilitate or impede system performance.

Exhibit 6.1 lists a number of performance measures that are commonly used by transit managers, governing boards, and funding agencies, grouped by performance dimension and relating directly to the program logic model. First, total expense is included in the list because managerial performance is often keyed in part to cost-containment objectives. Similarly, the standard outputs, such as vehicle-miles and vehicle-hours, are basic operational elements that are often included in monitoring systems as scale factors. Measures of various aspects of the quality of service, such as the percentage of bus trips that are operated on time according to published schedules or the percentage of passenger trips requiring transfers, reflect on how satisfactory the service is from the customers' point of view.

Following the logic model in Figure 6.1, the effectiveness of public transit systems is usually measured in terms of ridership. This is measured most directly by the number of passenger trips made on the system, but for comparative purposes the annual rides per capita in the service area might also be of interest. Consumption may also be measured by the amount of revenue generated by the system as well as by the revenue per passenger trip, as at least a partial reflection of the value of the benefit received by patrons. The overall productivity of a transit system can be viewed in terms of utilization rates, that is, the extent to which it is

EXHIBIT 6.1. TRANSIT PERFORMANCE MEASURES.

Resources and outputs
   Total expense
   Vehicle-hours
   Vehicle-miles
   Seat-miles

Labor productivity
   Vehicle-hours per employee
   Vehicle-hours per operator
   Vehicle-miles per maintenance
   employee

Vehicle productivity
   Vehicle-miles per vehicle
   Vehicle-hours per vehicle

Efficiency
   Expense per vehicle-mile
   Expense per vehicle-hour
   Variable cost per vehicle-mile
   Variable cost per vehicle-hour

Service quality
   Percent on-time trips
   Percent transfers
   Accidents per 100,000 vehicle-miles
   Service interruptions per 100,000
   vehicle-miles

Service consumption
   Passenger trips
   Annual rides per capita revenue
   Revenue per passenger trip

Utilization
   Passenger trips per vehicle-hour
   Passenger trips per vehicle-mile
   Passenger miles per seat-mile
   Revenue per vehicle-hour

Cost-effectiveness
   Cost per passenger trip
   Percent cost recovery (revenue/expense)
   Deficit
   Net cost per passenger trip

utilized relative to the amount of service provided. Thus, the number of passenger trips per vehicle-hour and passengers per vehicle-mile are often tracked as well as passenger-miles traveled per seat-mile provided, which is the percentage of capacity that is utilized. In addition, the ability of a transit system to generate revenue in relation to the amount of service provided is represented by the measure of revenue per vehicle-hour.

Labor productivity indicators relate outputs to the employees contributing to the production of those outputs. Because wear and tear on the vehicles is reflected more accurately by vehicle-miles rather than vehicle-hours, vehicle-miles operated per maintenance employee is an appropriate indicator of labor productivity for the maintenance program, whereas the vehicle-hours generated per vehicle operator better represents the labor productivity of the service component. Vehicle productivity can be measured by either vehicle-hours or vehicle-miles operated per active vehicle in the fleet. Operating efficiency is measured by unit costs of producing the outputs, such as the expense per vehicle-hour and the cost per vehicle-mile.

Finally, cost-effectiveness indicators relate the immediate or longer-term outcomes generated by a program to the cost of the resources going into it, most directly the cost per passenger trip. Although few public transit systems, if any, are expected to finance themselves fully from earned revenue, in the business enterprise sense of the bottom line, cost-effectiveness is expressed in terms of the relation of revenue to expense or the percent cost recovery. In addition, the operating deficit incurred and the net cost per passenger trip are other frequently used indicators of cost-effectiveness.

Trends over Time

Because performance monitoring systems track selected indicators of program performance at regular intervals over time, the data naturally accumulate in time-series databases that lend themselves most readily to gauging trends and making comparisons over time. For example, Figure 6.2 shows quarterly ridership data from 1993 through 1999 on the integrated bus and rail transit system operated by the Metropolitan Atlanta Rapid Transit Authority (MARTA) in Atlanta, Georgia. It is clear, first of all, that the bus system carries more passengers, in the range from nine to twelve million per quarter, than does the rail system, with some six to nine million passengers, with the exception of the steep spike in the rail ridership in the third quarter of 1996, which was due to the one-time unprecedented impact of the International Olympic Games held in Atlanta in July of that year.

FIGURE 6.2. MARTA REVENUE PASSENGERS.

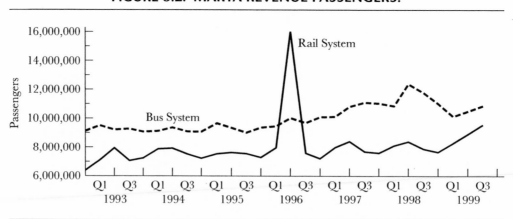

More important, the data reported in Figure 6.2 indicate positive long-term ridership trends on both the bus and rail systems over the six years in question. Although there is considerable up-and-down fluctuation in both series along the way, much of which appears to reflect seasonal variation in passenger levels, the series reflect very gradual but steady increases in ridership in both transit modes, but especially on the bus system since 1995. Whereas rail ridership in the early part of this period hovered around seven to eight million revenue passengers per quarter, toward the latter part of this series it appears to be up very slightly. Ridership on the bus system remained below ten million passengers per quarter through 1995, but since then has increased to eleven or twelve million passengers per quarter. Because maintaining or increasing ridership is so essential to transit system viability, this long-term view provides a very relevant strategic context.

However, while these trends provide an indication of the direction in which MARTA's overall ridership has been headed over the long run, the sharp fluctuations in both modes toward the end of the series also raise questions about the most current status of ridership on the system. Thus, a more precise reading of the most recent period might be more important from a managerial perspective.

Table 6.1 shows the same ridership data for both the bus and rail systems for the four most recent quarters. Because transit ridership is characterized by considerable seasonal variation, as is the case with outcomes in other program and policy areas as well, the most relevant comparison over time is not of the current quarter against the immediately preceding quarter but rather against the same quarter in the preceding year.

Most immediately, the data show that MARTA's bus system carried 1,772,652 *fewer* passengers in the third quarter of 1999 than in the third quarter of 1998, a drop of 14 percent. This steep a decline would be worrisome to any transit manager and would prompt an inquiry as to the causes and a concern with seeing whether bus ridership would rebound in the fourth quarter. The data suggest that drops in bus ridership over the most recent three quarters have been offset in part by increases in the number of passengers on the rail system. Whereas bus ridership is lower in three of the most recent four quarters than in those same quarters in the preceding year, ridership on the rail system was higher in each of the most recent four quarters as compared with the same quarters in the preceding year. Overall, then, over the most recent twelve months or four quarters, ridership on MARTA's bus system was down by 5 percent from the previous year, and ridership on the rail system was up by 4 percent over the previous year. Thus, the total number of revenue passengers on the MARTA system over the past four quarters decreased by 1 percent from the previous year.

TABLE 6.1. MARTA RIDERSHIP BY QUARTER.

Revenue Passengers	4th Quarter 1998	1st Quarter 1999	2nd Quarter 1999	3rd Quarter 1999	%	Four-Quarter Totals	%
Bus System	11,383,420	11,038,818	10,128,240	10,610,160		43,160,638	
Prior Year	11,057,038	11,058,056	10,842,331	12,382,812		45,340,237	
Gain/Loss	326,382	–19,238	–714,091	–1,772,652	–14	–2,179,599	–5
Rail System	7,909,413	7,610,955	8,184,452	9,166,253		32,871,073	
Prior Year	7,675,004	7,543,414	8,025,582	8,373,379		31,617,379	
Gain/Loss	234,409	67,541	158,870	792,874	9	1,253,694	4
Total	19,292,833	18,649,773	18,312,692	19,776,413		76,031,711	
Prior Year	18,732,042	18,601,470	18,867,913	20,756,191		76,957,616	
Gain/Loss	560,791	48,303	–555,221	–979,778	–5	–925,905	–1

Comparisons Against Standards

Monitoring systems often measure actual performance against program objectives, service standards, or budgetary targets in order to gauge the extent to which programs are meeting explicit expectations. For example, the Williamsport Bureau of Transportation, which operates a conventional public transit system known as City Bus in and around Williamsport, Pennsylvania, has defined a set of twenty-nine standards relating to labor productivity, operating efficiency, service quality, utilization, and cost-effectiveness, and annually assesses actual performance against these standards.

A selected set of these standards is shown in Table 6.2, along with City Bus's actual performance on these criteria for fiscal year 1999. Where the data are available, statewide averages for the other small and medium-size transit systems in Pennsylvania (in such urban areas as Reading, Harrisburg, Johnstown, Lancaster, Altoona, Erie, Wilkes-Barre, Scranton, State College, and York) are also shown as a basis of comparison. For example, one City Bus standard calls for operating 15,000 or more vehicle-miles per employee. In fiscal 1999 it actually exceeded this standard by some 1,799 vehicle-miles per employee and also substantially exceeded the statewide average of 14,635.

City Bus has set a standard of operating 95 percent of all bus trips within plus-or-minus five minutes of scheduled times during nonpeak periods and 90 percent during peak periods, and, according to sample check data, it exceeded both in fiscal 1999. It also outperformed the service quality standards concerning safety and service interruptions due to mechanical failures. However, with a 17.6 percent transfer ratio, City Bus fell far short of its standard of 10 percent or fewer passenger trips requiring transfers. With the opening of a new trade and transit center in the Williamsport central business district, the system hopes to reduce the number of transfers and meet this standard.

The internal operating efficiency standards are interesting in part because they are based after the fact on the other comparable systems in the state. The City Bus standard for expense per vehicle-mile is not to exceed the statewide average; the standard for expense per vehicle-hour is not to exceed the statewide average by more than 10 percent. In both cases, City Bus had lower unit costs than the statewide averages.

Regarding utilization standards, which really represent a broader conception of overall system productivity, the annual transit rides per capita in the service area is an indicator of the extent to which the transit system is used by the community. This measure reflects directly on the quality of transit service and the effectiveness of efforts to market this service to the community. In fiscal 1999 City

TABLE 6.2. CITY BUS PERFORMANCE STANDARDS.

	City Bus Standard	Actual 1999	Average for Statewide Class 3 Systems
Productivity Standards			
Vehicle-miles per employee	≥15,000	16,799	14,635
Vehicle-miles per operator	≥22,000	24,190	NA
Vehicle-miles per maintenance employee	≥80,000	100,793	NA
Vehicle-hours per vehicle	≥2,000	2,232	1,903
Vehicle-miles per vehicle	≥28,000	31,829	25,486
Efficiency Standards			
Expense per vehicle-mile	≤$3.63	$3.28	$3.63
Expense per vehicle-hour	≤$52.92	$46.34	$48.11
Service Quality Standards			
Percentage of trips ± 5 minutes			
Nonpeak periods	≥95%	97.4%	NA
Peak periods	≥90%	96.0%	NA
Percentage of transfers	≤10%	17.6%	NA
Collision accidents per 100,000 vehicle-miles	≤3.0	0.7	NA
Vehicle-miles between road calls	≥3,500	6,171	NA
Vehicle-miles between service interruptions	≥25,000	60,756	NA
Utilization Standards			
Annual rides per capita	≥15	16.2	11.4
Passenger trips per vehicle-mile	≥2	2.1	1.7
Passenger trips per vehicle-hour	≥28.0	30.5	22.3
Passenger miles per vehicle-mile	≥6.0	5.7	6.2
Cost-Effectiveness			
Cost per passenger trip	≤$1.85	$1.57	$2.14
Revenue per passenger trip	≥$.70	$0.58	$1.04
Net cost per passenger trip	≤$1.15	$0.99	$1.10
Percent cost recovery	≥35%	37%	49%

Source: Williamsport Bureau of Transportation, 2000. Used with permission.

Bus exceeded its own standard and outperformed the statewide average by a considerable margin. It also exceeded the standards and statewide averages in terms of the number of passenger trips per vehicle-hour and per vehicle-mile. However, actual performance fell a little below the standard of 6.0 passenger-miles per vehicle-mile and below the statewide average of 6.2 on that measure.

Finally, City Bus performed quite well in terms of its standards on cost-effectiveness in fiscal 1999, with the exception of its revenue generation standard. At $1.57, its operating cost per passenger trip was well under the standard of $1.85 and far below the statewide average of $2.14. However, with an average revenue of $.58 per passenger trip, it fell short of its standard of $.70 and the statewide average of $1.04. Although this is largely because, in keeping with a policy mandate to make the service affordable to all who need it, Williamsport has the lowest fare structure among the small and medium-size urban transit systems in Pennsylvania, City Bus was preparing to implement a modest fare increase in mid-2000 in an attempt to come up to this standard and maintain a reasonable balance between revenue and expense. In the meantime, it did recover 37 percent of its operating expense through the farebox, slightly exceeding its standard of 35 percent, but falling far below the statewide average of 49 percent. Collectively, then, City Bus met or exceeded most of its service standards in fiscal 1999, and it is taking action to strengthen performance in those few areas where it failed to achieve the standards.

Comparisons Among Subunits

Although tracking key performance indicators in the aggregate against service standards does provide a balanced picture of how well a local public transit system is performing overall, it can also be helpful to compare different parts of the system on a set of common measures to gain a deeper understanding of strengths and weaknesses and to identify where the system is performing well as opposed to areas that might be seriously underperforming. This is essentially the type of comparison MARTA makes when it breaks down data to track the performance of its bus and rail systems separately. Another transit authority, the Peninsula Transportation District Commission in Newport News, Virginia, tracks a set of performance indicators for five different services it operates: regular transit service, school bus service, work trippers, a shipyard express, and its paratransit system for elderly and disabled patrons.

Many transit agencies compare performance indicators across the various bus routes or rail lines they operate in order to distinguish between the stronger and weaker performers. The Williamsport Bureau of Transportation tracks passenger trips on each bus trip operated on each route during one sample week per year, in September or October, in order to analyze route performance. Table 6.3 shows selected performance indicators from fall 1998.

Clearly, the Newberry, Montoursville, Garden View, Loyalsock, and West Third Street routes are the backbone of the City Bus system; they account for two-thirds of the vehicle-miles operated on the system, and they carry nearly 80 percent of the passengers. Yet in terms of the number of passengers per vehicle-mile, some of the other routes, most notably the Market Street route and the two Nightline routes, hold up as well or even better than the aforementioned "workhorses."

In terms of the variable cost per passenger trip, not including the fixed costs of administrative overhead, the Nightline routes along with the Newberry route are the star performers; the least cost-effective routes are the Muncy/Mall Local route, the Lycoming Mall route, and the South Side route, followed by the "trippers" and assorted extra runs. In terms of the percentage of variable operating costs recovered through farebox revenue, the most problematic routes are the South Side, Market Street, and Muncy/Mall Local routes, followed by the trip-

TABLE 6.3. CITY BUS ROUTE STATISTICS.

Route	Vehicle-Miles Operated	Unlinked Passenger Trips	Passengers per Vehicle-Mile	Variable Cost per Passenger Trip ($)	Percent Variable Cost Recovery
Newberry	1,505.0	6,089	4.0	.66	57.69
Montoursville	1,866.0	3,437	1.8	1.23	30.52
Garden View	1,488.2	3,605	2.4	1.09	33.80
Loyalsock	1,365.0	2,991	2.2	1.28	29.64
Market Street	498.4	1,012	2.0	1.47	20.88
West Third Street	1,276.2	2,707	2.1	1.11	40.86
South Side	915.2	1,004	1.1	2.41	17.57
East End	912.6	1,523	1.7	1.58	27.29
Nightline East	127.8	331	2.6	.99	35.05
Nightline West	175.2	509	2.9	.78	45.92
Muncy/Mall Local	421.5	181	.4	4.38	20.74
Lycoming Mall	328.5	178	.5	2.98	30.57
Trippers/Extras	309.6	289	.9	2.03	23.49
Total	11,189.2	23,856	2.1	$1.17	33.80%

Source: Williamsport Bureau of Transportation, 2000. Used with permission.

pers and the East End route. Prompted in large part by these comparative performance data, City Bus has developed some route realignments and some reallocation of resources away from the Market Street, South Side, and East End routes in an effort to achieve a better balance between service levels and passengers across these routes and to make the overall system more productive.

External Benchmarking

As a final basis of comparison for performance measures, transit authorities, like other public and nonprofit agencies, often find it helpful to compare their performance against that of other similar organizations. Such peer-group comparisons help them gauge the performance of their own programs or operations within the context of the larger public service industry of which they are a part. This kind of external comparison of performance data is usually referred to as external benchmarking to distinguish it from internal comparisons among subunits or program components, which is sometimes referred to as internal benchmarking. In any case, the principal challenge in external benchmarking usually comes down to data reliability and ensuring that uniform definitions and data collection procedures are applied across the board in order to provide fair comparisons among different agencies and programs.

As we have seen, City Bus finds it useful to compare its performance on a number of key indicators against counterpart transit agencies in other small and medium-size urban areas in Pennsylvania. The statewide averages shown for some of the performance measures in Table 6.2 are based on uniform data reported annually by local transit agencies to PennDOT, which provides the local operators with both capital and operating financial assistance. Thus, these data are readily available to any local agency in Pennsylvania that wants to compare the performance of its transit system against others around the state. For City Bus, the data serve to confirm that its performance compares favorably with industry norms in most respects, but that there are a few areas where there may be considerable room for improvement.

Sometimes it is even possible to compare customer feedback on a uniform basis across different agencies or programmatic entities. In Pennsylvania, recent state legislation providing revenue enhancements for public transit included a provision requiring all grant recipients to conduct periodic surveys of their passengers to obtain a measure of customer satisfaction with the quality of service being provided. Although the surveys conducted by these agencies in responding to these requirements for the first time in 1998 differed somewhat from one system to the next, they did incorporate some common elements. Figure 6.3 shows the percentage of the respondents to these surveys who indicated that they were satisfied

FIGURE 6.3. PERCENTAGE OF PASSENGERS SATISFIED WITH VARIOUS ASPECTS OF TRANSIT SYSTEM PERFORMANCE.

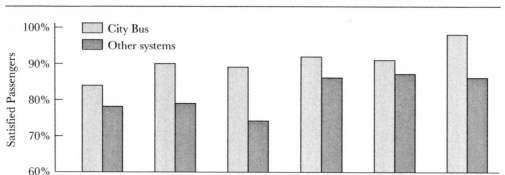

Source: On-board passenger surveys conducted in 1998.

with five common dimensions of transit service quality: on-time performance, cleanliness of the buses, fares, driver courtesy, and personal safety, in addition to an indicator of overall satisfaction. Although the statewide averages for the other small and medium-size systems listed earlier mask some fairly widespread variation in the levels of satisfaction, City Bus passengers on the average reported greater satisfaction with all these aspects of service quality than did the average respondent in these other systems.

Thus, external benchmarks provide one more type of comparison that can help public and nonprofit managers interpret the performance measures they observe on a periodic basis. In fact, some performance measurement systems are designed primarily for the purposes of statistical benchmarking, which is the subject of Chapter Twelve.

Other Comparisons

In addition to analysis of performance data over time, against targets, among operating units, or against external benchmarks, other kinds of comparisons are sometimes useful. Most frequently these focus on breakouts across clientele groups. For example, City Bus compares the aforementioned satisfaction measures across different age groups and between relatively new riders and long-time established passengers. Similarly, the DHHS tracks the percentage of the population defined as being obese as an indicator of physical fitness and compares the results across different age groups. Many public colleges and universities monitor the percentage of all students admitted as freshmen who are retained through their sophomore year, often breaking the data down by racial groups.

Breakouts based on environmental or operating conditions can be helpful in pinpointing strong performance or the incidence of problems. For example, City Bus compares many performance indicators related to its traditional routes serving urban and suburban areas versus those extending out to serve predominantly rural areas. Similarly, measurement systems designed to monitor health trends across the country routinely compare indicators among urban, rural, and suburban counties and among counties with different median income levels. Job training programs might compare employment-focused effectiveness measures across local jurisdictions with very different labor market conditions. Generally speaking, those who design or maintain performance measurement systems should always look for additional ways of breaking out the data in order to provide more useful information to decision makers.

A Concluding Word About Analysis of Performance Measures

When we consider the analysis of performance data, the issue of statistical reliability is sometimes a concern. More often than not, the data monitored by performance measurement systems are *population* data; that is, they are based on data for all relevant cases. Thus, assuming that the data are recorded accurately, entered the same way by all units in a decentralized reporting process, and entered into the software system correctly, then reliability is not an issue. However, sometimes data are reported on a *sample* basis. For example, the number of passenger-miles traveled on a transit system might be counted using a simple random sample of bus trips operated, or customer feedback might be solicited through surveys of a sample of passengers once each year. Sampling is used to save time, money, and effort in data collection, but with sampling there is always the possibility of error. When performance data are collected on a sample basis, therefore, the sample size should be large enough to provide an adequate level of statistical reliability— for example, plus-or-minus 10 percent at the 95 percent confidence level, and reports on the measures should state their level of statistical reliability.

In any case, whether they are based on the full population or on a sample, performance measures are meaningless on their own, without some context to help interpret what they actually show about program performance. Is performance improving or declining? Are we meeting specified standards and achieving our objectives? Are some parts of the operation—different field offices, organizational units, or various other system components, for example—performing better than others? How do we stack up against other similar agencies or programs? These are the relevant questions, and they are addressed by comparing the data generated by performance measurement systems over time, against established targets, across subunits, or against external benchmarks.

Yet we must acknowledge two points to help qualify this analysis of performance data. First, we need to recognize that the kind of comparisons illustrated in this chapter constitute only a surface-level analysis of program performance. Observing a set of indicators at periodic intervals over time provides performance data that are *descriptive* in nature, but not rigorously evaluative. When the data generated by ongoing performance monitoring systems show, for instance, that a program's intended outcomes are increasing, that can be taken as a matter of fact, but the data rarely *prove* that the program itself *causally produced* these beneficial results. Rather, we typically assume that the cause-and-effect relationship reflected in the program logic model are valid, and when the performance data show an increase in program output and a commensurate increase in effectiveness, for example, we conclude that the program really is effective. As a practical matter, this often makes sense, but when we are less certain about the causal connections in the logic underlying a program, these assumptions need to be tested with more intensive analysis using experimental or quasiexperimental designs before we can have faith in what the performance measures seem to be saying about program effectiveness. This is the function of intensive program evaluations rather than more descriptive performance measurement systems.

Second, external forces often exert heavy influence on the results of ongoing performance measurement systems, and these should be taken into account in examining the performance data. With respect to public transit systems, for example, large-scale special events in local communities might account for unusually strong ridership during one particular month, as was the case with the impact of the Atlanta Olympics on MARTA ridership in July 1996. Alternatively, unusually low ridership at certain points could be the result of a large local employer's taking a two-week "holiday" to cut costs and let sales catch up with inventory, or of severely inclement weather patterns that forced the closure of many schools and workplaces and kept people indoors much more than usual. The point is that any number of external factors that are far beyond a program's control may exert strong influence over its performance. These factors should be identified as part of the process of building a logic model, and they should be tracked at least in some informal way so as to shed additional light on the practical meaning of performance data. As we will discuss in Chapter Seven, many performance measurement reporting formats contain "comment fields" for just this purpose.

As long as we keep these two caveats in mind, then, concerning the essentially descriptive nature of performance monitoring data and the often overwhelming influence of external variables on performance, we can often use the kind of data produced by performance measurement systems to analyze program performance within reasonable bounds. This analysis comes from (1) making the kinds of comparisons discussed in this chapter, (2) developing a composite picture of performance by examining these kinds of comparisons and their interrelationships on a whole set of balanced indicators, and (3) keeping track of influential environmental conditions and external variables that might help us interpret trends in performance.

CHAPTER SEVEN

REPORTING PERFORMANCE DATA

Written with Julia Melkers

How do you effectively communicate the results of performance measurement? Which formats are best for displaying different kinds of performance data? Are graphics always necessary when communicating performance results? Once performance data are collected and measures are computed, managers and staff must decide on the most effective ways to communicate the results. This chapter addresses considerations that should be taken into account in the display of performance data and presents several examples of display formats. Chapter Eight discusses the software to support these reporting choices and overall design considerations of the performance measurement system.

Performance Data and Their Audience

Organizations implement measurement systems to monitor performance and communicate the results to managers, clients, governing bodies, and other stakeholders. The output of such a system, in fact, is focused on reporting results. To communicate performance effectively, managers and staff should take into account both the nature of the performance data and the needs of the audience for the data.

Nature of the Performance Data

As discussed in Chapter Three, a performance measurement system may include measures of effectiveness, efficiency, productivity, quality, and client satisfaction. Some of these measures may be expressed as raw numbers, others as averages, percentages, or ratios. In some cases, an index may have been created as a summary variable to represent, for example, overall program quality. Data may be collected on a monthly, quarterly, or annual basis. A program may be limited to a single office, or it may have geographically dispersed offices that provide data to the performance measurement system.

Because of their varied nature, there are three important aspects of the data that managers and staff should consider as they select from data display alternatives. First, what is the time orientation of the data? Is it desirable to display more than a single time period? Would it be effective to highlight the current time period or another specific time period? Second, is there a need to show actual performance against targets or to present their comparisons? For example, is it desirable to display the same measure for different program units, clientele groups, geographical locations, or external benchmarks? Third, are there aspects of the data that require additional explanatory information? For example, have there been variations in the data over time that are important to highlight? Have there been unusual occurrences that have affected performance? If so, it may be useful to integrate a comment field in the presentation of performance results. This would allow for explanation or comment on the data that may not be easily readily apparent through presentation of the numbers or graphics alone. The answers to these questions will help guide the choice of display format.

Needs of the Audience

The better that system designers understand the information needs of their intended audience, the more effectively they will be able to communicate performance results. The data should be displayed in a way that maximizes the audience's ability to easily, accurately, and quickly understand what the data represent. Managers and staff may accomplish this by communicating performance results in a way that is appropriate to the audience. Overall, the level of sophistication and interest of the audience must be considered. In some cases, the same data may be displayed differently for different groups. For example, it is likely that an audience internal to the organization or one very familiar with its activities would prefer more detail and perhaps more "breakdowns" of the data, whereas the general public would be better served with a simple, easily understandable display of the performance data. Elected officials often prefer information that is brief and easily understandable in a short period of time, whereas the media would prefer an easily understandable, attractive presentation of data. The audience may prefer to view only numerical performance results, or they may benefit from explanatory information to highlight different aspects of the performance data.

Reporting Formats

There are many different alternatives to choose from in terms of display formats. The remainder of this chapter presents several alternative formats for displaying performance data results and discusses the appropriate uses and advantages of each. Examples range from tabular to graphical to pictorial displays. Although these examples are useful for illustrating a range of data display formats, it is important to note that there are myriad ways in which any of these formats could be adapted to suit the reporting needs of both the organization and the audience.

Tabular Format: Basic Spreadsheets

Not all performance measurement systems involve elaborate databases. In fact, for some organizations, a performance data management system may simply involve detailed and well-organized spreadsheets. For example, Table 7.1 is an illustration of a simple spreadsheet design for performance reporting from the Telecommunications Division of Georgia's Department of Administrative Services, focusing on the resolution of customer-reported problems, or "trouble tickets," and the installation of new systems, or service orders. This particular spreadsheet report presents data on local telephone service programs for state agencies for each of the state's eight districts, affording the opportunity for comparison from district to district, as well as a "roll-up" for the state overall. The report also shows breakout categories of completion times, along with percentages to track on-time performance.

Spreadsheet designs can also be useful for displaying performance data for different time periods, thereby allowing comparisons to be made by month, quarter, or year. In another example of a simple tabular design, the State of Texas provides reports in tabular format for all agencies as part of their annual performance measures report. Columns display not only performance data by quarters but also targeted performance levels for the year, year-to-date performance, and the percentage of the annual target that has been met to date. Stars are used to highlight measures for which the performance varies more than 5 percent from its targeted performance level. This can be a useful way to draw attention to an individual item.

Performance reports generated directly from a spreadsheet or database have the advantage of being convenient and easy to access for users. They are also

TABLE 7.1. EXAMPLE OF A BASIC SPREADSHEET: DATA BY REGION.

State of Georgia Department of Administrative Services
Telecommunications Performance Report

Local Telephone Service   January 1998

Performance Measures	District 1 Atlanta	District 2 Milledgeville	District 3 Augusta	District 4 Athens	District 5 Rome	District 6 Savannah	District 7 Albany	District 8 Columbus	Total
Telephone Lines Served	46,310	12,368	9,355	18,166	11,415	13,935	12,032	7,936	131,517
Trouble Tickets									
Carryover from Previous Month	5	0	12	0	2	5	0	3	27
Tickets Received This Month	1,896	211	392	296	276	312	305	174	3,862
Total Tickets	1,901	211	404	296	278	317	305	177	3,889
Trouble Tickets Closed Out									
N Within 24 Hours	1,395	146	241	252	245	171	210	131	2,791
%	99%	72%	63%	91%	88%	55%	73%	75%	84%
N Within 24–48 Hours	10	5	131	16	7	92	41	35	337
%	1%	2%	34%	6%	3%	29%	14%	20%	10%
N over 48 Hours	8	53	11	10	26	49	37	8	202
%	1%	26%	3%	4%	9%	16%	13%	5%	6%
Total Closed Out	1,413	204	383	278	278	312	288	174	3,330

TABLE 7.1. EXAMPLE OF A BASIC SPREADSHEET: DATA BY REGION, Cont'd.

Performance Measures	District 1 Atlanta	District 2 Milledgeville	District 3 Augusta	District 4 Athens	District 5 Rome	District 6 Savannah	District 7 Albany	District 8 Columbus	Total
Service Orders									
Carryover from Previous Month									
Routine (10 lines or less)	44	27	37	14	20	35	24	24	225
Complex (11 lines or more)	9	0	9	11	0	6	0	1	36
Received This Month									
Routine (10 lines or less)	371	158	94	138	185	164	104	69	1,283
Complex (11 lines or more)	24	3	0	6	0	2	6	3	44
Routine Completion Times									
Total for Current Month	415	185	131	152	205	199	128	93	1,508
Total Worked This Month	326	155	116	144	120	102	109	73	1,145
N Within 10 Working Days	278	100	93	138	100	73	87	44	913
%	85%	65%	80%	96%	83%	72%	80%	60%	80%
N over 10 Working Days	48	55	23	6	20	29	22	29	232
%	15%	35%	20%	4%	17%	28%	20%	40%	20%
N by Due Date	268	126	89	11	113	80	16	37	740
%	82%	81%	77%	8%	94%	78%	15%	51%	65%

economical to produce and allow for rapid, regular updating. Once the spread-sheet is designed, it requires no special intervention or command to generate the report. This sort of report is especially useful for performance items that need to be viewed regularly. The spreadsheet may be designed once, and as data are up-dated, the report spreadsheet is also updated and ready to be used as a perfor-mance report.

Tabular displays of performance data do not always provide the most desir-able format for all audiences, however. They are most suited for audiences who are very familiar with the program activities detailed in the spreadsheet and who wish to see detailed figures. For individuals who do not view the spreadsheet re-port on a regular basis, understanding the data may be very time consuming. Some individuals may be interested in only a few summary items, in which case graphical formats could be preferable.

Enhanced Tabular Format

Additional information can be integrated in a tabular format, including creative symbols and graphics to enhance the communicability of the information. The Council for School Performance in Georgia issues "report cards" on schools and school districts in the state. The reports are available on the Internet and are aimed at policymakers, parents, and other stakeholders in the education commu-nity. Table 7.2 shows a report card for one particular school in Appling County, Georgia. Data are presented in an easy-to-understand format, using percentages and graphical symbols. Because a goal of these performance reports is to offer comparability across time and against similar schools as well as all schools in the state, the report includes columns offering comparative ratings, using easy-to-read symbols. A detailed legend and description of the report card are featured at the top of the report and provide information important for understanding the sym-bols and the report overall.

Performance reports using an enhanced tabular format have distinct advan-tages. A great deal of data can be presented in a way that is accessible to a broad range of audiences. In the school performance example in Table 7.2, some audi-ences may gravitate only to the graphical symbols, using the arrows to ascertain a school's standing quickly and easily. Users who are more interested in particu-lar numbers have easy access to them, including figures for categories. By dis-playing a combination of numbers and symbols, the report allows users to easily integrate and understand comparative information. The user can quickly scan a report to look for particular symbols, such as a downward arrow. Although en-hanced tabular formats may often be generated in an automated way similar to that of the simple spreadsheet design, producing the report is likely to involve ad-ditional steps and therefore will probably require more expertise than is necessary

TABLE 7.2. EXAMPLE OF AN ENHANCED TABULAR FORMAT: COUNCIL FOR SCHOOL PERFORMANCE.

Appling County Schools: Altamaha Elementary School
Council for School Performance Elementary School Performance Report (1997–98)

This performance report provides information that can be used for school improvement and accountability. *Please note:* (1) Indicators and comparisons are not equally meaningful to every school. Use your judgment on the importance of any given indicator or comparison. (2) More stars or checks means better performance relative to similar schools or the entire state. For indicators where lower scores are desirable, such as dropout rates, *more* stars or checks means *lower* dropout rates. (3) Comparisons are not possible if data are missing or if numbers are too small to maintain student confidentiality. (4) Trends compare 1997–98 data to 1996–97 data. Comparisons are not possible if data are missing, schools are new, or if the indicator is new or has changed. (5) Visit our website at http://arcweb.gsu.edu/csp/ to see reports on other Georgia schools or to see last year's reports.

Legend

*****	School is in upper 20% of similar schools.	✓✓✓✓✓ School is in upper 20% in Georgia.
****	School is in upper 40% of similar schools.	✓✓✓✓ School is in upper 40% in Georgia.
***	School is in the middle range of similar schools.	✓✓✓ School is in the middle range in Georgia.
**	School is in lower 40% of similar schools.	✓✓ School is in lower 40% in Georgia.
*	School is in lower 20% of similar schools	✓ School is in lower 20% in Georgia.
Note:	*Community indicators in italics*	TFC Too few cases to report
		DNR Data not reported

↑↑	Improved more than 5 percentage points this year
↑	Improved more than 2 percentage points this year
←→	Performance within 2 percentage points of last year's
↓	Declined more than 2 percentage points this year
↓↓	Declined more than 5 percentage points this year
◆	Performance comparison not possible
†	Lower score is better.

Rating with Similar Schools	Rating with Entire State	Indicator	GA School Median	Your School	Two-Year Trend
		Academic Preparation			
***	✓✓✓	1. *Percent of kindergartners who were in preschool/organized child care prior to kindergarten.*	64.5%	62.0%	→
*****	✓✓✓✓✓	2. Percent of kindergartners passing all 5 sections of the Georgia Kindergarten Assessment Program	89.0%	97.7%	←↑
*****	✓✓✓✓✓	3. Percent of 3rd grade above national median: Iowa Test of Basic Skills in Reading	50.0%	73.0%	↑↑
*****	✓✓✓✓✓	4. Math	55.6%	86.5%	↑↑
*****	✓✓✓✓✓	5. Science	50.0%	83.8%	↑↑
*****	✓✓✓✓✓	6. Social Studies	51.6%	73.0%	↑↑
*****	✓✓✓✓✓	7. Language Arts	54.5%	81.1%	↑↑
*****	✓✓✓✓✓	8. Sources of Information	52.1%	75.7%	↑↑
*****	✓✓✓✓✓	9. Percent of 3rd grade scoring: in the upper quarter on Iowa Test of Basic Skills in Reading	19.3%	40.5%	↑↑
*****	✓✓✓✓✓	10. in the upper three-quarters on Iowa Test of Basic Skills in Reading	78.1%	91.9%	↑↑
*****	✓✓✓✓✓	11. in the upper quarter on Iowa Test of Basic Skills in Math	30.2%	67.6%	↑↑
****	✓✓✓	12. in the upper three-quarters on Iowa Test of Basic Skills in Math	82.9%	91.9%	↑
****	✓✓✓	13. Percent of 5th grade above national median: Iowa Test of Basic Skills in Reading	51.3%	58.1%	↓↓
*	✓✓	14. Math	54.9%	46.7%	↓↓
*****	✓✓✓✓✓	15. Science	55.7%	74.2%	↕→
****	✓✓✓✓✓	16. Social Studies	53.2%	71.0%	↑
***	✓✓✓	17. Language Arts	57.0%	58.1%	↑↑
****	✓✓✓	18. Sources of Information	53.7%	64.5%	↕→
**	✓✓	19. Percent of 5th grade scoring: in the upper quarter on Iowa Test of Basic Skills in Reading	16.9%	12.9%	↓↓
****	✓✓✓	20. in the upper three-quarters on Iowa Test of Basic Skills in Reading	84.0%	90.3%	↑↑
*	✓	21. in the upper quarter on Iowa Test of Basic Skills in Math	26.1%	13.3%	↓↓
***	✓✓✓✓	22. in the upper three-quarters on Iowa Test of Basic Skills in Math	81.5%	86.7%	↕→

to generate a simpler report. However, with the continuing advances in available software, integrating simple symbols using an embedded formula is becoming increasingly easy.

Common Graphical Displays

Many software packages make it easy and quick to display data in a variety of graphical formats. Graphical displays of data have the advantage of quickly communicating performance results without requiring in-depth knowledge of the raw numbers. Graphics are especially useful for showing trends over time, or the relationship of different groups to one another. Perhaps most important, graphical displays allow information to be easily disseminated and quickly absorbed by a wide range of audiences. They have the advantage of easy readability for audiences who are intimidated by or uninterested in the actual numbers. Displaying performance data in any of these simple graphical formats is appropriate for dissemination to both internal groups and external stakeholders, such as policymakers or the media. The general public and even policymakers may be most interested in trends or comparisons of groups; these are easily communicated using graphical displays. Graphical displays can also be memorable; individuals may be more apt to remember a trend illustrated by a line graph, or a relative comparison illustrated by a bar chart, than the actual numbers.

Common graphical display formats include pie charts, bar charts, and line graphs. Bar charts are especially useful ways to display performance data. They may be used individually as simple bar charts that show data for an individual measure, or they may be constructed as "cluster" charts with individual bars for breakout groups within the data to allow for comparisons across groups or across time. Examples of different graphical formats are shown in Figure 7.1. The State of Texas combines agency budget and performance information in a single performance measurement report that is available both in hard copy for the Texas Department of Economic Development and on the Internet.

The format shown in Figure 7.1 is representative of the reports of other Texas agencies that provide similar budget information and key performance measures. On the second page, performance data (target and actual) are shown for a five-year period in line graphs for four key economic development measures. For example, the first measure, Job Opportunities Announced by Businesses Receiving Assistance, shows an increase from 1997 to 2001. Because these reports are used in the budgeting process, certain budgetary and staff data are also provided in the report. Because Texas has required performance information from its agencies for a number of years, multiyear data are included, which allows for comparisons to be made across time. In addition to the graphical display of data, the Texas report also includes a second page for each agency, offering additional descriptive information

FIGURE 7.1. EXAMPLE OF A GRAPHICAL DISPLAY: BUDGET AND PERFORMANCE SUMMARY, TEXAS DEPARTMENT OF ECONOMIC DEVELOPMENT.

TEXAS DEPARTMENT OF ECONOMIC DEVELOPMENT

SELECTED BUDGET INFORMATION

ALL FUNDS, 2001 BUDGETED

General Revenue - Dedicated 2.5%
Federal Funds 7.3%
Other Funds 7.9%
General Revenue 82.3%

Total: $31,422,230

FULL-TIME-EQUIVALENT POSITIONS

Cap 195, Cap 195, Cap 179, Cap 179
180, 175, 178, 164, 164
1997 1998 1999 2000 2001

MAJOR CONTRACTS REPORTED, 2001

Despacho Travel SC *
  Accounting services, Mexico City office
  $527,550
Garza, Gonzalez & Associates *
  Auditing services
  $40,000
Read-Poland, Inc. *
  Mission strategy development
  $14,500

* Known multi-year contract

LAWSUITS REPORTED, 2000-01

One lawsuit with an unspecified potential liability amount.

BUDGET HIGHLIGHTS

General Revenue Funds accounted for over 82 percent of the agency's expenditures in fiscal year 2001, which included $1 million in unexpended balance authority for Defense Dependant Communities from fiscal year 2000.

Approximately $20.3 million in General Revenue Funds (Hotel Occupancy Tax) was expended in fiscal year 2001. That amount represents one-twelfth of the state's 6 percent hotel occupancy tax revenue which is dedicated for funding a statewide tourism marketing effort.

The agency expended approximately $0.8 million in Capital Access Funds in fiscal year 2001. These funds were used to induce lending institutions to make small loans to businesses. The state was able to use a small sum of money from these funds to facilitate larger loan amounts.

As the administrator of the Federal Empowerment Zones/ Enterprise Communities, the agency distributed over $2.3 million in Federal Funds to local communities in Texas, which provided incentives for businesses to create and retain jobs.

Because the Smart Jobs Program was frozen from entering into new contracts, approximately $48.8 million in Other Funds was not expended in fiscal year 2001.

FULL-TIME-EQUIVALENT EMPLOYEES

The agency <u>did not</u> exceed its cap for full-time-equivalent (FTE) positions for fiscal year 2001 as a result of a turnover rate of 28.6 percent and leaving some positions vacant.

RELATED REPORTS AND REVIEWS

In the *Texas Department of Economic Development Financial Profile* issued in February 2001, the State Auditor's Office (SAO) reported that the agency did not spend or obligate approximately $58 million of its fiscal year 2000 budget. It overestimated expenditures by approximately $4 million for two strategies. In addition, during fiscal year 2000, the agency transferred approximately $93 million from the Smart Jobs Fund to the Unemployment Compensation Fund to comply with Government Code, Section 481.154(i).

In *A Review of Projections for the Smart Jobs, the Unemployment Compensation Trust Fund, and the Smart Jobs Holding Fund*, the SAO estimated that the ending balance in the Smart Jobs Fund would be $101.6 million when the Smart Jobs program would conclude on December 31, 2001. This amount is significantly higher than the agency's estimated fund balance of $71.6 million. After an October 2001 transfer of $83.4 million to the Unemployment Insurance Fund and a $10.2 million appropriation to the Higher Education Coordinating Board in 2002–03, the agency reports that the Smart Jobs Fund will have a remaining balance just large enough to cover outstanding obligations.

FIGURE 7.1. EXAMPLE OF A GRAPHICAL DISPLAY: BUDGET AND PERFORMANCE SUMMARY, TEXAS DEPARTMENT OF ECONOMIC DEVELOPMENT, Cont'd.

TEXAS DEPARTMENT OF ECONOMIC DEVELOPMENT

An August 1997 SAO *Audit Report on Performance Measures at 26 Agencies* certified without qualification all three of the 1996 performance measures reviewed when the agency was known as the Department of Commerce.

PERFORMANCE HIGHLIGHTS
During fiscal year 2001, the agency attained (within 5 percent) or exceeded 63 percent of its 16 established key performance targets.

The agency attained or exceeded three of its seven outcome targets and seven of its nine output/efficiency targets.

The fiscal year 2001 target for *Number of Job Opportunities Announced by Businesses Receiving Assistance* was not met, which indicated a decline in economic growth and, therefore, slowed new job announcements in the second half of fiscal year 2001. Companies actively seeking information on Texas were reluctant to make business location decisions because of a softening in the national economy.

The *Number of Smart Jobs Participants Trained for New Jobs* dropped to 10.1 percent of the target. Because of loss of statutory authority effective December 31, 2001, Smart Jobs program activity was limited to contract administration, closeout, and reporting. A larger than anticipated number of businesses did not meet contractual terms under stricter enforcement, which resulted in fewer than anticipated trainees completing training.

The agency exceeded its target for *Number of Businesses Developed as Expansion/Recruitment Prospects* as companies continued to show a high degree of interest in seeking assistance in their expansion efforts. Specific information was provided regarding tax issues, permitting, sites, and financing.

In fiscal year 2001, the agency exceeded its target for *Number of Consumer Inquiries in Response to Advertising for Tourism.* The 1.8 million consumer inquiries received also exceeded the previous peak year of 1999. The tourism advertising campaign, which included a sweepstakes promotion with travelocity.com and Internet and website programs, was successful in generating inquiries for Texas travel information.

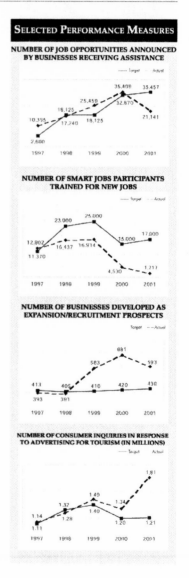

SELECTED PERFORMANCE MEASURES

NUMBER OF JOB OPPORTUNITIES ANNOUNCED BY BUSINESSES RECEIVING ASSISTANCE

NUMBER OF SMART JOBS PARTICIPANTS TRAINED FOR NEW JOBS

NUMBER OF BUSINESSES DEVELOPED AS EXPANSION/RECRUITMENT PROSPECTS

NUMBER OF CONSUMER INQUIRIES IN RESPONSE TO ADVERTISING FOR TOURISM (IN MILLIONS)

Source: Legislative Budget Board, State of Texas, 2001a.

useful for highlighting accomplishments and offering explanatory information. For example, this illustration notes the attainment of targeted levels of performance for business development and job creation. Comment fields such as these are useful for conveying additional qualitative information or descriptions of the data that are especially important to communicate.

Creative Graphical and Pictorial Displays

Graphical displays of data such as those described in the preceding section are common and familiar to most groups. It is useful to display data using a scale and a graphic that is easily understood by the audience. However, for audiences that might be intimidated by even simple bar or pie charts, the creative use of pictorial items from everyday life makes the data display more accessible and less threatening. For example, Figure 7.2 shows the use of a thermometer to illustrate the "overall quality of care" for a particular public hospital as solicited in brief interviews with recent patients. Using the thermometer, "hotter" is better in terms of quality, whereas "cooler" implies poorer-quality care. In this example, a number of comparative items are also displayed on the thermometer, such as the benchmark "goal" level, the system mean for twenty hospitals, and the low score from the survey results. It is a nonthreatening, efficient way to show not only the performance results but also their relationship to other key figures. The patient feedback shown in the thermometer is also displayed in tabular format, along with ratings from other dimensions, including overall nursing and overall physician quality, willingness to return, willingness to recommend, and helpfulness of visit. Other data useful to the audience are also shown in a bar graph ("Reasons for visits" to the Healthcare Center) to add an additional level of respondent information to the report.

In another example, Figure 7.3 illustrates a "dashboard" display with an automotive flavor to convey performance results for a Department of Juvenile Justice. In this example, both the current status of certain performance items, represented by the arrows, as well as target levels, shown with solid lines, are displayed on each gauge. For example, the actual number of escapes is above the target level, as are cases of reported abuse, whereas the recidivism rate of discharged juveniles is lower than the target. Here, the arrow on the dashboard is implied to be moving in an upward direction. Below the dashboards, "traffic signals" (best displayed in color) are used to indicate how well a number of ongoing operations are moving along. Red is used to indicate a problem for an individual item, yellow to indicate a warning, and green to indicate that the item is within an acceptable range, or cruising. This pictorial example allows users to quickly scan the display and see where trouble spots may be.

There is a wide range of options to choose from in pictorial graphical displays. For example, for programs or organizations that serve a broad geographical

FIGURE 7.2. EXAMPLE OF A CREATIVE GRAPHICAL DISPLAY: HOSPITAL PATIENT FEEDBACK.

The Healthcare Center
Inpatient Survey Results
THIRD QUARTER
From patients discharged August 21st thru September 30th

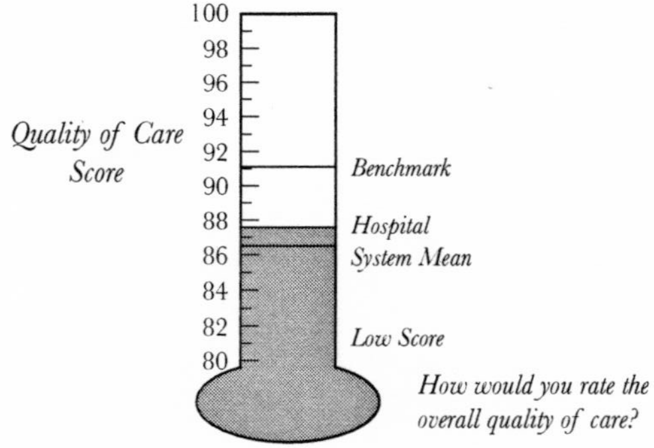

Quality of Care Score

100
98
96
94
92 — Benchmark
90
88 — Hospital
86 — System Mean
84
82 — Low Score
80

How would you rate the overall quality of care?

Summary of Outcomes

400 completed interviews

	Benchmark	Hospital
Quality of Care Score	91.1	87.7
Overall Nursing	95.1	91.8
Overall Physician	95.9	95.9
Willingness to Return	96.9	93.5
Willingness to Recommend	96.7	93.2
Helpfulness of Visit	95.7	94.8

Overall Assessment

The overall quality of care score for the hospital is

87.7

This puts the hospital 8th among 20 hospitals measured.

The aggregate score (computed by taking the average score for all attributes and functional area items) is

92.0

Reasons for Visits

Reason	Hospital	System
Physician	31.9%	48.5%
Convenient	15.8%	33.0%
Friend recommend	17.4%	14.8%
Care better	39.4%	29.4%
Insurance	15.8%	12.3%
Cost lower	1.3%	0.5%
Only hospital in area	5.5%	5.4%

Percent of respondents

0.0% 10.0% 20.0% 30.0% 40.0% 50.0% 60.0%

■ Hospital □ System

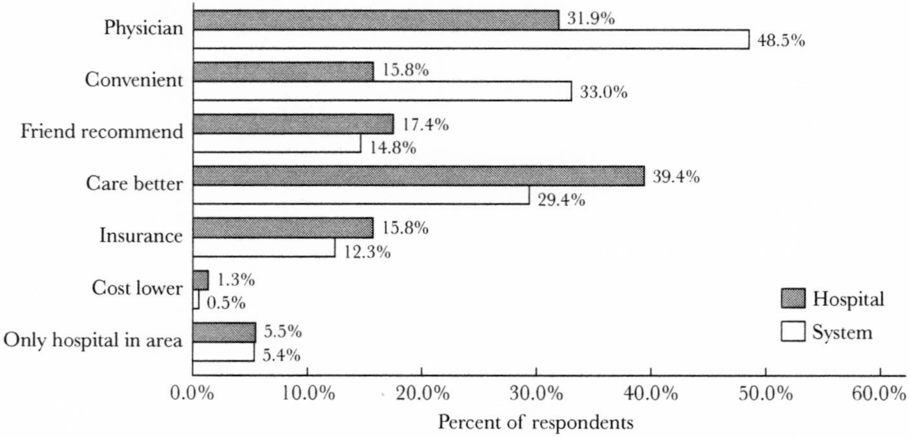

Source: SatisQuest℠. Reprinted with permission.

FIGURE 7.3. EXAMPLE OF A PICTORIAL DISPLAY: DASHBOARD.

Department of Juvenile Justice

Regional Youth Detention Centers

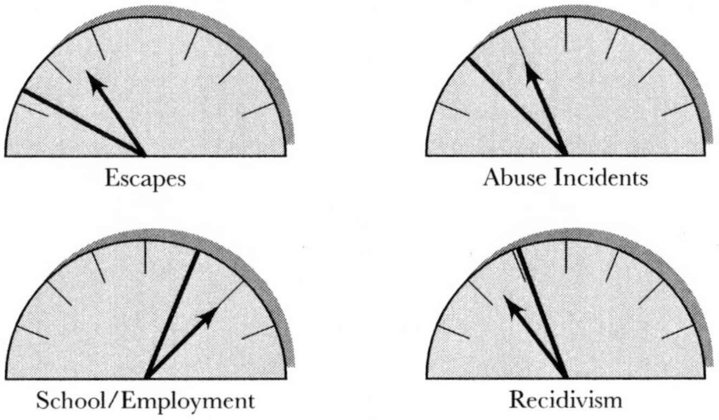
Escapes
Abuse Incidents
School/Employment
Recidivism

Service Areas QA	**Unsatisfactory**	**Status vs. Targets**
Mental Health	3%	Cruising
Medical	7%	Problem
Education	12%	Cruising
Behavior Management	5%	Warning
Transition Planning	29%	Problem
Admissions and Orientation	4%	Cruising
Food Service	8%	Cruising
Facility Maintenance	15%	Warning
Community Relations	9%	Problem

Cruising Warning Problem

area, it is sometimes desirable to indicate changes by geographical area to facilitate comparisons across or between areas. The creative use of mapping can be particularly useful in displaying performance results. With advances in geographic information systems (GIS), maps can be increasingly integrated in performance reporting. For example, the Fund for the City of New York (FCNY) (www.fcny.org) has used maps extensively to communicate performance results both in hard copy and on the Internet. Street smoothness is displayed for each of the fifty-nine community

FIGURE 7.4. EXAMPLE OF A MAP DISPLAY: FUND FOR THE CITY OF NEW YORK.

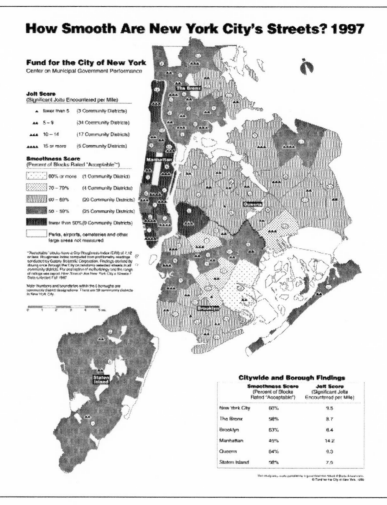

districts in New York City, using shading to indicate the degree of street smooth-ness and other marks to indicate significant jolts encountered per mile. The map is accompanied by a small table that summarizes the performance for these two variables by borough, as shown in Figure 7.4. The online version of the map also allows the viewer to click on an individual borough or community district and ac-cess additional performance results for that specific area. FCNY also has an ex-tensive program that addresses a range of street-level quality issues in its Computerized Neighborhood Environment Tracking (ComNET) program. Data on a broad range of street conditions—such as litter, potholes, graffiti, and bro-

FIGURE 7.4. EXAMPLE OF A MAP DISPLAY:
FUND FOR THE CITY OF NEW YORK, Cont'd.

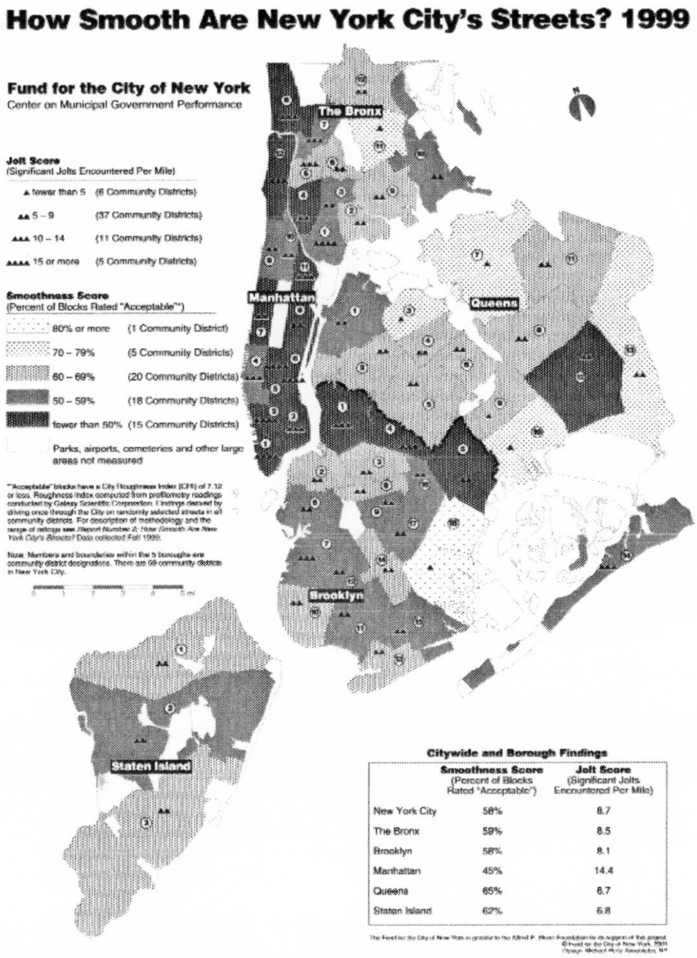

How Smooth Are New York City's Streets? 1999

Source: Fund for the City of New York. http://www.fcny.org/cmgp/streets/pages/map.htm.
© Fund for the City of New York, 2001. Printed with permission.

ken streetlights—are gathered by community representatives using handheld computers that feed data directly into the ComNET database. This use of mapping provides data on a block-by-block area, showing precisely where various poor street conditions occur. Using this system, detailed reports, graphics, and neighborhood maps may easily be displayed, and government and community groups can address the problem more efficiently. The maps can also be used for longitudinal comparisions as additional years of data are collected, as shown in the two parts of Figure 7.4.

Creative graphical displays, such as the thermometer or dashboard, are particularly advantageous for communicating performance results in a way that attracts attention to the data in a nonthreatening way. Maps can also be used creatively to display not only basic differences between areas but also additional detail by integrating the use of symbols, as shown in Figure 7.4. Overall, creative graphical and pictorial displays can be especially useful for communicating with the media, in press releases, and in annual reports or news briefs that are read by a variety of audiences. Organizations should choose pictorial displays that make sense to their audience and that are appropriate for the services they provide. Like other graphical displays, the results can be memorable to some individuals who are not likely to recall the precise numbers. However, unlike the simpler graphical displays discussed earlier, displays such as these do require some expertise in graphics and may not be easily generated by all staff. More specialized software or graphical design may be required.

Concluding Thoughts on Reporting Performance Results

The output of a performance measurement system is generally a performance report of one form or another. Organizations are interested in demonstrating their performance to stakeholders and the policymaking community, often offering comparisons among time periods or to other organizations. The overall utility of a performance measurement system resides in large part in the accessibility and understandability of its results—in how quickly, easily, and accurately the intended audiences are able to understand and absorb the performance reporting.

In deciding the best way to communicate their organization's performance results, managers and staff need to consider not only the nature of the data but also the information needs of the audiences for the information. For many organizations, it makes sense to use more than one type of display format because their performance measurement system will include a variety of measures and types of performance data. It is not unusual to report the same data in different formats to different audiences. Organizations should be creative in their choice of display, and they need not feel restricted to the easiest, most common formats. Combining display formats may also be useful—displaying some items in bar graphs, others in more creative pictorial displays.

To be creative, organizations need to be familiar with and take advantage of software technologies. The range of display options continues to increase as advances in software technology greatly improve the ease and accessibility of different display formats for even the relatively unsophisticated computer user.

CHAPTER EIGHT

PROCESSING PERFORMANCE DATA

Julia Melkers

O nce performance measures have been established, what is the best way to maintain the performance measurement data? Typically, an organization maintains data in an electronic format, in what is known as a performance data management system. This term refers to the integrated hardware and software environment that may provide links between databases, an interface to allow easy access and reporting from the databases, or both. What are the characteristics of a useful performance data management system? What considerations should you take in the selection or design of such a system? Establishing an electronic platform for maintaining performance data presents issues of data quality, integrity, and accessibility. This chapter first addresses the design or selection of a performance data management system. It then provides an overview of software selection, concluding with guidelines for establishing a high-quality system.

Selecting or Designing the Data Management System

The quality and ease of use of the data management system have profound implications for the ability to use and communicate performance information effectively. Although it is not possible to point to a "single best" database system here, the goal should be to establish a performance data management system that

- Allows for safe, effective, and accessible data entry
- Is designed to minimize data entry errors and for ease of data entry and verification
- Is integrated with other data collection systems within the organization
- Is cost-effective
- Is designed to accommodate multiple reporting formats, depending on the request of the user
- Is adaptable as data and reporting needs change
- May be easily integrated with Web-based applications to allow for various options in the dissemination of data

Data management needs vary tremendously among organizations, depending on a number of characteristics: their size; the number, complexity, and diversity of their programs; their reporting requirements; and their level of technical sophistication. Ideally, you will address issues of data management and access as you refine the measures themselves. The decisions you will need to make in the process of selecting or designing a performance data management system are listed here. We will discuss them in the sections that follow.

Important Decisions in Selecting or Designing a Software
Platform for Performance Measurement Data

- Clarify the time frame of the data and integrate it into the selection or design of the data management system.
- Decide on and plan for the level of detail required for analysis of the performance data.
- Clarify and plan for the interface between the performance database and both new and existing data sources and data collection instruments.
- Decide on the level of sophistication required for the most effective data entry to the system.
- Decide on which formats and platforms you will use for reporting performance data.
- Identify data safety measures and integrate them in the system design.

Data Time Frames

Your organization is likely to have a broad range of measures gathered and reported on a longitudinal basis; the data system must be able not only to differentiate between the different time frames the data represent but also to allow the user to request different time frames in data reporting, if desired. For example, some data will be most appropriately viewed on a monthly or quarterly basis, whereas other data would be most meaningful viewed and analyzed only twice a year. The viewer of the data may also want to select particular time frames for comparison. The ability to do this should be planned for in the system development phase and integrated in the system design so that data are collected and maintained in a way that is most useful to the viewer.

Level of Analysis

It is important to decide and plan for the required level of analysis of the performance data. For example, will only summary data be needed, or would users also like to be able to specify different time frames or categories within the data? Would the users like to select performance data for a geographical region or a particular regional office? For client satisfaction data, will it be important to input all response categories in the database or simply to know only how many are "very dissatisfied"? Will it be important to calculate or report percentages of respondents as well as the raw data?

Interface with Other Data Systems

In addition to the characteristics of the data, there are also features of the data collection process that feed into the design of the performance data management system. Thus, it is important to clarify and plan for the interface between data sources and the databases and systems. A performance data management system can be designed to accommodate different information types and sources, as well as be designed to allow for information linkages between sources. Because performance data are likely to come from a number of sources—some new (such as a newly designed client response card) and others already existing (such as a financial or budget database)—a performance data management system will need to integrate existing and newly constructed databases. For newly created data collection instruments, the linkage with the performance data management system may be developed as it is designed. For example, online data entry and access to performance reports are becoming increasingly important as technology changes and administrators and the public alike become more comfortable with Internet technology and have easier and cheaper access to it. However, you need not always create new data collection instruments or processes. You may also explore using *existing* data collection forms, such as financial reporting or customer response cards, adapting or changing them to better suit the data system if necessary. Establishing linkages between databases (new and old) should be addressed in the design process in order to maximize the cost-effectiveness, ease of use, and accuracy of data in the system.

Appropriate Data Entry Systems

You will also need to decide on the level of sophistication of the data entry system. For some organizations, it will be appropriate to design a fairly complex and sophisticated system. This is especially true of larger decentralized organizations, such as federal or state agencies, or even large programs with multiple offices. In these cases, a database system that allows for multiple data entry and access points may be most appropriate. The challenge is to integrate data from multiple sources in a useful and useable way. The effort to design a performance data management system for a highly decentralized organization is complicated by the fact that many programs are not housed in a single location. Program activities may be scattered geographically across a locality, state, or region, yet performance measurement of a program overall requires collecting and coordinating data across these locations. In this scenario, additional communication and work are required to ensure consistency in data quality and reliability. At the very least, the performance data management system should allow for easy importation of data from existing systems. Smaller, centralized organizations, in contrast, are likely to have less complex data management needs. Individual programs or organizations may be interested in tracking performance data for their activities, but may not have an extensive operation nor detailed reporting requirements.

Data Reporting Formats

Although data maintenance issues are part of the day-to-day activities in managing a performance data management system, the ultimate goal of establishing such a system is generally focused on reporting results. Thus, another critical decision in the system design or selection process is to address the reporting of performance data. For example, which formats (as discussed in Chapter Seven) are desirable for reporting results? Are reporting preferences limited to hard copies only, or are accessible electronic copies also desirable? Is access to the reports restricted to individuals within the organization, or should others outside have easy access? Is it desirable to publish performance data on the Internet? The software selected or designed for the performance data management system should take these needs into account.

As discussed in Chapter Seven, many organizations find reports generated directly from a spreadsheet or database to be the most convenient and easy to access, especially when users need to view the performance items regularly. It is easy to embed formulas in spreadsheet programs (such as Microsoft Excel) to generate graphics or tables from specified cells. The spreadsheet or database may also be configured to allow either active links to other software packages (such as Powerpoint) or other graphics packages to automatically generate graphics, tables, and reports. Either of these two approaches may be especially useful in satisfying regular reporting needs and requirements—particularly if the same data fields are required each time.

Traditional reporting formats are changing, however. With rapid advances in computing technology, it is not only acceptable but expected that government and nonprofit organizations use the Internet for providing and gathering information relevant to their operations, and the design of performance data management systems needs to take this into account. Web-based formats may be used both internally and externally. For example, some reports may be generated for access through an internal local area network (LAN) for use by employees or special groups of employees. A LAN may be useful for circulating performance information among internal task forces or for limiting access to certain levels of management or even within selected departments. It may also be a way to disseminate performance data prior to wider dissemination on an outside network.

Generally, however, it is important to disseminate performance information to outside stakeholders, and the Internet allows for an inexpensive and rapid way to communicate information to large groups of individuals. Government and nonprofit organizations may wish to publish performance information on their organization's Web page. This platform has become even more acceptable as household Internet use and access to computing technologies by the general public have increased. Websites can be designed to allow simple viewing of reports or even easy downloading of reports and charts. Adobe Acrobat Reader has become a popular way to provide reports in an easily viewable, downloadable format, without risking changes to the original format.

Although the Internet is becoming an increasingly popular mode of access, organizations do vary in the level of sophistication of the data they disseminate on the Web. For example, the State of Texas uses the Adobe Acrobat Reader format to provide an online report each year that includes budget and performance data for all state agencies. The Council for School Performance in Georgia allows users to read online and download an individual school report card or even an entire spreadsheet for a selected school. Plans are under way to make the system even more interactive so that users would be able to compare their selected school to other schools around the state on a single performance measure.

Data Safety Measures

It is crucial to integrate data safety measures in the design of your organization's performance data management system. In spite of your best efforts to hire the right data manager, to employ careful, competent data entry staff, and to design a sophisticated yet user-friendly performance data management system, the over-all quality of these efforts depends on the quality and accuracy of the data itself. To put it simply, *mistakes happen*. Errors in the recording of performance data or in the data entry process itself must be uncovered and repaired so that the performance data being reported and used are accurate. Most often, errors occur due to operator or data entry failure. Sound procedures are needed to ensure data accuracy, because open access to the system creates multiple points at which data entry errors can occur or, worse, existing data may be altered, even unknowingly, by another user. In anticipation of these potential problems, you should take great care in selecting the individuals who will have access to the system. The number of these individuals should be kept to a minimum, and you should establish a mechanism for identifying them, such as a password or user ID. These safeguards should be considered in the design process.

Additional data verification techniques should of course be addressed in the overall management of a performance measurement system, but verification items can also be integrated in the system design itself. "Safety doors" can be built into the system as variable fields are defined. For example, for some items that may never exceed a certain value, the cell in which those data would be entered could be limited to figures within a specified range. For some items, this would be fairly easy to integrate (for example: no client numbers greater than a certain value). Additional "red flags" for the data entry staff can be integrated into the system through the labels that are used in the data entry page, such as maximum or minimum values for particular fields. These would serve as visual reminders for data entry staff and thus as additional safeguards for the integrity of the system overall.

Selecting the Right Performance Data Management Software

Choices of the software platform for maintaining and accessing the performance database are changing frequently. In general, an organization may choose to purchase a commercial performance measurement database, design a custom database, or adapt an existing software package to process, report, and disseminate the data.

Commercial Programs

If an organization's performance measurement data management needs are large and complex, it may opt to purchase a commercial performance measurement database. An "off-the-shelf" performance measurement software package will typically allow an organization to install the software and select options that adapt it to the organization's needs. A number of commercial performance measurement data applications exist, such as FlexMeasures, pbviews (used by the State of Illinois and several divisions of the military, among others), Comshare (used by the Internal Revenue Service), and dbProbe (used by the National Archives and Records Service), each designed for various aspects of performance measurement processes. All are marketed to both public and private organizations and are Web enabled. Figure 8.1 shows sample screen shots from the pbviews® software package, illustrating an overview of a range of measures alongside a summary of customer satisfaction data for a hypothetical government agency. The visuals show actual versus targeted performance for a range of measures, and a summary of the customer satisfaction data is provided in bar graph format.

As the example shows, the visuals are constructed so that users can move easily between screens, using buttons similar to those you would find in a binder for hard copies. For some, these commercial packages serve as useful and easily adaptable data management systems. The advantages of purchasing such a system are that it is designed specifically for maintaining and reporting performance data, and therefore often includes user-friendly data entry, update, and reporting options. When problems arise, software support is usually available through the vendor. As mentioned, users are generally able to make selections from within the

FIGURE 8.1. SCREEN SHOTS OF A COMMERCIAL PERFORMANCE MEASUREMENT SOFTWARE PACKAGE: pbviews®.

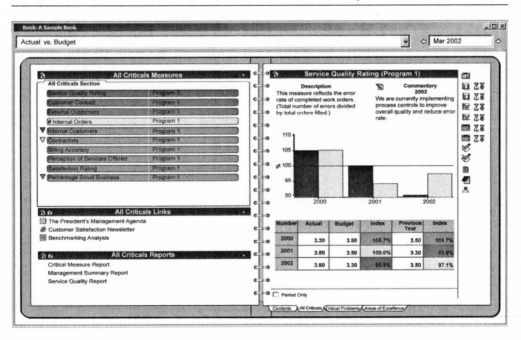

FIGURE 8.1. SCREEN SHOTS OF A COMMERCIAL PERFORMANCE MEASUREMENT SOFTWARE PACKAGE: pbviews®, Cont'd.

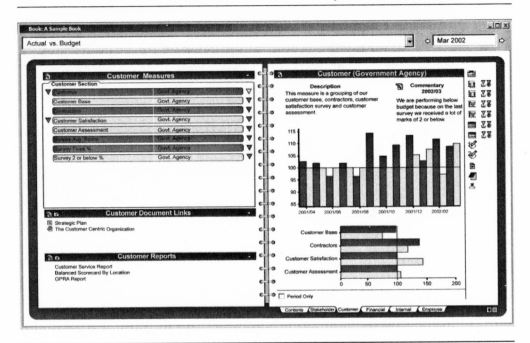

Source: pbviews. Printed with permission of Panoramic Business Views, Inc.

software to adapt it to, for example, the terminology used in their organization. The main disadvantage of off-the-shelf packages is that they may not suit the specific data collection and reporting needs of your organization.

Customized Systems

If an organization cannot afford or is unhappy with the commercial applications available, another option is to design a customized system, either using in-house expertise or hiring a database consultant. The costs associated with this would vary depending on the qualifications of the consultant and the complexity of the system requested. The primary disadvantage of designing a system "from the ground up" is that hiring an outside consultant can be very costly. However, the advantage of such an approach is that the organization can customize a system specifically to its needs, adapting it during a trial period. For example, the State of Texas used internal software experts to design the statewide Automated Budget and Evaluation System of Texas, which is maintained on the Texas mainframe computer and accessed via the Internet. It is a menu-driven system that provides space for managers and staff to input data and allows the agency to explain variance in the performance data. (In explaining variance, agencies are required to describe both the factors that caused the changes in performance as well as the methods by which the agency plans to deal with that variation.)

Generic Software

Even if its data needs are fairly complex, an organization can design and implement a software platform to maintain performance data by using existing packages that the organization already has and even uses on a regular basis. It is impossible to say which software will work best for any one organization because that decision is dependent on the needs of the specific organization, the types and sources of the data, and the reporting formats desired. The software and technology alternatives are rapidly changing, with new and improved packages coming onto the market regularly. Often the easiest and most cost-effective approach to establishing a data management system is to adapt one of these existing software packages; this is perhaps the most common approach for state and local governments to take in the development of a performance-based data management system. The primary advantages of this approach are that, because most organizations already have suitable software, it is inexpensive, and members of the organization are likely to be familiar with the application; also, the existing software can be adapted quickly and easily for maintenance of performance data. The disadvantage of using these types of software is that because they are not designed to be an integrated performance measurement data system, you may need to take additional steps or create new linkages in order to have efficient and effective data entry and reporting processes.

Several software packages may be adapted to performance measurement database use, including database programs, such as Microsoft Access and Oracle; spreadsheet programs, such as Microsoft Excel, Corel Quattro Pro, or Lotus 1-2-3; or Web-based software, such as SQL Server. For smaller, centralized organizations, spreadsheet programs may offer a useful framework for maintaining performance data. For these organizations, creating a performance data management system may involve little more than adapting a spreadsheet program. In this case, the "design" process would entail little more than assigning designations (time frame, category of service, geographical, or other categories) to the spreadsheet columns and performance measures to the spreadsheet rows, and perhaps writing some simple formulas to calculate percentages and sums in some of those rows and columns. The resulting spreadsheet may look something like the example in Table 8.1, which is from PennDOT's quarterly report. Employees of various local

TABLE 8.1. EXAMPLE OF A SPREADSHEET FORMAT: PENNDOT'S TRANSIT PROGRAM QUARTERLY REPORT.

PennDOT Operating Reports Version 7	Systemwide Total	Fixed-Route Vehicle Operation	Fixed-Route Vehicle Maintenance
PASSENGER INFORMATION			
Fixed-Route Originating Farepaying Passengers			
Free Transit Senior Citizen Passengers			
Shared Ride Senior Citizen Passengers			
ADA Complementary Paratransit Passengers			
Other Originating Passengers			
Total Originating Passenger Trips			
Transfer Passengers			
TOTAL PASSENGER TRIPS			
Average Trip Length			
TOTAL PASSENGER MILES			
SERVICE INFORMATION			
Total Actual Vehicle-Miles			
Total Actual Vehicle-Hours			
Total Actual Vehicle-Revenue-Miles			
Total Actual Vehicle-Revenue-Hours			
Total Vehicles Operated in Maximum Service			
Total Vehicles Available for Maximum Service			
Average Age of Vehicles Available for Maximum Service			
Total ADA Accessible Vehicles in Available Fleet			

public transit systems in Pennsylvania access this screen via the Internet, enter their data for the current quarter, and submit the data electronically back to PennDOT. This sort of design could easily be accomplished by someone in the organization familiar with spreadsheet programs.

Larger, more decentralized organizations may opt for a menu-driven system, where persons responsible for data input enter data in response to questions or other cues on the screen. This type of system is also easily adapted for multiple data entry and access points. The State of Virginia, for example, chose initially to use an existing database program (Microsoft Access) to meet its performance data needs rather than purchasing an off-the-shelf performance data management system. As this system was used, however, additional data management needs became apparent. Virginia's system is now a fully Web-based system, Virginia Results, and is directly accessible from the state's home page, emphasizing the importance of performance management in the state and making results-oriented information of all types directly accessible. Using forms available on the site, agencies are able to directly submit strategic planning and performance measurement information to central state performance management databases. The system was developed using Microsoft's SQL Server, using in-house expertise and personnel, which in turn helped create a completely customized system. Figure 8.2 provides an example that shows a data input screen for Virginia's statewide performance data management system. Users of this system are able not only to input data but also to add explanatory information or comments to expand on the performance data in the spaces provided. For example, a space is provided to allow agencies to indicate any problems in attaining performance targets. The database allows the following information to be displayed for any state agency: baseline performance data, performance targets, measurement methodology, and interim performance levels. Interested parties may then access performance reports for any Virginia state agencies, as shown in Figure 8.3, which shows the performance reporting for the Virginia Department of Mines, Minerals and Energy. Users may view details of the performance measures as well as request graphic displays of specified measures.

Summary Guidelines for Establishing a High-Quality Performance Data Management System

To summarize, the quality of a performance data management system has a profound impact on its ease of use. For some organizations with extensive data support staff, the performance data management system can be easily integrated into

FIGURE 8.2. EXAMPLE OF A MENU-DRIVEN DATA INPUT SCREEN: STATE OF VIRGINIA.

<u>**Modify, Delete**</u>, or <u>**Add**</u> performance measures to ensure that your measures are:

- Relevant to your agency's mission, key customers, and critical issues.
- Understandable to the non-expert.
- Mutually supportable (i.e., do not contradict one another).
- Focused on one issue (produce only one quantitative result).
- Acceptable to the agency's key stakeholders.
- Balanced (taken together, they document the key work of the agency).

Each agency is required to have at least one performance measure. There is no maximum limit to how many measures an agency can list on Virginia Results, as long as the measures meet the above criteria.

Modify/Delete Current Performance Measures

Add New Performance Measure

Add a new performance measure by submitting information in the fields below.

(?) **New performance measure:**

┌──┐
│   ∧ │
│   │
│   ∨ │
└──┘

┌──────────┐
│ 250   │ characters left (maximum allowed = 250)
└──────────┘

(?) **Current data for selected measure:**

Performance data entries:

- Must be numeric (cannot contain any text or commas).
- Are displayed/rounded to one decimal point.
- Cannot use more than five digits (ten thousands). If necessary, change your performance measure to indicate that data is in thousands, ten thousands, millions, etc.

Fiscal Year	Data
1996	_____
1997	_____

FIGURE 8.2. EXAMPLE OF A MENU-DRIVEN DATA INPUT SCREEN: STATE OF VIRGINIA, Cont'd.

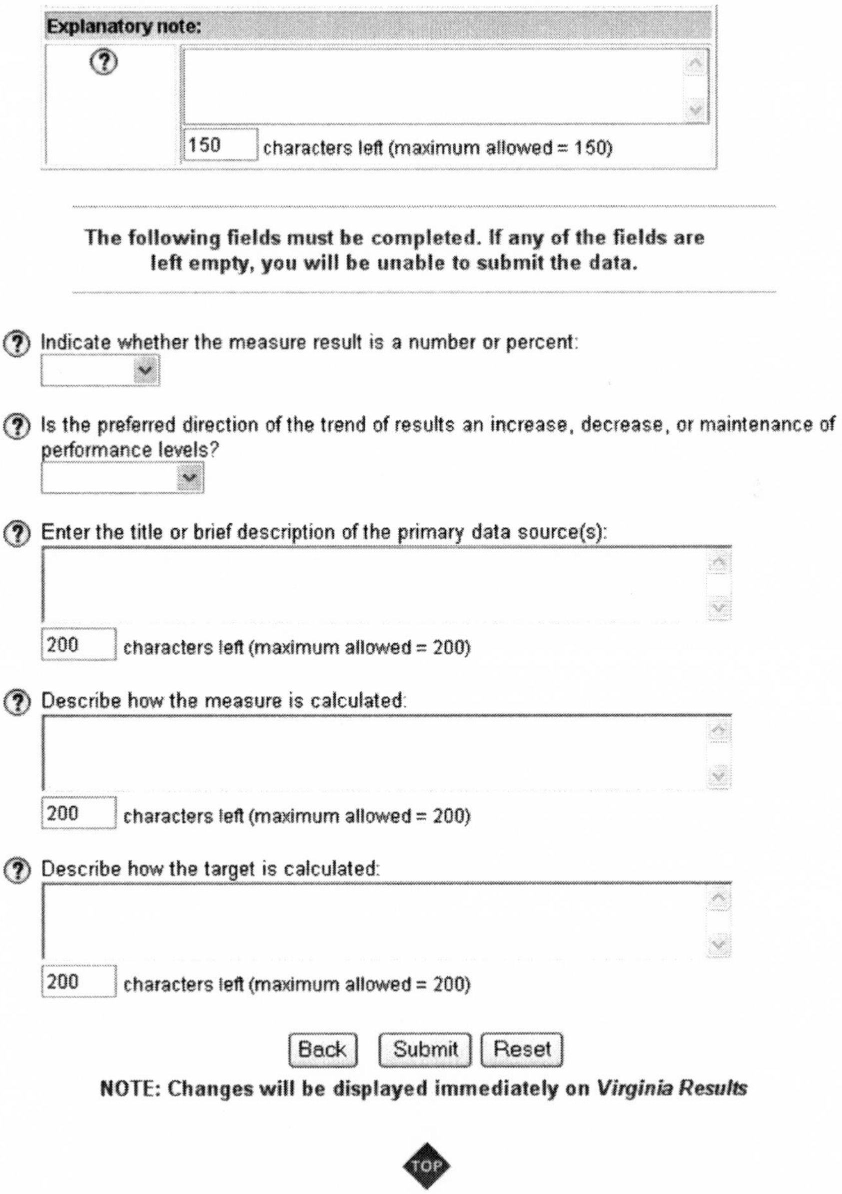

Explanatory note:

(?)

150   characters left (maximum allowed = 150)

The following fields must be completed. If any of the fields are left empty, you will be unable to submit the data.

(?) Indicate whether the measure result is a number or percent:

(?) Is the preferred direction of the trend of results an increase, decrease, or maintenance of performance levels?

(?) Enter the title or brief description of the primary data source(s):

200   characters left (maximum allowed = 200)

(?) Describe how the measure is calculated:

200   characters left (maximum allowed = 200)

(?) Describe how the target is calculated:

200   characters left (maximum allowed = 200)

Back   Submit   Reset

NOTE: Changes will be displayed immediately on *Virginia Results*

Source: State of Virginia, 2003. Printed with the permission of the Virginia Department of Planning and Budget.

FIGURE 8.3. PERFORMANCE MEASURE DATA: DEPARTMENT OF MINES, MINERALS AND ENERGY, STATE OF VIRGINIA.

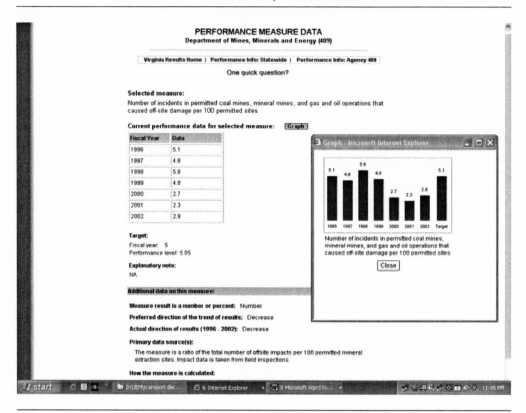

Source: State of Virginia, 2003. Printed with the permission of the Virginia Department of Planning and Budget.

existing systems. Others may need outside assistance to design or select the appropriate software and components. Working through the decisions involved in the design or selection process, which we discussed in this chapter, should guide you.

A word of caution: it may be tempting to develop or select all the bells and whistles in a performance data management system. However, organizations should be realistic about their data and reporting needs. The costs of establishing the system should not go beyond what is appropriate to your organization's needs. Going through the decisions involved in each of the steps outlined in this chapter will help in determining what is most appropriate. The following additional guidelines should be helpful to those working to establish a software system for maintaining performance data:

- Identify existing capabilities and processes within the organization for data collection, data entry, and reporting of performance data.
- Identify database needs in terms of the types of data to be collected and the format of reports to be generated. This should include identifying desired data access priorities, such as variables to be accessed most frequently.
- Attempt to modify existing software in order to save costs, but be aware that outside database assistance can be highly beneficial and cost-effective in the long run.
- Select a data manager who can assist in the measurement refinement phase as well as be accountable for the system overall and play a role in data verification.
- Establish data entry processes that minimize data entry errors or unauthorized altering of existing data.
- Establish data verification responsibilities and procedures as you develop the system itself.
- Plan for reporting requirements and preferences in the design of the system.

It is also important to note that the development of the database will be incremental. Although the users and stakeholders can address many of the decisions discussed in this chapter, there is no substitute for testing the data needs and data system in real time. Only after using the data system for a year or so will users be able to accurately identify problems and other data needs. Organizations should not only be open to the possibility that changes will be made to the data system after a certain trial period but also should *expect* that the system will be refined at some point. Nonetheless, it will be to their benefit to anticipate and plan for these needs as much as possible in the initial design phase.

PART THREE

STRATEGIC APPLICATIONS OF PERFORMANCE MEASUREMENT

Performance measurement systems serve a variety of purposes in public and nonprofit agencies. Whereas some are stand-alone reporting systems, many are designed specially to support other important management and decision-making processes. Although the approach to developing measurement systems discussed throughout this book is appropriate for all types of applications, Part Three discusses five principal types of applications that are of strategic value to many public and nonprofit agencies.

First, Chapter Nine discusses the critical role performance measures play in successful strategic planning efforts; it focuses on the need to track progress in implementing strategic objectives and accomplishing strategic goals and objectives. Chapter Ten discusses approaches to injecting performance measures into budgeting processes, focusing on both advantages and limitations. Chapter Eleven examines the role of performance measures in performance management systems designed to direct and control the work of organizational units and individual employees. Chapter Twelve then looks at the use of performance measures in process improvement efforts aimed at improving service quality, productivity, and customer service. Finally, Chapter Thirteen discusses the use of comparative performance measures to benchmark program or organizational performance against other agencies or programs. Emphasized throughout this part of the book is the notion that performance measurement systems developed to support these different applications will tend to vary systematically in terms of the kinds of measures used, level of aggregation, and reporting frequencies, as well as other design features.

CHAPTER NINE

USING PERFORMANCE MEASURES TO SUPPORT STRATEGIC PLANNING AND MANAGEMENT

W hy are performance measurement systems essential for supporting public and nonprofit agencies' strategic planning and management processes? Clearly, strategic management requires good information on performance, but what kinds of performance indicators are most useful in strategic planning and management, and how can they be used most advantageously to strengthen strategic management and decision making? This chapter briefly overviews the processes of strategic planning and management, defines the role of performance measurement in these processes, and discusses the development and use of measurement systems to support them.

Strategic Planning and Management

The terms *strategic planning* and *strategic management* are often used interchangeably, but in fact they are not the same thing. Strategic planning is the process of clarifying mission and vision, defining major goals and objectives, and developing long-term strategies for moving an organization into the future in a purposeful way and ensuring a high level of performance in the long run. Strategic management, in contrast, is the larger process that is responsible for the development of strategic plans, the implementation of strategic initiatives, and the ongoing evaluation of their effectiveness. Thus, strategic planning is a critical component or the corner-stone of strategic management, which is necessarily a more encompassing process.

Strategic planning has been defined as "a disciplined effort to produce fundamental decisions and actions that shape and guide what an organization is, what it does, and why it does it (Bryson, 1995, pp. 4–5). It blends futuristic thinking, objective analysis, and subjective evaluation of goals and priorities to chart future courses of action. In contrast to more closed-system traditional long-range or program planning processes, strategic planning is a "big picture" approach that

> Is concerned with identifying and responding to the most fundamental issues facing an organization in terms of long-term viability and performance
>
> Addresses the subjective question of basic purposes and the often competing values that influence mission, vision, and strategies
>
> Emphasizes the importance of external trends and forces as they are likely to affect the organization and its mission
>
> Attempts to be politically realistic by taking into account the needs, concerns, and preferences of internal and, especially, external stakeholders
>
> Relies heavily on the active involvement of senior-level managers and sometimes elected officials or governing boards, assisted by staff support where needed
>
> Requires key participants to confront candidly the most critical issues facing an organization or program in order to build commitment to plans
>
> Is action oriented and stresses the importance of developing plans for implementing strategies
>
> Focuses on implementing decisions now so as to position the organization favorably in the future

Whereas strategic planning is typically undertaken to create or update an organization's strategic agenda, strategic management is the central management process that integrates all major activities and functions and directs them toward advancing that strategic agenda. It is concerned with strengthening the long-term viability and effectiveness of public and nonprofit organizations in terms of both substantive policy and management capacity. Strategic management integrates all other management processes to provide a coherent and effective approach to establishing, attaining, monitoring, and updating an agency's strategic objectives. Indeed, a thorough strategic management system "embraces the entire set of managerial decisions and actions that determine the long-run performance of an organization" (Koteen, 1989, p. 8).

A strategically managed public or nonprofit organization is one in which budgeting, performance measurement, human resource development, program management, and all other management processes are guided by a strategic agenda that has been developed with buy-in from key actors and communicated widely among external constituencies as well as internally. Strategic management is concerned with implementing strategies and measuring performance as well as monitoring trends and identifying emerging issues that might require strategic responses. Thus, the strategic management process as illustrated in Figure 9.1 places heavy emphasis on implementation as well as planning. To ensure that strategic plans will indeed become the driving force behind operating-level decisions and activities throughout the organization, strategic managers must develop processes for allocating resources, managing people, and measuring performance that are geared to moving the strategic agenda forward.

Once strategic plans have been formulated, the resources for implementing them must be committed. As indicated in Figure 9.1, some type of results-oriented budgeting system in which funds can be tied to particular programs, projects, or activities and related to planned outputs and impacts can facilitate the allocation of resources so as to maximize their impact in advancing the strategic agenda. Such a

FIGURE 9.1. THE STRATEGIC MANAGEMENT PROCESS.

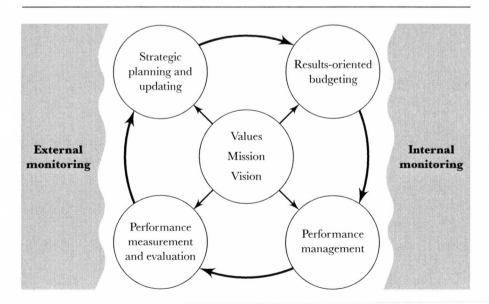

budgeting process can ensure that specific strategic initiatives are adequately funded and provide incentives for supporting the strategic agenda wherever possible.

Similarly, strategic management requires assigning implementation responsibilities for particular strategic initiatives to specific individuals and organizational units and holding them accountable for the results. In MBO-type performance management systems, for example, performance contracts with specific higher-level managers can incorporate lead and support responsibilities regarding particular strategic initiatives. These managers can, in turn, use the performance management process to link these responsibilities to their subordinates, and so on down through the ranks, with individuals' respective efforts on these tasks weighing in heavily in annual performance appraisals, recognition programs, and the rewards system in general. By incorporating strategic plans into this type of performance management process, strategic managers can establish clear lines of accountability for implementing strategies, and managers and employees at all levels of the organization become personally invested in advancing the strategic agenda.

Finally, as will be discussed in this chapter, the strategic management process also incorporates the monitoring and evaluation of the results of strategic initiatives. In addition, public and nonprofit managers concerned with overall strategy should monitor both the internal organization and its external environment on an ongoing basis, as indicated in Figure 9.1. Although much of this will be accomplished through a variety of sources—published reports, professional associations, customer feedback, advisory committees, surveys, debriefings, site visits, brown bag lunches, and informal conversations and management by walking around—to some extent this monitoring activity may be well served by regular management information systems and ongoing performance measurement activities.

Performance Measurement in the Strategic Management Process

Performance measurement needs to be a critical element of both strategic planning and the overall strategic management process. Although existing measurement systems are likely to serve the purpose of many strategic planning exercises, effective strategic management often requires new or revised systems to track particular indicators that are tailored to the specific strategic initiatives that are being implemented and monitored.

Strategic Planning

Although every strategic planning effort is apt to be unique in some respects, most will incorporate a basic set of common elements. Figure 9.2 shows a conventional process that reflects the way many public and nonprofit organizations go about

FIGURE 9.2. CONVENTIONAL STRATEGIC PLANNING PROCESS.

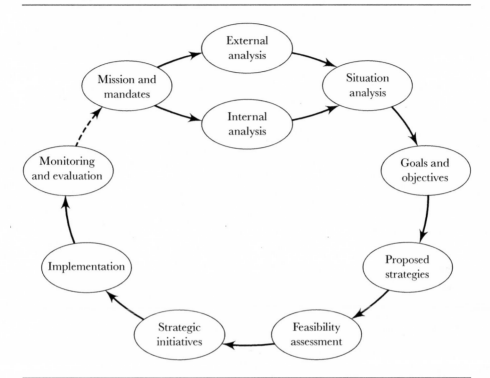

strategic planning. Strategic planning typically begins by clarifying mission and mandates for the organization or program and conducting both external and internal analyses in light of these. As the process continues, planners conduct situation analyses to identify strategic issues, those that are likely to impact heavily on future viability and performance, and to define strategic goals and objectives to resolve these issues productively and pursue the mission more effectively. Then strategic planners focus on developing and assessing strategies for achieving the goals and objectives as well as action plans for implementing the strategies. The final step in this iterative process involves continual, regular monitoring and evaluation that should seek to keep strategic plans closely linked to environmental change.

Performance measures play an important role in two phases of the typical strategic planning process: internal analysis and ongoing monitoring and evaluation.

Internal Analysis. Internal analysis consists primarily of identifying and analyzing major strengths and weaknesses of the organization or program. These strengths and weaknesses, which in conjunction with external threats and opportunities are critical for identifying strategic issues, may relate to any aspect of performance, such as resource availability, management capacity, employee skills and morale, technology use, and external relations as well as quality, productivity, service delivery, program effectiveness, and customer satisfaction. Strategic issues may arise from problems in any of these areas, but in most public and nonprofit service industries, issues of quality, productivity, program effectiveness, and client satisfaction are of critical importance. Thus, performance measures—available, one hopes, in existing systems—that track performance in terms of this "bottom line" of service delivery are often crucial for successful strategic planning.

These kinds of data are often helpful in constructing a situation analysis, which is a critical element of most public and nonprofit agencies' strategic planning efforts. Often, cumulative data on services, participation rates, scope and scale of operations, costs, and the like give an indication of the overall parameters that help "size up" an agency's or program's strategic situation. When these measures have been tracked systematically over time, they also provide trend data that can help an agency understand where it has been coming from and in what direction it is headed.

For example, the American Red Cross uses its Field Operations Consolidate Information System (FOCIS) to track a set of performance measures concerning the delivery of "must" services (for example, emergency communication, international tracing, multifamily disaster operations, and disaster education) and a variety of other "should" and "may" services, along with data on staff, volunteers, and financial resources. The data input is submitted by the 990 local chapters of the Red Cross electronically via the Internet; then FOCIS reports that track all these measures over the most recent five-year period are produced for each local chapter, each state, multistate regions, and the nation. In addition, for each of the measures, the reports benchmark a given state or local program against a reference group of other comparable geographical areas selected on the basis of similar demographics. These FOCIS data are used by management and governing boards at several levels in the Red Cross structure in planning, evaluation, and resource allocation.

Ongoing Monitoring and Evaluation. The monitoring and evaluation phase of the strategic planning process borders on strategic management, as discussed in the next section. However, because strategic planning is best thought of as an ongoing process aimed at maintaining the most appropriate "fit" between the agency or program and the environment in which it functions, continuing performance monitoring is needed to confirm that strategic directions still make sense or to determine that some updating is in order. At a minimum this means monitoring program effectiveness on a regular basis, but it might also entail tracking environmental conditions—crime rates, health status indicators, highway fatalities, unemployment rates, or air quality indexes, for example—that have implications for policies or programs or are targeted to be affected by them.

Strategic Management

As discussed earlier, strategic management systems need to incorporate strategic planning, results-based budgeting, performance management processes, and performance measurement systems and tie them together in a coherent manner. Performance measures play a critical role in both results-based budgeting and performance management systems, as will be discussed in Chapters Ten and Eleven, respectively. However, whereas budgeting and performance management are essential for implementing strategic initiatives effectively, the performance measurement component of the strategic management process shown in Figure 9.1 is concerned with tracking and evaluating the success of these initiatives. That is, performance measures are essential for monitoring progress in implementing strategic initiatives and assessing their effectiveness in producing the desired results.

These strategic initiatives often focus on service delivery, but they may also involve any other aspect of the organization's operations or management, as indicated by the strategic management model presented in Figure 9.3. At its core

FIGURE 9.3. STRATEGIC MANAGEMENT MODEL.

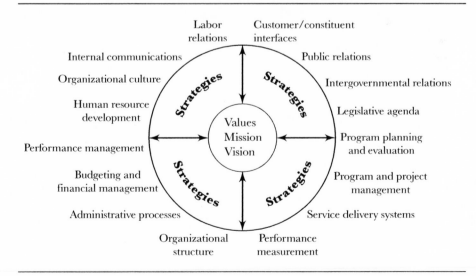

are the values that are most important to the agency, its mission and the communities or constituencies it serves, and a vision of what the agency will be in the future. Around the outer ring of the model are a number of management responsibilities (intended to be illustrative rather than exhaustive) that must be coordinated in terms of their strategic implications. As indicated in Figure 9.3, there are two-directional relationships between all these elements and the values, mission, and vision that drive the strategic management process. The model is best thought of as a constellation of key management functions orbiting around the core values, mission, and vision of any public or nonprofit organization, and the force that keeps them in orbit consists of the strategies that are formulated, implemented, and evaluated on an ongoing basis pursuant to the agency's mission, vision, and values.

For example, programs, projects, and service delivery systems (as shown in the lower right quadrant of the model) are often the vehicles for implementing strategic plans. Similarly, strategic managers must also ensure that organizational structure, budgeting, and financial management systems, performance management, and other administrative processes (as shown in the lower left quadrant) are designed to reinforce the focus on the strategic agenda throughout the organization. In addition, as suggested in the upper left portion of the model, strategic management must be critically concerned with human resources and the relational aspects of managing the organization. Finally, strategic managers must be concerned with building and maintaining the support of various external stakeholders, as illustrated in the upper right quadrant. Thus, strategic management may at times work through all these elements in a coherent fashion to advance an agency's strategic agenda, and performance measures may be needed, therefore, to track progress in any or all of these areas.

Strategic Performance Measures

In contrast to program planning, project planning, or operations planning, strategic planning in the public and nonprofit sectors tends to take a global perspective, consider long-term implications, and focus on the organization as a whole, or at least major components or major programs. Thus, the kinds of performance measurement systems that tend to be the most appropriate for supporting strategic planning and management efforts are those that portray the "big picture," using macro-level indicators that track performance in the aggregate and relating to the whole organization or major units rather than to detailed operating data broken down by numerous subunits. Strategic performance indicators also tend to be observed over longer time frames, more commonly providing annual or possibly semi-annual or quarterly data rather than more detailed daily, weekly, or monthly data.

Outcome Measures

Because strategic planning is concerned ultimately with maintaining and improving organizational effectiveness, it is not surprising that often the most important performance measures used in the strategic management process are outcome indicators. These outcome indicators are most often designed to track the effectiveness of services delivered, but they may also focus on other aspects of performance, such as the effectiveness of a change in organizational structure in improving customer relations, the performance of a training program in terms of strengthening employees' skills, or the impact of a public relations initiative on positive coverage by the media.

Some of the broadest strategic planning efforts undertaken in the United States are statewide planning processes such as Florida Benchmarks, Minnesota Milestones, and Texas Tomorrow, which involve the private and nonprofit sectors as well as government and encompass a wide range of policy issues. One of the pioneers in this arena is the Oregon Benchmarks program led by the Oregon Progress Board, which was created by the Oregon state legislature in 1989. This program involves business executives, community leaders, educators, and nonprofit service representatives as well as elected officials in developing, updating, and implementing a statewide strategic plan called Oregon Shines, which is aimed at expanding economic opportunities and improving the quality of life for all Oregonians. All agencies of state government in Oregon are directed to undertake initiatives designed to support the strategies enumerated in the plan, and all other relevant entities—the corporate sector, local governments, school systems, colleges and universities, service organizations, community associations, and nonprofit agencies—are also encouraged to take actions to advance the state's overall strategic agenda.

To keep track of the state's progress in achieving a wide range of strategic objectives identified by this comprehensive plan, the Progress Board monitors a total of ninety-two measures of success, called benchmarks, which are divided into the following seven categories: economy, education, civic engagement, social support, public safety, community development, and environment. Representative benchmarks in these areas include the following indicators:

- The percentage of Oregon workers with earnings of 150 percent or more of the poverty level

- The percentage of Oregonians who report they use a computer to create and edit documents or graphics or to analyze data
- The percentage of Oregonians who volunteer at least fifty hours of their time per year to civic, community, or nonprofit activities
- The percentage of babies whose mothers received early prenatal care
- The total number of juvenile arrests per thousand juvenile Oregonians per year
- The percentage of Oregonians who commute during peak hours by means other than a single-occupant vehicle
- The percentage of assessed ground water that meets drinking water standards

The Oregon Progress Board reports performance on these measures to the legislature every two years. Table 9.1 excerpts data for selected indicators in the social support category from the 1999 report. Many of the measures in Oregon Benchmarks are taken from existing data compilations, but most of the data for these particular indicators shown in Table 9.1 are gathered through biennial sample surveys of the population. The data show trends over the past decade as well as targeted levels for both the year 2000 and 2010. In addition, a grade ranging from A to F is assigned to each benchmark based on recent trends and current performance as graded against the targets. Although the measures employed by Oregon Benchmarks are for the most part surface-level social indicators, the overall report on all ninety-two benchmark measures does provide a composite picture of the economic vitality, community robustness, and quality of life in Oregon. Within this framework, state and local government agencies, as well as other entities committed to advancing the Oregon Shines vision, monitor more specific measures designed to track the progress of their own particular strategic initiatives along these lines.

Agency-Based Strategic Goals

At the agency level, where most strategic planning is actually done, it is essential to define and monitor performance indicators that are tied directly to missions and strategies in order to be sure that programs are on track. Public and nonprofit agencies are increasingly concerned with monitoring their performance in light of their mission, and the linkages usually run through goals and objectives. An organization's mission and vision are the driving forces in defining performance indicators. In order to be justified, programs must be aligned with the organization's mission, and goals and objectives are defined that support the mission and basic program purpose. When an organization has a clear understanding of what the goals need to be to support the mission, and of what more operational objectives need to be accomplished in order to reach the goals, then it can determine how

TABLE 9.1. SAMPLE OREGON BENCHMARKS: SOCIAL SUPPORT.

Protection	1990	1992	1994	1996	1998	2000	2010	Grade
53. Percentage of 8th grade students who report using:								D+
a. Alcohol in the previous month	23%	26%	30%	30%	26%	26%	21%	B–
b. Illicit drugs in the previous month	14%	11%	19%	22%	29%	15%	12%	F
c. Cigarettes in the previous month	12%	15%	19%	22%	20%	15%	12%	F
54. Number of children abused or neglected per 1,000 persons under age 18	11	11	10	10		9	6	F
55. Reported elder abuse rate per 1,000				14		12	12	F
56. Percentage of infants whose mothers used:								A
a. Alcohol during pregnancy (self-reported by mother)	22%	20%	18%	18%		15%	12%	A
b. Tobacco during pregnancy (self-reported by mother)	22%	20%	18%	18%		15%	12%	A

Poverty	1990	1992	1994	1996	1998	2000	2010	Grade
57. Percentage of Oregonians with incomes below 100% of the federal poverty level	11%	13%	15%	12%	12%	11%	9%	C
58. Percentage of Oregonians without health insurance	16%	18%	14%	11%	11%	9%	4%	B+
59. Number of Oregonians that are homeless on any given night		7,607	7,262	6,819	7,050	5,196	5,196	D+
60. Percentage of current court-ordered child support paid to families	50%	50%	60%	68%	68%	72%	80%	A

Independent Living	1990	1992	1994	1996	1998	2000	2010	Grade
61. Percentage of seniors living independently		97%	97%	98%		98%	98%	A

Source: Adapted from Oregon Progress Board, March 1999. Printed with permission.

to measure the success of particular programmatic activities and be confident that the performance indicators are consistent with its mission.

Strategic Goals and Objectives: U.S. Department of Education

The notion of direct linkages from mission to performance indicators is indispensable. For example, the stated mission of the U.S. Department of Education is "To ensure equal access to education and to promote educational excellence throughout the Nation." Like many federal agencies, the Department of Education is not engaged for the most part in direct service delivery, but rather pursues this mission through advocacy, standard setting, student loans, and a mix of financial, technical, and programmatic assistance provided to state education agencies, local school systems, higher education institutions, and other entities.

Table 9.2 shows the framework of high-level goals and objectives developed through the department's strategic planning process. These goals and objectives are department-wide rather than program specific, and they identify basic purposes and things that need to be accomplished through approximately 175 operating programs in order to move toward the department's vision of educational excellence for the country as a whole. The goal statements are quite general in nature, but they do point to what is deemed important in terms of academic standards, learning outcomes, access to postsecondary education and beyond, and excellence within the education department itself. Although the objectives are not stated as SMART objectives as defined in Chapter Four, they do provide a clear sense of direction in terms of what has to be done to achieve the goals and advance the overall mission.

These objectives, however, are further specified through multiple performance measures and standards that have been defined for each one of the objectives identified in Table 9.2. For instance, goal 1 is to "help all children reach challenging academic standards, so that they are prepared for responsible citizenship, further learning, and productive employment," and Objective 1.2 calls for local schools to "help all students make successful transitions to college and careers" in support of this goal. Programmatically, the primary vehicle for achieving this objective is the education department's School-to-Work system. At the next level, then, six performance indicators have been identified for monitoring progress in achieving this objective, with target values for the year 2000 and beyond. These are actually specified as SMART objectives, as follows:

- By fall 2000, one million youths will participate annually in School-to-Work systems.
- By fall 2000, the percentage of vocational concentrators completing core curriculum standards will double from baseline data.

TABLE 9.2. FRAMEWORK OF STRATEGIC PLAN GOALS AND OBJECTIVES: U.S. DEPARTMENT OF EDUCATION.

Mission: To ensure equal access to education and to promote educational excellence throughout the Nation.

Goal 1 Help all children reach challenging academic standards, so that they are prepared for responsible citizenship, further learning, and productive employment.	Goal 2 Build a solid foundation for learning for all children.	Goal 3 Ensure access to postsecondary education and lifelong learning.	Goal 4 Make ED a high-performance organization by focusing on results, service quality, and customer satisfaction.
Objectives 1. States develop challenging standards and assessments for all students in the core academic subjects. 2. Schools help all students make successful transitions to college and careers. 3. Schools are strong, safe, disciplined, and drug-free. 4. A talented and dedicated teacher is in every classroom in America. 5. Families and communities are fully involved with schools and school improvement efforts. 6. Greater public school choice will be available to students and families. 7. Schools use advanced technology for all students and teachers to improve education.	*Objectives* 1. All children enter school ready to learn. 2. Every child reads well and independently by the end of the third grade. 3. Every eighth-grader masters challenging mathematics, including the foundations of algebra and geometry. 4. Special populations participate in appropriate services and assessments consistent with high standards.	*Objectives* 1. Secondary school students get the information, skills, and support they need to prepare successfully for postsecondary education. 2. Postsecondary students receive the financial aid and support services they need to enroll in and complete a high-quality educational program. 3. Postsecondary student aid delivery and program management is efficient, financially sound, and customer-responsive. 4. All educationally disadvantaged adults can strengthen their literacy skills and improve their earning power over their lifetime through lifelong learning.	*Objectives* 1. Our customers receive fast, seamless service and dissemination of high-quality information and products. 2. Our partners have the support and flexibility they need without diminishing accountability for results. 3. An up-to-date knowledge base is available from education research to support education reform and equity. 4. Our information technology investments are sound and used to improve impact and efficiency. 5. The Department's employees are highly skilled and high-performing. 6. Management of our programs and services ensures financial integrity. 7. All levels of the agency are fully performance-driven.

Source: U.S. Department of Education, 2000.

- By fall 2000, the percentage of high school graduates, including vocational concentrators, who make a successful transition into employment, further education, or the military will increase to 90 percent.
- By fall 2000, 10 percent of students in local School-to-Work systems will earn skill certificates.
- By fall 2000, two hundred high schools will receive and twenty-five hundred will be working toward department recognition for implementing New American High School strategies that combine career and academic preparation.
- By fall 2000, 350,000 employers participating in School-to-Work systems will offer work-based learning opportunities.

Figure 9.4 shows data from the Department of Education's *1999 Performance Report and 2001 Annual Plan* for one of these indicators, concerning the percentage of high school students concentrating on vocational training who also complete core academic criteria in English, math, science, and social studies. The data, which are collected on a sample basis by the National Assessment of Educational Progress and validated by review procedures and statistical standards of the National Center for Education Statistics every four years, show a very positive trend that prompted the department to increase the standard for the year 2002 from 33 percent to 50 percent.

The real point here, however, concerns the development of an overall measurement system: a systematic hierarchy of relatively few strategic goals, each sup-

FIGURE 9.4. EXAMPLE OF PERFORMANCE DATA:
U.S. DEPARTMENT OF EDUCATION.

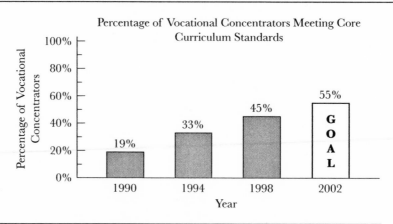

Source: U.S. Department of Education, 2000.

ported by a few more specific objectives, each one of which is monitored with several indicators comparing actual performance against standards. Such a system can be very useful in providing a composite picture of how well the nation's large and complex education system is performing in light of the U.S. Department of Education's overall mission.

Managing the Strategic Agenda with Measures: PennDOT

As another example of performance measures developed in support of strategic plans, PennDOT, in its most recent iteration of strategic planning in 1999, established eight strategic focus areas—such as putting top priority on maintenance of existing transportation facilities, enhancing the quality of life, improving safety, and increasing mobility and access—then thirteen high-level goals nested within those focus areas and twenty-one strategic objectives to support those goals. Although the objectives are somewhat more specific than the goals, the strategic performance measures to be incorporated in PennDOT's overall scorecard are keyed to the thirteen high-level goals.

Table 9.3, PennDOT's scorecard, summarizes the department's strategic focus areas, the thirteen high-level goals, the measures to be used in tracking progress on these goals, and targets to be achieved in 2002 and 2005. For instance, one high-level goal that is tied to the maintenance-first priority is to maintain smoother roads, to be measured in terms of better ride conditions on major (national highway system, or NHS) state highways. The measurement tool to be used will be the international roughness index (IRI), and targets have been set to reduce the median IRI value for NHS roads to 104 by the year 2002 and down to 99 by the year 2005. Similarly, a major goal that is tied to the safety focus is to reduce highway accident fatalities by 5 percent in the year 2002 and by 10 percent in 2005.

As would be expected from a comprehensive strategic planning process, some of PennDOT's major goals focus internally, at the way the department does its work. Thus, complementing measures concerned with service delivery, the plan also includes goals that address the implementation of an asset management system, the reduction of work-related injuries, innovation and the use of technology, and leadership within the organization. These goals are seen as being essential to strengthen the organization's capacity for delivering services to the public, and performance indicators and targets have been established for them as well. It is also worth noting that although the performance measures for most of PennDOT's high-level goals consist of single indicators, in certain other cases—the ISO environmental standards and the organizational climate survey of employees, for example—a set of related indicators is used.

TABLE 9.3. SCORECARD OF MEASURES: PENNSYLVANIA DEPARTMENT OF TRANSPORTATION.

STRATEGIC FOCUS AREA	High Level Goals *Pledge to Customers*	How Success Will Be Measured	External (Customer)	Internal (Support)	Measurement Tool (Metric)	Target 2002	Target 2005
Maintenance First	Smoother roads	Better ride conditions on major (NHS) highways	X		International Roughness Index (IRI)	104 for NHS roads	99 for NHS roads
	Cost-effective highway maintenance investment	Reduction in outstanding maintenance needs		X	Condition Assessment for highways and bridges	Complete asset management system	Meet target established in 2002
Quality of Life	Balance social, economic, and environmental concerns	Timely decisions based on public and technical input on project impacts	X		Highway project environmental approvals meeting target dates	75% meeting target dates	90% meeting target dates
	Demonstrate sound environmental practices	Attaining world class environmental status		X	ISO 14001 environmental criteria	Implement a pilot program	Meet ISO standards
Mobility and Access	Delivery of transportation products and services	Honoring commitments on scheduled transportation projects	X		Dollar value of 12-Year Program construction contracts initiated	$1.3 billion per year	$1.4 billion per year
	Efficient movement of people and goods	Reduced travel delays	X		2002—peak period work zone lane restrictions 2005—travel delays on selected corridors	Set baseline in 2000 for reduced 2002 lane restrictions	Meet target set in 2002 to reduce corridor travel delays
Customer Focus	Improve customer satisfaction	Competitiveness on Malcolm Baldrige Criteria for Excellence		X	Baldrige Organizational Review Package Scores—Customer Criteria	80 Department average	100 Department average
	Improve customer access to information	Prompt answers to telephone inquiries	X		Answer rate of calls to the Customer Call Center	94% of calls answered	94% of calls answered

		Competitiveness on Malcolm Baldrige Criteria for Excellence			500 level	600 level
Innovation and Technology	World class process and product performance	Competitiveness on Malcolm Baldrige Criteria for Excellence	X	Baldrige Organizational Review Package Scores—All Criteria	500 level met by lead organizations	600 level met by lead organizations
Safety	Safer travel	Fewer fatalities from highway crashes	X	Number of fatalities per year	5% reduction in fatalities	10% reduction in fatalities
	Safer working conditions	Fewer work-related injuries	X	Injury rate per 100 employees working one year	8.25% injury rate	7.5% injury rate
Leadership at All Levels	Improve leadership capabilities and work environment	Positive trends in employee feedback on job related factors	X	Organizational Climate Survey (OCS)—Selected Items	48% positive rating	54% positive rating
Relationship Building	Cultivate effective relationships	Effectiveness of partnerships to achieve business results	X	PennDOT/Partner business effectiveness survey scores	Establish metric, baseline, and target	Meet target established in 2002

Source: Pennsylvania Department of Transportation, 2000. Reprinted with permission.

PennDOT's strategic management committee monitors the scorecard data on these strategic goals and objectives every six months on a rotating basis, focusing on a couple of goals each month. In addition to this "enterprise" level scorecard, each of the department's six deputates and eleven engineering districts has developed its own scorecard that is responsive to PennDOT's department-wide strategic goals and objectives, and in some parts of the department, lower-level organizational units have their own scorecards as well. Each of these organizational scorecards, complete with strategic goals and objectives, performance measures, and targets, is reviewed quarterly, with the results reported up to the "owners" of the objectives, usually members of the strategic management committee, who ultimately are held accountable for hitting the targets. When the performance data show that progress is behind schedule or that results are not meeting expectations, these owners are responsible for redirecting resources, changing tactics, or otherwise adjusting plans in order to get particular strategic initiatives back on track.

Focus on Outputs

Strategic planning in the public and nonprofit sectors quite naturally tends to focus on producing or improving programmatic outcomes. Thus, the performance measures used in strategic management systems often constitute direct effectiveness measures—for example, academic proficiency achieved or gainful employment resulting from education programs, or indicators of reduced travel times or decreased highway accident fatalities in the case of transportation programs. However, because strategic plans are often concerned with bringing about change in what public and nonprofit organizations actually do or how they go about doing these things, strategic managers may need to rely heavily on *output* measures, in addition to real outcome measures, to determine whether their organizations are implementing their strategic initiatives effectively. Indeed, output indicators often serve as proximate measures of outcomes, but they can also be critical indicators of success in their own right, particularly in the earlier stages of implementing strategic initiatives.

For example, the Sexually Transmitted Disease (STD) Prevention Division of the Centers for Disease Control (CDC) is attempting to refocus the national STD prevention effort and develop a performance measurement system to help monitor the effectiveness of a strategic change in programmatic approach. The goals of the program are to eradicate certain STDs and contain others at minimal levels throughout the United States, and the effectiveness measures are well established. As illustrated by the following sample indicators and targets, the indicators of "bottom line" outcomes focus primarily on the incidence and prevalence of certain diseases:

- Prevalence of *Chlamydia trachomatis* among high-risk females under twenty-five to be reduced from 11.7 percent to 8 percent by 2000
- Incidence of gonorrhea in females ages fifteen to forty-four to be reduced from 292 per 100,000 to 250 per 100,000 by 2000
- Incidence of congenital syphilis in the general population to be reduced from 27.5 per 100,000 to 20 per 100,000 by 2000
- Percentage of U.S. counties with an incidence of primary and secondary syphilis in the general population of less than or equal to 4 per 100,000 to be increased from 87 percent to 90 percent or higher by 2000

Traditionally the STD prevention program has operated through direct service delivery—screening, diagnosis, treatment, and partner services—provided by dedicated STD clinics supported in part with CDC funding channeled through state and local STD programs. However, as a result of environmental and program assessments, CDC program staff are convinced that this approach will no longer be adequate, due largely to increasingly fragmented health care delivery systems, the lack of coordination among related health programs at the local level, and the fact that the clinics do not have a strong track record in reaching some of the most critical target populations. Thus, they have concluded that STD prevention programs need to implement a broader range of strategies to leverage impact on a variety of other stakeholders—managed care organizations, private medical practices, schools, detention and corrections facilities, and community-based organizations, for example—in order to reach out to at-risk persons and effectively contain the spread of these infectious diseases.

Figure 9.5 shows a logic model for the STD prevention system; it is important to note that this is the comprehensive national STD prevention *system* rather than the CDC STD prevention *program* itself. This model represents the logic by which a variety of system components bring about intermediate outcomes involving safer sex behaviors; increased use of condoms; and decreased duration of STD infections, which in turn leads to decreased prevalence, decreased exposure, and reduced incidence. These longer-term outcomes continue to be monitored in terms of incidence and prevalence rates; however, interest now focuses on the earlier-stage outputs and immediate outcomes so that the CDC can begin to monitor the extent to which state and local STD prevention programs are impacting on the larger *system* in a productive way.

Thus, regarding the awareness-building component, for example, the CDC might want to track such outputs as the percentage of existing HIV prevention programs that provide appropriate STD information to their clients, the number of local school systems offering appropriate STD prevention curricula, and the number of patients receiving appropriate STD information from their managed

FIGURE 9.5. STD PREVENTION SYSTEM.

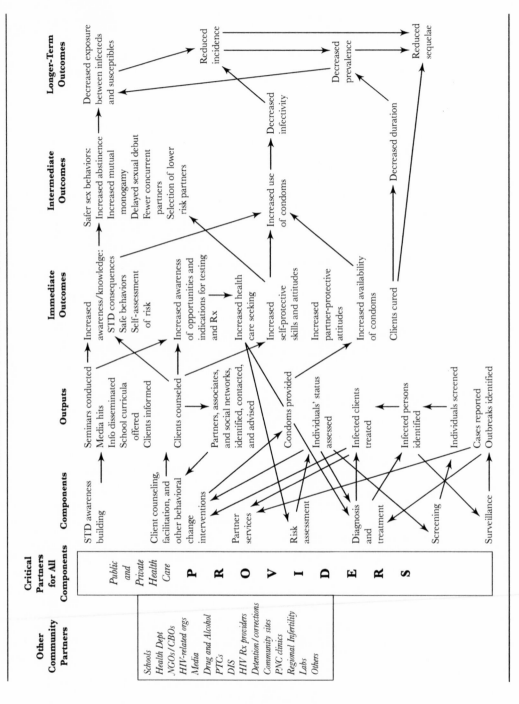

care organizations. Useful indicators for the counseling component might include the percentage of patients with newly diagnosed STDs who receive recommendations for reducing risk from client-centered counseling or the percentage of patients at STD clinics receiving skill-building interventions aimed at reducing risks. For monitoring the effectiveness of the screening component, the percentage of sexually active females enrolled in school who are tested for chlamydia would be an important output measure.

The point here is that to monitor progress in broadening the CDC's strategic response to the threat of STDs, program managers at the CDC need to track system outputs to determine the extent to which health care providers and other stakeholders far beyond the CDC's control are in fact engaged in the requisite activities. From a performance measurement perspective, the next issue will necessarily be to focus on what state and local STD prevention programs are doing to leverage their effort through these health care providers and other critical partners. Thus, for instance, these programs might report data on the number of successful attempts to encourage providers to provide appropriate materials to their patients or the number of successful efforts to convince school districts to include appropriate STD content in their curricula.

Balanced Scorecard Models

One useful framework that emphasizes the linkage between strategic objectives and performance measures is the balanced scorecard model developed by Kaplan and Norton (1996). Designed originally for private sector applications, this model was based on the premise that corporations need to look beyond such traditional financial measures as return on investment, profit and loss, and cash flow so as to get a more balanced picture of performance. As shown in Figure 9.6, the balanced scorecard incorporates four perspectives: the customer perspective, the internal business perspective, the innovation and learning perspective, and the financial perspective. Corporate entities establish goals in each of these domains and then define measures to track their performance against these goals.

The kinds of measures typically used to track performance from the customer perspective include market share of products or services sold, on-time delivery, rankings by key accounts, and customer satisfaction indexes. Measures pertaining to the innovation and learning perspective tend to focus on the development and sales of new products and services as well as on employee attitudes, capabilities, and involvement. The internal business perspective tends to emphasize such elements as engineering efficiency and unit costs, actual production versus business

FIGURE 9.6. THE BALANCED SCORECARD MODEL.

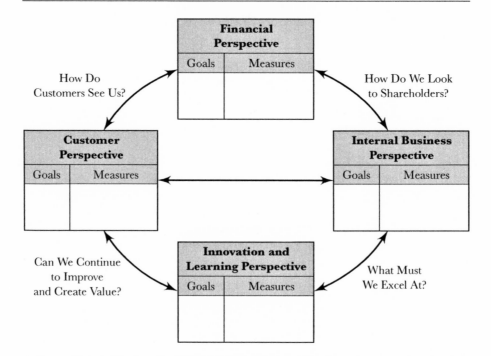

Source: Reprinted by permission of *Harvard Business Review,* figure titled The Balanced Scorecard Links Performance Measures. From "The Balanced Scorecard: Measures that Drive Performance," by R. S. Kaplan and D. P. Norton. *Harvard Business Review,* Jan./Feb. 1992. Copyright © 1992 by the Harvard Business School Publishing Corporation; all rights reserved. Kaplan and Norton, 1992, p. 72.

plans, rework, safety incidents, and project management. All of these measures obviously have been used by business firms in the past, but the contribution of the balanced scorecard model is to encourage managers to consider these four perspectives as a comprehensive package.

The Balanced Scorecard Approach: City of Charlotte, North Carolina

For quite some time, the City of Charlotte, North Carolina, has been on the leading edge among local governments in terms of developing its capacity for results-oriented management through MBO, program budgeting, performance measurement, and other similar approaches. In 1995, Charlotte began experimenting with the balanced scorecard method as a comprehensive approach to strategic planning and performance measurement. This effort began with the city council's identifying seven broad, overarching goals it wanted to establish as top-level priorities for the city as a whole.

Because the council's priorities—including reducing crime, strengthening neighborhoods, promoting safe and convenient transportation, and promoting economic opportunities—all target substantive outcomes intended to benefit the citizenry at large, they were adopted as representing the customer perspective, as shown in Figure 9.7. With the help of other top city officials, the council then identified goals regarding financial accountability, internal processes, and organizational learning and growth. The priorities from the other perspectives—expanding noncity funding, improving productivity, and closing the skills gap, for example—are seen as being important in their own right, but moreover they are viewed as strategies for accomplishing the customer-oriented priorities, which represent the real "bottom line" in this plan.

Performance measures have been established for each of the council's customer-oriented priorities. For the goal of strengthening neighborhoods, for instance, the city council identified the following indicators: (1) change in the proportion of owner-occupied housing units in target neighborhoods, (2) the number of businesses created or retained in targeted business corridors, (3) employment rates in targeted neighborhoods, and (4) Part I and Part II crime rates per 1,000 population in these neighborhoods. Various city departments and programs will have to focus resources and activities on the goal of strengthening these neighborhoods in order to bring about improvement on these indicators.

The actual development of performance measures to support the balanced scorecard was piloted by the Charlotte Department of Transportation (CDOT), which at that time had responsibility for both city streets and the public transit system. Thus, CDOT has established a set of objectives from each of the four perspectives, although they have not yet been defined and formatted as SMART objectives. For each objective, CDOT defined at least one "lead" measure and one "lag" measure, as shown in Table 9.4. The lead measures represent performance dimensions that must be achieved in order to achieve the objectives; the lag measures represent the broader impact of attaining the objective. CDOT has since defined operational indicators and begun to collect data for each of the performance measures on a regular basis.

Balanced Scorecard and Logic Models

The balanced scorecard has been catching on in both public and nonprofit agencies because it serves as a very straightforward and comprehensive framework for strategic planning and performance measurement. Whereas the kinds of measures that end up being incorporated for the most part are the same kinds of

FIGURE 9.7. BALANCED SCORECARD: CHARLOTTE, NORTH CAROLINA.

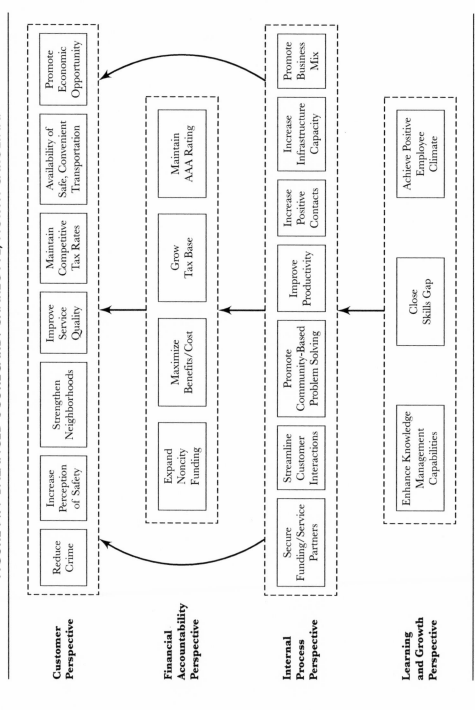

Source: Charlotte Department of Transportation, City of Charlotte, North Carolina. Reprinted with permission.

Perspective	Objective	Lead Measures	Lag Measures
Customer	C-1 Maintain the transportation system C-2 Operate the transportation system C-3 Develop the transportation system C-4 Determine the optimal system design C-5 Improve service quality	C-1 Repair Response: repair response action C-1 Travel Speed: average travel speed by facility and selected location C-2 Commute Time: average commute time on selected roads C-2 On-Time Buses: public transit on-time C-3 Programs Introduced: newly introduced programs, pilots, or program specifications C-5 Responsiveness: % of citizen complaints and requests resolved at the CDOT level	C-1 High Quality Streets: condition of lane miles ≥90 rating C-2 Safety: citywide accident rate; no. of high-accident locations C-3 Basic Mobility: availability of public transport C-4 Plan Progress: % complete on 2015 Transportation Plan
Financial	F-1 Expand noncity funding F-2 Maximize benefit/cost	F-2 Costs: costs compared to other municipalities and private sector competition	F-1 Funding Leverage: dollar value from noncity sources F-1 New Funding Sources: dollar value from sources not previously available
Internal Process	I-1 Gain infrastructure capacity I-2 Secure funding/service partners I-3 Improve productivity I-4 Increase positive contacts with community	I-1 Capital Investment: $ allocated to capital projects in targeted areas I-2 Leverage funding/service partners: new funding/resource partners identified I-3 Cost per Unit: cost per unit I-3 Competitive Sourcing: % of budget bid I-3 Problem Identification: source and action I-4 Customer Communications: no., type, frequency	I-1 Capacity Ratios: incremental capacity built vs. required by 2015 Plan I-2 No. of Partners: number of partners I-3 Street Maintenance Cost: cost/passenger I-4 Customer Surveys: survey results concerning service quality
Learning	L-1 Enhance automated information systems L-2 Enhance "field" technology L-3 Close the skills gap L-4 Empower employees	L-1 IT Infrastructure: complete relational database across CDOT L-3 Skills Identified: key skills identified in strategic functions L-4 Employee Climate Survey: results of employee survey	L-1 Information Access: strategic information available vs. user requirements L-2 Information Tools: strategic tools available vs. user requirements L-3 Skills Transfer: skill evidence in task or job performance L-4 Employee Goal Alignment: training/career development alliance with mission

Source: Charlotte Department of Transportation, City of Charlotte, North Carolina. Reprinted with permission.

indicators presented earlier in this chapter—with the addition of internally oriented measures representing such aspects as employee development and satisfaction, use of technology, and management capacity—the balanced scorecard
simply encourages taking a holistic view. The balanced scorecard model is by no
means incompatible with the program logic models emphasized in Chapter Three
and used throughout this book. The real difference is that the balanced scorecard
is a framework for measuring *organizational* performance, whereas the program
logic model focuses on *program* performance per se.

Thus, where the purpose of a performance measurement system is to track
the performance of specific operating programs, as is the case under the federal
Government Performance and Results Act of 1993 and similar legislation in many
states, the program logic model provides an essential methodology for determining the important dimensions of performance to measure. However, where large,
multifunctional public or nonprofit agencies wish to monitor their overall performance, the balanced scorecard can be very useful. Of course, even with a balanced scorecard framework, an agency would probably want to track program
effectiveness as "external results," and a program logic model will be helpful in
ensuring that the agency is focusing on the most relevant outputs and outcomes.

Performance Measurement and Strategic Management

Increasingly, both public and nonprofit organizations are developing strategic
plans and disciplining their management processes to ensure organizational follow-
through in implementing strategic initiatives and accomplishing strategic objectives. Adhering to the principle that "what gets measured gets done," these
agencies define measures of success for each strategic goal or objective in order
to focus attention on these top management priorities and to track progress in
achieving results in strategic focus areas. Therefore, the measurement systems that
are developed to support strategic planning efforts

Tend to focus on a mix of output and outcome measures that are of fundamental importance to the organization

Emphasize global measures that pertain to the organization as a whole, although they may consist of roll-ups from decentralized divisions and units

Employ measured scales on some indicators but may also include nominal
measures and more qualitative indicators

Often establish target levels on indicators of key results and then track actual performance against these targets

Sometimes "cascade" performance measures down to major divisions and other organizational units to track strategic results at those levels, particularly in the case of multimission, multifunctional, or highly decentralized agencies

Thus, performance measures are critical elements of the strategic management process designed to create, implement, and evaluate strategic agendas. In larger, more complex agencies, an essential linkage in this process is to tie divisions' business plans or annual operating plans to the overall strategic plan and then, on a shorter time frame, monitor performance measures that are directly tied to the overall indicators of strategic results. In addition, there are two important tools for drilling strategic plans down into organizations and making sure that they are given priority at the operating level: the budgeting process and the performance management process, the latter for ensuring that individual-level work objectives are responsive to the agency's overall strategic objectives. Performance measures are indispensable elements in both of these processes, as will be discussed in Chapters Ten and Eleven, respectively.

CHAPTER TEN

INCORPORATING PERFORMANCE MEASURES INTO THE BUDGETING PROCESS

Julia Melkers

How are performance measures used to make decisions about allocating financial resources in organizations? A major impetus for the implementation of performance systems in public and nonprofit organizations is the need to improve accountability. This becomes an even greater issue when resources and funds are widely dispersed. This chapter addresses the realities of integrating performance measurement into public and nonprofit budgetary systems. It defines the role of performance measurement in budgetary decision making, provides examples of current performance budgeting activities, and discusses the issues in implementing performance-based budgetary systems.

Performance Budgeting

Although it seems intuitive that aspects of performance should be included in decisions about the allocation of resources, this is often not the case. Today, however, governments and nonprofit organizations are moving away from a line-item approach and adopting performance budgets, establishing a link between allocated funds and what an organization will achieve with those funds. Line-item budgets encourage decision-making processes that focus on individual items in a short-term framework with little or no explanatory information. Performance budgeting efforts take a broader approach, encouraging a long-term perspective with an emphasis on what will be achieved in the future. Using performance data in the budgetary process means *integrating information about outcomes and impacts in decisions about the allocation of funds, where the goal is to use performance information to make more informed decisions about resource allocations.*

The use of performance data in budget processes and budget decision making is increasingly becoming the norm in public and nonprofit organizations. In fact, governments are not merely *encouraging* but *requiring* the integration of performance data in the budgetary process. As mentioned elsewhere, the Government Performance and Results Act of 1993 requires the establishment and use of performance measures in federal agencies. At the state level, all but three states (Arkansas, Massachusetts, and New York) have legislative or administrative requirements for the integration of performance data in the budget process; most of these requirements were established in the 1990s (Melkers and Willoughby, 1998). A similar trend toward the use of performance measurement information in the budget process is taking place in local governments; many municipal and county governments require performance measurement and then its integration in the budgetary process.

Why the push to include this information in budget decision making? In a word, *accountability.* An important thrust of current budget reform efforts is to develop structures that improve communication both among government and nonprofit entities and with citizens. Reflecting the trend toward use of performance measures in budgetary processes in this era of budget reform and government reinvention, the term *performance-based budgeting* (PBB) has become increasingly popular. However, what may be described as PBB is actually a more diverse set of requirements that blends various aspects of current public management trends, including outcome measurement, performance measurement systems, strategic planning, and benchmarking. Although PBB may be the most common term for this process, the actual terminology varies a great deal as organizations and governments design the process and "make it their own." In fact, these variations are reflected in the performance-based requirements used in different governments and organizations. Some state and local governments refer explicitly to *performance-based budgeting, performance-budgeting, results-based budgeting,* or *outcome-based budgeting system.* Others are more general, using such terms as *program performance reports, performance measures, outcome measures,* and *performance standards and measures.* The essence of these different requirements does not vary, however: each indicates that performance measures should be actively incorporated in the budgetary process. Specifically, these performance budgeting initiatives involve

• Identifying broad performance measures for selected organizations (programs, departments, agencies), with an emphasis on outcomes

- Linking of outcome measures to organizational activities and their respective budgets
- Targeting performance levels and budget levels together

Although the current requirements for the use of performance measures in performance-based budgeting are relatively recent, they are not completely new (Joyce, 1997). Integrating performance goals into budget decision making has been attempted in prior budgetary reform efforts. In general, these attempts were not successful and were often abandoned. The current efforts reflect two important changes. First and foremost is the integration of PBB-like efforts with other public management initiatives, most notably strategic planning. This integration creates momentum within organizations that can lead to a greater understanding and support of the use of performance measures. There is also a change in philosophy about the role that performance data plays in the decision-making process. In earlier efforts, it was viewed as a more linear process. Today's reform, however, acknowledges the complexity of not only public programs but also the budget process itself. For example, in the State of Washington, the budget guidelines are clear that performance data inform, but do not drive, budgetary decision making. The actual budget or policy decision involves performance measures, but is also affected by a variety of other factors, such as financial realities and public sentiment.

The second change is that technological advances over the last two decades have dramatically improved the way that performance data can be maintained and examined over time. User-friendly spreadsheets and databases that are capable of linking data sources have revolutionized our ability not only to maintain and track performance data but also to integrate it with budget data.

Identifying Appropriate Measures for the Budget Process

Although performance budgeting on its own does not have quite the long-term or global perspective that strategic planning does (as discussed in Chapter Eight), the performance measures it uses do require characteristics similar to those of measures used in strategic planning. Performance budgeting processes work best when performance measures reflect the "big picture" or summarize a program's or agency's activities. They are sometimes referred to as roll-up measures that summarize a group of activities or a group of measures that may be used at a more operational level. The Government Finance Officers Association (Tigue and Strachota, 1994) suggests that financial, service, and program performance measures be developed and used as an important component of decision making and incorporated into governmental budgeting; it recommends that performance measures should

- Be based on program goals and objectives that tie to a statement of program mission or purpose
- Measure program results or accomplishments
- Provide for comparisons over time
- Measure efficiency and effectiveness
- Be reliable, verifiable, and understandable
- Be reported internally and externally
- Be monitored and used in decision-making processes; and
- Be limited to a number and a degree of complexity that can provide an efficient and meaningful way to assess the effectiveness and efficiency of key programs.

In an ideal performance budgeting process, output measures are included to show the level of work accomplished, but it is efficiency and effectiveness measures that are most relevant and may be most informative in the budgeting process, where decision makers are looking for links to actual funds. Taking output, outcome, and efficiency measures together gives policymakers a full view of activities completed, the cost and value of the outputs and outcomes, and what has actually been accomplished with the actual expenditures. Helping government become more efficient is an important aspect of the current state of government reform. In this vein, incorporating performance measures in the budgetary process is important for identifying the relative efficiency of services. Efficiency measures are important in the budget process because they help answer the question, how much output is there for a given input? These measures are especially important in making fiscal decisions because they yield information on the cost of providing services and, when linked to output measures, provide information on the cost of obtaining given outputs.

The rationale behind performance budgeting processes is that people will make better resource allocation decisions if they can use information that indicates how well an entity is performing. For many governments, this performance is linked to agency or program goals and objectives. Therefore, performance budgeting should indicate how well an agency or program is meeting its goals and objectives. It is imperative that performance measures in the budgeting processes not be limited to measures of outputs but rather include actual outcomes.

Although it seems straightforward to select certain categories of measures most useful for budgetary decision making, it is not a uncomplicated process. In addition to the challenges discussed earlier in this volume related to identifying and selecting performance measures, there are three important additional challenges in selecting measures for budget processes: (1) the nature of the budget cycle, (2) the perspective and attention span of policymakers, and (3) the pressure to demonstrate macro-level results.

Chapter Nine describes a global, long-term perspective for strategic planning, but because of their nature, budget cycles require a much more limited view of performance results. Typically, most budget cycles are annual, although some governments adopt a biennial budget. Because of this relatively short time frame, integrating performance measures in the budget process means selecting measures that can show some change within that time frame. Measures cannot be so global as not to be meaningful within the budgetary calendar. One problem with measuring outcomes within the budgeting cycle is that the outcomes of most government and nonprofit programs and services occur in a much longer time frame. This is perhaps the greatest challenge in integrating performance measures in the budgetary process. Because of this challenge, it is important to identify intermediate outcomes that show progress toward or a contribution to the ultimate projected outcome. In addition, to create a context for performance information, budget reports can include performance targets or goals.

The second important challenge is that policymakers and others involved in the budget process typically have to review budgets and measures for a large number of programs and departments. Further, these individuals will have varying levels of familiarity with the individual budgetary entities. For this reason, it is important to include only key measures in the budget process. More detailed measures are more appropriate for the departmental level. For example, in Florida, the guidelines for its performance budgeting initiative, PB^2 (performance-based program budgeting), note that only measures of broad program results should appear in the budget documents, whereas detailed output and outcome measures should be maintained and used at the agency level. Similarly, the guidelines of the State of Washington stress that only key summary measures appear in the budget documents: "Agencies should include performance measures in the strategic plan, generally measuring accomplishments in relation to each major strategic plan goal. Only a core set of useful and verifiable performance measures relating to agency goals should be submitted to OFM [Office of Financial Management]. Agencies may utilize performance measures to track accomplishment of more detailed objectives or operations for internal management purposes, but such performance measures need not be submitted to OFM" (State of Washington, 2001).

The third challenge is that there may be pressure from policymakers to identify measures that reflect macro-level governmental policy goals, such as "lower infant mortality rate" or "healthier society." However, it is important that performance measures in the budget be tied to activities and results that the agency can actually affect. It is important then that interim measures be selected that show progress toward those larger policy goals, where performance is related to agency strategy and goals.

It is important for an agency or program to work with guidelines for the selection, reporting format, and use of performance measures that are incorporated into the budget, in order to ensure consistency across agencies or programs, but also to inform stakeholders about the changes and the related requirements associated with the new process. In some cases, such as in the State of Florida, there are elaborate review procedures of the measures themselves to ensure the consistency and quality of measures across agencies. In most cases where performance measures are required in the budget process, general guidelines are provided in budget preparation guidelines prepared by a central budget office or government body, indicating the types of measures that are to be included.

Integrating Measures into the Budget Process

The way that performance measures are actually integrated into the budget process varies from organization to organization. In some cases, performance data are presented alongside budget figures, suggesting a more direct link between expenditures and outcomes. In other scenarios, performance measures are presented so as to suggest that they are intended to inform the budget process but not to directly link outcomes and budget allocations. Two examples from the state governments of Texas and Florida and a local government example from Fairfax County, Virginia, illustrate the different ways that performance measures are incorporated into the budget process.

The influence of a strategic planning framework is apparent in the State of Texas, where department mission, program goals, and outcomes are presented in the budget documents. The budget is organized by mission, goals, and related strategies, and outputs are identified for each strategy. For example, with regard to the Texas Department of Agriculture's mission, "To make Texas the nation's leader in agriculture while providing efficient and extraordinary service," the budget document lays out several goals. The first goal, "Markets and Public Health: To enable Texas farmers, ranchers, and agribusinesses to expand profitable markets for their agricultural products while protecting public health and natural resources," is shown in Table 10.1.

In this example, there are four individual strategies for the articulated goal. Outcomes are defined for the goal, and each strategy has related outputs. Budget figures are shown broken out by individual strategy for years 1999 to 2003, and there is a summary of the total budget figures for each goal. For example, under strategy A.1.2., Regulate Pesticide Use, the related output—the "number of

TABLE 10.1. PERFORMANCE BUDGET DOCUMENT: TEXAS DEPARTMENT OF AGRICULTURE.

Susan Combs, Commissioner
Mission: The Department of Agriculture's mission is to make Texas the nation's leader in agriculture while providing efficient and extraordinary service.
Statutory Reference: Texas Constitution and VTCA, Agriculture Code, Title 2, 11, and 12.

	Expended 1999	Expended 2000	Budgeted 2001	Requested 2002	Requested 2003	Recommended 2002	Recommended 2003
A. Goal: MARKETS AND PUBLIC HEALTH To enable Texas farmers, ranchers, and agribusinesses to expand profitable markets for their agricultural products while protecting public health and our natural resources.							
Outcome (Results/Impact):							
Percent increase from the 1996 level in the number of marketing opportunities for Texas farmers, ranchers, and agribusinesses	68%	87.3%	78.7%	84%	89.6%	87%	89.6%
Percent reduction from the 1994 level in the number of pesticide-related violations	(2.54)%	(33.1)%	3%	3%	7%	3%	7%
Percent of communities assisted by TDED and TDA		115.2%	85%	85%	85%	85%	85%
A.1.1. Strategy: GENERATE MARKETS Generate marketing opportunities for Texas farmers, ranchers, and agribusinesses.	$7,151,336	$7,487,738	$10,120,410	$12,841,983	$7,660,562	$9,532,971	$7,619,000
Output (Volume):							
Number of acres inspected for seed certification	195,962	187,362	190,000	190,000	190,000	190,000	190,000
Number of rural communities assisted by TDED and TDA		670	600	600	600	680	680
Rural development activities and events held by TDA and TDED		144	120	120	120	120	120
Businesses developed as expansion and recruitment prospects in rural Texas		1,390	1,300	1,300	1,300	1,300	1,300
A.1.2. Strategy: REGULATE PESTICIDE USE Regulate pesticide use through registration, certification, education, and enforcement.	$5,485,424	$6,068,081	$6,104,922	$8,470,206	$6,081,178	$5,988,659	$5,839,380

Output (Volume):							
Number of pesticide complaint investigations conducted	213	216	250	250	250	225	225
A.1.3. Strategy: INTEGRATED PEST MANAGEMENT	$26,831,794	$27,047,886	$27,003,690	$27,745,888	$27,001,757	$26,976,673	$26,914,473
Assist farmers with integrated pest management practices to reduce pesticide use.							
Output (Volume):							
Hours spent informing producers and surveying cotton for compliance with cotton stalk destruction deadlines	10,512	11,339	10,000	12,500	12,500	12,500	12,500
Number of inspections to verify compliance for organic or other crop production certification programs	1,040	1,138	1,268	1,307	1,320	1,307	1,320
A.1.4. Strategy: CERTIFY PRODUCE	$278,580	$225,369	$265,167	$320,273	$261,372	$233,015	$254,014
Certify fruits, vegetables, peanuts, and nuts to enhance their marketability.							
Output (Volume):							
Number of pounds of fruits, vegetables, peanuts, and nuts inspected (in billions)	3.4	3.4	3.0	3.0	3.0	3.1	3.2
Total, Goal A: MARKETS AND PUBLIC HEALTH	$39,747,134	$40,829,074	$43,494,189	$49,378,350	$41,004,869	$42,731,318	$40,626,867

B. Goal: ENFORCE STANDARDS
To protect consumers by establishing and enforcing standards for agricultural commodities.

Outcome (Results/Impact):							
Percent of seed samples found to be in full compliance with state and federal standards	97%	96%	96%	96%	96%	97%	97%
B.1.1. Strategy: NURSERY/FLORAL REGULATION	$2,293,127	$1,990,080	$2,174,489	$2,833,250	$2,201,979	$2,028,372	$2,095,910
Inspect and register nursery and floral production and retail outlets.							
Output (Volume):							
Number of nursery and floral establishment inspections conducted	12,211	10,361	11,500	11,500	11,500	11,500	11,500

TABLE 10.1. PERFORMANCE BUDGET DOCUMENT: TEXAS DEPARTMENT OF AGRICULTURE, Cont'd.

	Expended 1999	Expended 2000	Budgeted 2001	Requested 2002	Requested 2003	Recommended 2002	Recommended 2003
B.1.2. Strategy: VERIFY SEED QUALITY Verify that farmers, ranchers, and home gardeners receive the quality and type of seeds desired.	$1,888,514	$1,872,347	$1,906,530	$2,569,643	$1,911,182	$1,958,743	$1,849,382
Output (Volume):							
Number of seed samples analyzed	20,539	19,937	20,500	20,500	20,500	20,500	20,500
B.1.3. Strategy: AGRICULTURAL COMMODITY REGULATION Regulate agricultural commodities through verification, licensing, inspection, and enforcement of state standards for eggs, grain warehouses, perishables, and other agricultural commodities.	$1,147,034	$1,258,044	$1,456,967	$1,983,965	$1,469,129	$1,481,161	$1,420,225
Output (Volume):							
Number of egg producer, dealer, wholesaler, and retailer inspections conducted	3,885	3,500	3,500	3,500	3,500	3,500	3,500
Number of grain warehouse inspections, reinspections, and audits conducted	653	576	650	650	650	650	650
Total, Goal B: ENFORCE STANDARDS	$5,328,675	$5,120,471	$5,537,986	$7,386,858	$5,582,290	$5,468,276	$5,365,517
C. Goal: ENSURE PROPER MEASUREMENT To increase the likelihood that goods offered for sale to Texas consumers are properly measured, priced, and marketed.							
Outcome (Results/Impact):							
Percent of total weights and measures inspections conducted that are found to be in full compliance with state and federal standards	94%	95%	95%	95%	95%	96%	96%

C.1.1. Strategy: INSPECT MEASURING DEVICES

Inspect weighing and measuring devices and remove inaccurately measured, priced, or marketed goods from sale.

Output (Volume):

Number of weights and measures inspections conducted	111,225	136,091	120,000	120,000	120,000	123,000	123,000

D. Goal: FAIR PARK STRUCTURE RESTORATION
Oversee structural building improvements within the Agrarian District at Fair Park.

D.1.1. Strategy: FAIR PARK STRUCTURE RESTORATION

Prioritize, monitor, and manage the use of appropriated funds for structural building improvements within the Agrarian District at Fair Park.

C.1.1. Strategy: INSPECT MEASURING DEVICES	$3,467,557	$3,479,209	$3,488,799	$8,414,424	$3,463,994	$3,502,488	$3,356,758
D.1.1. Strategy: FAIR PARK STRUCTURE RESTORATION	$1,110,682	$39,488	$1,935,112	$1,974,600	$0	$1,974,600	$0
Grand Total, DEPARTMENT OF AGRICULTURE	**$49,654,048**	**$49,468,242**	**$54,456,086**	**$67,154,232**	**$50,051,153**	**$53,676,682**	**$49,349,142**

Method of Financing:

General Revenue Fund

General Revenue Fund	$47,254,524	$45,836,887	$49,345,742	$59,150,754	$47,246,436	$48,673,204	$46,344,425
Earned Federal Funds	263,317	363,238	442,317	382,363	382,363	382,363	382,363
Subtotal, General Revenue Fund	$47,517,841	$46,200,125	$49,788,059	$59,533,117	$47,628,799	$49,055,567	$46,726,788

General Revenue (GR) Fund—Dedicated

GR Dedicated—Young Farmer Loan Guarantee Account No. 5002	68,180	100,000	100,000	100,000	100,000	100,000	100,000
GR Dedicated—GO TEXAN Partner Program Account No. 5051	0	124,546	875,454	1,000,000	0	1,060,000	60,000
Subtotal, General Revenue Fund—Dedicated	$68,180	$224,546	$975,454	$1,100,000	$100,000	$1,160,000	$160,000
Federal Funds	1,261,585	1,652,109	1,536,789	1,477,394	1,477,394	1,477,394	1,477,394

TABLE 10.1. PERFORMANCE BUDGET DOCUMENT: TEXAS DEPARTMENT OF AGRICULTURE, Cont'd.

	Expended 1999	Expended 2000	Budgeted 2001	Requested 2002	Requested 2003	Recommended 2002	Recommended 2003
Other Funds							
Farm and Ranch Finance Program Fund							
Account No. 575	38,516	76,631	76,991	76,632	76,991	76,632	76,991
Appropriated Receipts	556,685	600,733	1,320,978	408,000	408,000	1,348,000	348,000
Texas Agricultural Fund No. 683	201,161	250,089	249,969	250,089	249,969	250,089	249,969
Interagency Contracts	10,080	311,509	507,846	509,000	110,000	309,000	310,000
Bond Proceeds—Revenue Bonds	0	0	0	3,800,000	0	0	0
Governor's Emergency and Deficiency Grant	0	152,500	0	0	0	0	0
Subtotal, Other Funds	$806,442	$1,391,462	$2,155,784	$5,043,721	$844,960	$1,983,721	$984,960
Total, Method of Financing	$49,654,048	$49,468,242	$54,456,086	$67,154,232	$50,051,153	$53,676,682	$49,349,142
Number of Full-Time-Equivalent Positions (FTE):	502.5	505.5	505.5	508.5	508.5	505.5	505.5
Number of FTEs in Riders:	0.0	0.0	0.0	1.0	1.0	0.0	0.0
Schedule of Exempt Positions:							
Commissioner of Agriculture, Group 4	$92,217	$92,217	$92,217	$92,217	$92,217	$92,217	$92,217
Supplemental Appropriations Made in Riders:	$0	$0	$0	$556,550	$502,200	$42,950	$0

Source: Legislative Budget Board, State of Texas, 2001b.

pesticide complaint investigations conducted"—is shown alongside budget allocations for each year. Fluctuations in pesticide complaints investigations can then be viewed together with changes in budget outlays for that particular strategy. In this case, the cost of implementing the four strategies to accomplish the Markets and Public Health goal in 1999 was $39,747,134. Portraying performance measures alongside budget figures, as shown here, also provides target information, as budget figures are projected through the following budget cycle.

Not all performance budgets combine performance and budget figures in a detailed, integrated fashion, as shown in the Texas example. In Fairfax County, Virginia, performance data and budget figures are presented in one document, but in separate tables. The budget document for each department begins with a statement of departmental mission and is then organized by "cost centers" or divisions. For example, the mission of the Fairfax County Economic Development Authority (EDA) is "To encourage and facilitate business and capital attraction, retention and development in Fairfax County; to promote the County's cultural, historical, and recreational attractions to business travelers; and to attract business meetings, conferences, and seminars to the County's meeting facilities in order to expand the County's nonresidential tax base." To accomplish this mission, the Fairfax County EDA is organized into two cost centers—Administration and the Convention and Visitor's Bureau. It states the goal for the cost center, followed by the cost center's objectives and performance measures.

In this example, the EDA Administration cost center's goal is "To foster and promote the governmental, social, educational, and environmental infrastructure in order to make Fairfax County a world-class, 21st century business center and the global capital of the knowledge industry." To accomplish this goal, the EDA has defined the following objectives:

> To increase the number of businesses announcing location to Fairfax County by 4.0 percent, from 125 in fiscal year (FY) 2000 to 130 in FY 2001 in order to increase the number of new jobs created by 1.0 percent from 11,000 new jobs in FY 2000 to 11,100 new jobs in FY 2001
>
> To increase the number of new business prospects by 6.7 percent, from 375 in FY 2000 to 400 in FY 2001, in order to increase the amount of venture capital attracted by 9.4 percent, from $64 million in FY 2000 to $70 million in FY 2001

The budget document also includes additional descriptive information reviewing agency activities overall as well as details of budget adjustments (not shown in this example). Unlike the Texas example, Fairfax County's budget does not show as clear a link between budget categories and strategies or performance measures. The EDA's expenditures are provided only in broad categories of personnel, operating, and capital expenses. However, this example illustrates the use of global measures in performance budgets. Performance indicators are organized by the three categories of output, efficiency, and outcome, listing actual and estimated figures for a period of five years. Presenting performance budget information in this way does not show a link between a particular line-item expenditure and a projected output or outcome. Instead, measures are looked at as a grouping for the organization overall.

In another example, the State of Florida operates with two related documents: the actual budget document and the "Governor's Budget Recommendations Performance Ledger." The performance ledger is included in the budget process and is presented alongside budget data. In the performance ledger, data are organized by agency and program. Each agency articulates its overall purposes and provides performance measures and data for a range of years, including an initial baseline year. It is not unusual for governmental bodies to integrate performance data in the budget process while retaining separate budget documents and performance reports. The State of Washington also asks agencies to submit performance measures and data separately, which are then combined by the Office of Financial Management. For each major agency goal, each agency submits the related performance measure and the relevant data for the prior, current, and future biennium.

Implementing Performance Budgeting

Implementing performance budgeting means changing the way that agencies submit budget requests as well as changing the way that policymakers make decisions. The formalization of performance-based budgeting requirements creates a framework or process so that performance data are considered in the budgetary process. It goes without saying that it is a complex process that is sometimes difficult to implement. What is the best way to proceed in formalizing the use of performance measures in budgetary decision making? The examples in this chapter show the diversity of presentations of performance and budget data. The processes that governments have gone through to implement these systems are just as diverse.

Because most governments and nonprofits have not been collecting performance data as a regular activity, implementing performance budgeting means not only refining the budget process but also developing a parallel or concurrent process that identifies performance measures and collects and reports data such that they coordinate with the existing budget cycle. Thus, implementing performance budgeting often means initiating performance measurement activities in the first place. Many governments that have adopted performance budgeting processes have done so in a multistage process: different programs or agencies are selected to pilot the use of performance measures in the budget process before the process is implemented government-wide. Adopting a performance budgeting system in this way allows for learning, adaptation, and integration with existing systems.

For example, the State of Florida implemented its PB^2 initiative over a period of several years, adding new departments and programs each budget cycle. An important advantage of a pilot process is that as new agencies or departments or programs begin performance budgeting, they are able to look at and communicate with other entities within their government as examples. The list that follows shows the steps involved in implementing performance budgeting in the Florida Department of Business and Professional Regulation. As mentioned earlier, performance budgeting efforts today are often closely linked to other public management initiatives. Thus, calendars such as the one shown in the list may also coincide with time frames for other reporting and requirements, such as those associated with a strategic planning schedule.

Time Frame for PB^2 Implementation for Florida's
Department of Business and Professional Regulation (DBPR)

September 1997 DBPR begins process by holding internal workshops to identify PB2 programs and measures.

September 1998 DBPR proposes programs and measures to governor's office, which consults with legislature and will include proposed programs and measures in budget recommendations.

January-April 1999 Legislative committees will review proposal and provide feedback to DBPR.

September 1999 DBPR will submit PB2 budget request based on PB2 programs and measures. The agency must provide one year of actual performance data and recommend a specific level of performance (standard) for each measure.

January 2000 PB^2 proposal will be included in the governor's FY 2000–01 budget recommendation, which will include measures and performance standards for DBPR programs.

March-April 2000 Legislature will designate approved DBPR programs, measures, and standards in the FY 2000–01 General Appropriations Act or the implementing act.

July 2000 DBPR will begin to operate under PB^2. The agency will collect performance data and report its actual performance levels in its next budget request.

July 2001 The Office of Program Policy Analysis and Government Accountability (OPPAGA) will begin evaluation of DBPR programs. OPPAGA's program evaluation and justification review of DBPR programs will be completed by June 2002.

An important fiscal issue arises in this implementation process. If performance measures are meant to be used in budgetary decision making, what happens when programs or agencies do not meet their targets? If they exceed their targets, are they allocated more funds? If they fall below their targets, are they "punished" with fewer allocations? In implementing a performance budgeting process, it is important to consider how or if performance data will be used in terms of punishments and rewards. A handful of state governments provide explicit guidelines for actual agency attainment or nonattainment of goals and objectives as part of their legislated performance budgeting requirements. These are guidelines that define rewards to public managers who attain the performance goals that they have identified in their strategic planning or other process. For example, agency personnel in California, Florida, Georgia, and Texas may receive financial rewards in the form of gain sharing or a proportion of savings; Mississippi adds public commendation with a monetary reward for cost savings, and Louisiana provides incentives through an existing employee incentive program.

Only two states, Florida and Texas, provide specific guidelines for agencies or programs that do not meet performance goals or targets. The Texas 1996–1997 general appropriations guidelines state that if an agency fails to meet its goals, the Legislative Budget Board and the governor may adopt a budget execution order, which may result in the "reduction, elimination, restriction, or withholding of funding or . . . transferability, in addition to possible reorganization." Florida's guidelines allow for a number of budget execution and management restrictions in the event of poor performance, which is not defined. It is part of the planning and design process for an organization to determine whether it is useful or necessary to articulate incentives and disincentives for performance at either the individual or organizational level. For most governments, it seems easier and more realistic not to have anything explicitly defined, leaving the door open to amending the process at a later date.

As discussed in earlier chapters, implementing a comprehensive performance measurement system requires coordination with existing organizational practices. In the budgeting process, this involves creating linkages with existing accounting practices and systems. Links between costs and activities have traditionally been the responsibility of the organization's accounting divisions. With the adoption of a performance measurement system, accounting and performance measurement systems may become blended. The challenge lies in the fact that traditional accounting systems often do not support this blending because they are limited to dealing with costs and inventory on a broad organizational scale that may be difficult to link to certain activities. Specifically, in traditional accounting procedures it is difficult to address the broader concepts addressed in performance measurement, such as cause-and-effect relationships (Brown, Myring, and Gard, 1999).

Activity-based accounting practices have increasingly been adopted in public organizations. This approach to accounting involves tracking the costs associated with various organizational activities and services. Cost centers may be located within an individual division or may cross divisions. Managers use activity-based accounting systems to access information about cost management, which in turn is used for organization planning and control. Ideally, a managerial accounting system will link to planning and control activities, existing accounting practices, and budgets. This approach to accounting is relevant to the development of performance budgeting because as part of the activity-based accounting process, managers and staff identify measurable activities. In a comprehensive performance measurement and budgeting system, these measures could form all or some portion of the system's activity measures. The performance budgeting system would then involve the development of performance measures that are logically linked to the activity measures. Activity-based accounting systems can overcome the problem of blending existing accounting systems with newer performance measurement systems because they focus on precise groups of activities and allocate costs according to those activities, rather than to the organization overall (Brown, Myring, and Gard, 1999). Thus, as performance measures for particular activities are formulated, they may be linked with existing cost data that are also organized in terms of those activities.

If an organization uses a form of activity-based costing, it adds another layer of coordination within the overall system that is required for implementing a performance measurement system. However, organizations with an activity-based accounting system have developed some of the framework from which a performance budgeting system can be developed. Cost data could be used to add additional detail and depth to measures of level of service and other measures so that costs can be easily and accurately examined alongside performance measures and data in the budget process. Thus, in the developmental stages of creating a performance budgeting system, managers and staff should pay attention to existing accounting systems so that the two can be blended for shared purposes.

Making It Work: Helping Policymakers Understand Performance Budgets

Overall, there is little evidence to show that performance data are affecting actual budget appropriations. This is neither surprising nor disturbing, as the implementation of performance budgeting is still in the early phases for many governments and nonprofit organizations. Integrating performance data in the budget process can help decision makers make better, more informed decisions along the way. Specifically, performance data are useful for helping decision makers in a number of areas:

- Understanding the activities and objectives of funded programs by viewing summary measures of performance
- Understanding changes in performance over time compared to budgetary changes
- Having more meaningful dialogues with public managers about agency activities, goals, and performance
- Identifying poorly performing and high-performing programs and departments
- Justifying fiscal decisions using evidence rather than anecdotes or impressions.

Implementing a performance budgeting system means changing the way in which policymakers make decisions. If policymakers have been accustomed to making budgetary decisions without explicit performance data, how can you present performance data such that policymakers will be comfortable with them and able to understand them easily? There are four important things that budgeters and agency or department staff can do to ease this process:

1. Carefully select a reasonable number of measures.
2. Include performance targets when possible.
3. Include explanatory information in the budget document.
4. Personally communicate with decision makers about agency or department activities and performance.

First, when including performance measures in a budget document, it is important to select only a few key, meaningful measures. Policymakers will generally have neither the time nor the patience to sort through a long list of performance measures in addition to other budgetary data. Therefore, it is critical that only the most useful and most explanatory or summary measures appear in the budget document. Ideally, these will be roll-up measures that summarize performance for a particular goal, program area, or activity. Other, more detailed measures can be used internally in the program or unit.

Second, because performance data on their own do not always give an adequate picture of an organization's activities, a budget document that shows performance targets or goals, including some information on progress toward those goals, can be extremely useful to the reader and assist the policymaker in understanding the performance data quickly and easily.

Third, numbers do not always speak for themselves, particularly to an audience not completely familiar with the details of the program or department activity. It is useful to the readers of the budget document to include some explanatory information to indicate changes in performance, extenuating factors or problems, and progress toward targets or goals.

Finally, personal contact with key policymakers can give agency or department staff an opportunity to explain details of performance and provide additional insight to performance data presented in the budget. This is especially useful when policymakers are unaccustomed to reading performance data and may be unsure of how to use them. Making these contacts is time consuming and may not always be possible, but it can be a very useful way to increase the comfort of policymakers with performance data that has been incorporated into the budgetary process.

CHAPTER ELEVEN

SUPPORTING PERFORMANCE MANAGEMENT SYSTEMS

H ow can you ensure that managers and employees focus their attention on strategic goals and objectives and that top management's priorities are driven down through the management layers to the workforce at the operating level? To what extent can you use performance measures to help direct and control the work of people in the agency so as to channel their energy and efforts toward accomplishing important organizational goals? What kinds of performance management systems are used in public and nonprofit organizations, and what kinds of performance measures can support them? Whereas Chapter Ten discussed the incorporation of performance measures in systems for budgeting an agency's financial resources, this chapter examines the use of performance measures in processes for managing programs and an organization's most important resources: its *human* resources.

Performance Management Systems

In order for an agency to function effectively, it is essential for managers, employees, programs, and organizational units to direct their work toward meeting targets and accomplishing objectives that are consistent with higher-level goals and objectives, top management priorities, strategic initiatives, and the agency's mission. How can this be accomplished? By setting more specific goals and objectives, developing operational plans and providing the wherewithal, monitoring progress and evaluating results, and taking appropriate follow-up actions that are aligned with overall organizational goals.

The term *performance management* has come to refer to processes for managing the work of people and organizational units so as to maximize their effectiveness and enhance organizational performance. The principal approaches to performance management are MBO-type systems, which are focused directly on individual managers and employees. However, performance monitoring systems, which focus more generally on programs or organizations, are also considered to be performance management systems (Swiss, 1991).

Management by Objectives

MBO systems have been used in the private sector for the past fifty years as a way of clarifying expectations for individuals' work and evaluating their performance accordingly. MBO was introduced in the federal government by the Nixon administration and has become widespread in state and local government over the past three decades (Poister and Streib, 1995). Generally speaking, it has been found to be effective in boosting employee productivity and channeling individual efforts toward the achievement of organizational goals because it is based on three essential elements of sound management of personnel: goal setting, participative decision making, and objective feedback (Rodgers and Hunter, 1992). Although the terms *management by objectives* and *MBO* have not been in vogue for quite some time, MBO-type systems are in fact very prevalent in the public sector, usually under other names. For example, the performance management system used by the State of Georgia, called Georgia Gain, is an MBO-type system.

MBO systems are tied to personnel appraisal processes and thus usually operate on annual cycles, although in some cases they may operate on a six-month or quarterly basis. In theory, at least, the process involves the following four steps:

1. In negotiation with their supervisors, individual managers or employees set personal-level objectives in order to clarify shared expectations regarding their performance for the next year.
2. Subordinates and their supervisors develop action plans to identify a workable approach to achieving each of these objectives. At the same time, supervisors commit the necessary resources to ensure that these plans can be implemented.
3. Supervisors and subordinates monitor progress toward implementing plans and realizing objectives on an ongoing basis, and midcourse adjustments in strategy, resources, implementation procedures, or even the objectives themselves are made if necessary.

4. At the end of the year, the supervisor conducts the individual's annual performance appraisal, based at least in part on the accomplishment of the specified objectives. Salary increases and other decisions follow from this, and individual development plans may also be devised, if necessary.

Thus, the MBO process is designed to clarify organizational expectations for individuals' performance, motivate them to work toward accomplishing appropriate objectives, and enable them to do so effectively. For an example, we can look at an action plan developed for a deputy manager in a medium-size local jurisdiction aimed at increasing traffic safety on city streets. The plan is associated with the following MBO objective: "To reduce the number of vehicular accidents on city streets by a minimum of 15 percent below 1999 levels, at no increase in departmental operating budgets." (Note first that the objective is stated as a SMART objective, as discussed in Chapter Four.) The following list, adapted from Morrisey (1976), outlines the action plan, which serves as a blueprint for undertaking a project aimed at achieving the stated objective.

Sample Action Plan

1. Determine locations of highest incidence and select those with highest potential for improvement.
2. Set up an ad hoc committee (to include representatives of local citizens, traffic engineers, city planning staff, and police officers) to analyze and recommend alternative corrective actions, including but not limited to education, increased surveillance, traffic control equipment, and possible rerouting of traffic.
3. Establish an information-motivation plan for police officers.
4. Inform the city council, city manager, other related departments, and the media about plans and progress.
5. Test proposed plan in selected locations.
6. Implement plans on a citywide basis.
7. Establish a monitoring system.
8. Evaluate initial results and modify implementation plans accordingly after three months.

For this effort to be successful, it will be the responsibility of the city manager, the direct supervisor, to ensure the requisite resources in terms of cooperation from the participating departments.

Performance measures play a role at two stages in this one MBO example. First, the action plan calls for establishing a monitoring system and using the data to evaluate initial results after three months. This monitoring system, which in all likelihood will draw on existing traffic enforcement reporting systems, will also be used after the close of the year to determine whether the expected 15 percent reduction in vehicular accidents has been accomplished. These data may be broken out by various types of accidents (for example, single vehicle, multiple vehicle, vehicle-pedestrian) to gain a clearer understanding of the impact of this MBO initiative.

Alternatively, breaking the accident data out by contributing factors—such as mechanical failures, driver impairment, road conditions, or weather conditions—would probably be useful in targeting strategies as well as tracking results. In addition, depending on the kinds of interventions developed in this project, it may be helpful to track measures regarding patrol hours, traffic citations, seat belt checks, safety courses, traffic engineering projects, and so forth to provide further insight into the success or failure of this initiative. Thus, performance measurement plays an integral role in the MBO process.

Performance Monitoring Systems

At one level, performance monitoring is what this whole book is about: tracking key sets of performance measures over time to gauge progress and evaluate the results of public and nonprofit programs and activities. More specifically, however, performance monitoring systems constitute performance *management* systems designed to direct and control organizational entities, again by clarifying expectations and evaluating results based on agreed-on objective measures. Unlike MBO systems, though, performance monitoring systems do not focus so directly on the performance of individual managers and employees.

Although both MBO and performance monitoring systems seek to enhance performance through establishing clear goals and objective feedback, there are some key differences between these two approaches, as summarized in the following list, adapted from Swiss (1991):

Key Characteristics of "Pure" MBO and Performance Monitoring Systems

Dimension	MBO Systems	Performance Monitoring Systems
Principal focus	Individual managers and employees	Programs or organizational units
Orientation	Usually projects	Ongoing programs or continuing operations
Goal setting	Through face-to-face negotiations	Often unilateral, based on past performance

Performance measures	Outputs and immediate outcomes, along with quality and productivity	Outcomes emphasized, along with quality and customer service
Changes in measures	Frequent changes as objectives change	Usually continuing measures with only rare changes
Data collection and monitoring	Done by individual managers and reviewed with supervisors	Done by staff and distributed in regular reports

The most crucial difference between these systems is in focus: whereas MBO systems focus attention directly on the performance of individual managers and employees, performance monitoring systems formally address the performance of programs or organizational units. Thus, MBO is a much more personalized process, bringing incentives to bear directly on individuals, whereas with performance monitoring processes the incentives tend to be spread more diffusely over organizational entities. In terms of the overall management framework, MBO systems are usually rooted in personnel systems, whereas performance monitoring is usually carried out as part of strategic management, program management, or operations management.

Based on the principle of participative goal setting, MBO objectives are usually negotiated in face-to-face meetings between pairs of supervisors and subordinates, often in tiers from the executive level down to first-line supervisors, whereas targets for performance monitoring systems may be set unilaterally by higher-level management. In addition, whereas performance monitoring systems are usually oriented to ongoing programs, service delivery, or operations, MBO systems often focus on a changing mix of projects or specific one-time initiatives. Thus, MBO and performance monitoring represent two different approaches to performance management. It should be understood, however, that such "pure" versions of these systems are not always found in practice and that elements of these two approaches are often combined in "hybrid" systems.

Measures for Performance Management Systems

Measurement is a particularly interesting phenomenon with respect to the concept of performance management because the measures are intended to have an impact on behavior and results. Although researchers are usually interested in nonreactive measures, performance measures have a more overt purpose in monitoring systems. Performance measures are designed to track performance, and in performance management systems, they are used to provide feedback on performance in real time. For both MBO and performance monitoring systems, this feedback—usually in conjunction with targets or specific objectives—is designed to focus managers and employees' efforts and to motivate them to work "harder and smarter" to accomplish organizational objectives. These systems are predicated on the idea that people's intentions, decisions, behavior, and performance will be influenced by the performance data and how they are used.

Both these approaches are usually considered to be outcome oriented, but because MBO systems are so directly focused on the job performance of individuals, they often emphasize output measures as opposed to true effectiveness measures. Managers in public and nonprofit organizations often resist the idea of being held personally accountable for real outcomes because they have relatively little control over them. Thus, MBO systems often use output measures, and perhaps some *immediate* outcome measures, along with quality indicators and productivity measures over which managers typically do have more control. Performance monitoring systems, in contrast, because they are less personalized, often emphasize real outcomes along with efficiency, productivity, and quality indicators and, especially, measures of customer satisfaction.

One basic difference between these two approaches to measurement is that because MBO systems are often project oriented, with a varying mix of initiatives in the pipeline at any one time, the measures used to evaluate a manager's performance tend to change frequently over time. In contrast, performance monitoring systems tend to focus on ongoing programs, service delivery systems, and operations, and therefore the measures used to track performance are fairly constant, allowing trend analysis over time. Finally, the measures used to assess individuals' performance in MBO systems are usually observed or collected by those individuals themselves and reported to their supervisors for the purpose of performance appraisal, whereas performance monitoring data are usually collected by other staff who are assigned to maintain the system and report out the data.

MBO Measures

The measures used to evaluate performance in MBO systems address different kinds of issues because those systems often specify a variety of objectives. During any given MBO cycle, an individual manager is likely to be working on a mix of objectives, some of which may well call for improving the performance of ongoing programs or operations, and in fact the appropriate measures for these kinds of objectives may well be supplied by ongoing performance monitoring systems. In addition, though, managers often specify objectives that focus on problem solving, troubleshooting particular issues, implementing new projects, undertaking special initiatives, or engaging in self-development activities intended to strengthen work-related knowledge and skills. For the most part, the measures defined to evaluate performance on these kinds of objectives will be substantively different from those tracking ongoing programs or activities, and they are likely to be shorter-term indicators that will be replaced by others in subsequent MBO cycles.

In some cases, MBO systems focus largely on ongoing responsibilities and employ continuous measures to track the performance of individual managers. For example, Table 11.1 shows the first page of numerous specific objectives established for one fiscal year for the commander of the Planning and Research Bureau of the Phoenix, Arizona, police department. The objectives are clustered in different areas of responsibility and are weighted by their relative importance. This example is also notable for its specification of maximum attainment, target levels, and minimum acceptable levels of performance. With respect to the first objective, regarding the processing of certain statistical reports, for instance, the target level is to process 95 percent of these reports before the deadline, the minimum level is set at 90 percent, and the maximum is 100 percent.

Most of the measures in this particular example are expressed as percentages or raw numbers. They are fairly typical performance indicators calibrated in scale variables that can be evaluated against target levels, and most of them can probably be tracked as going up or down over time because they concern ongoing responsibilities of this particular officer. However, one of these objectives, concerning the administration of an internal employee survey within the department, sets alternative dates as targets, and the indicator is operationalized as a discrete measure of whether a given target date is attained or not. It is also interesting to note that all the objectives in this particular example relate to outputs or quality indicators, not to outcomes or effectiveness measures.

Individual Targets and Actual Performance: Community Disaster Education Program

Some MBO-type performance management systems will prorate targets over the course of a year and then track progress on a quarterly or monthly basis. For example, local chapters of the American Red Cross conduct community disaster education (CDE) programs through arrangements with public and private schools in their service areas, primarily using volunteer instructors. In one local chapter, which uses an MBO approach, the director of this program has a number of individual objectives she is expected to achieve during the 2002 fiscal year, including such items as the following:

- Launch professional development training for teachers in CDE.
- Institute Red Cross safe schools training packages in schools.
- Initiate a new CDE training program and recruit five volunteer instructors.

TABLE 11.1. PERFORMANCE ACHIEVEMENT PROGRAM: CITY OF PHOENIX.

PERFORMANCE ACHIEVEMENT PROGRAM
PERFORMANCE PROGRAM _____ FY

Signature of Employee			Signature of Supervisor		
1995/96		Planning and Research Bureau Commander		06/09/95	Page 1 of 6
FY	Name	Position		Date	

Responsibilities	Priority	Results	Observable Standards Min./Target/Max.	Weight	Responsible Person
Basic Police Services	21	1A. Percentage of requests for statistical reports received from and processed for line bureaus and precincts before deadline	90/95/100	5	Sergeants Henderson and Pitzer
		1B. Number of police facility inspections to identify problems that could reduce the building's life expectancy	2/4/64	4	Mr. Brueggeman
		1C. Percentage of on-site inspections during significant repairs or possible disruptive construction projects (power test)	90/95/100	5	Mr. Brueggeman
		1D. Percentage of timely notifications issued to the user bureau of an upcoming warranty expiration	90/98/100	4	Mr. Brueggeman
		1E. Number of facilities examined for major improvements or renovations; plan assistance for the improvement (example: academy range)	2/3/4	3	Mr. Brueggeman
Employee Safety, Morale, Effectiveness	12	2A. To receive feedback as to bureau service levels, meet with users ____ times	3/5/7	3	Commander Buchanan
		2B. Administer internal bureau Employee Morale/Satisfaction Survey by ____	06-01/05-01/04-01		Sergeant Henderson
		2C. Conduct ____ quality circle meetings within the bureau involving representation from all employee levels to improve bureau operations	4/5/6	4	Sergeant Fisher

Source: City of Phoenix, 2001. Reprinted with permission.

- Upgrade the CDE curriculum.
- Launch the Masters of Disaster curriculum kits.
- Train twenty-two thousand youth in CDE.
- Continue to develop and implement program outcome measures.

Most of these objectives are stated in general terms, and there is not a clear indication of precisely what will constitute success in accomplishing them. Only two of them have established target levels, but others could be reformulated as SMART objectives. Performance on others will be determined based on periodic reviews of progress in activity intended to realize the objectives; in the director's annual performance evaluation, judgments will have to be made by her supervisor regarding whether or not she accomplished certain of these objectives. Thus, it is not surprising that one of the director's objectives for this year is to "continue to develop and implement program outcome measures."

In contrast, the objective to train twenty-two thousand youth in CDE programs can be monitored very directly. As shown in Figure 11.1, the overall number of youth targeted to receive this training has been prorated over the course of the twelve-month fiscal year, based in part on seasonal patterns in this activity in prior years, as well as on the director's understanding of the feasibility of training particular numbers of youth in different months. Thus, this outcome measure can be tracked on a monthly basis and compared against the monthly targets in order to track her progress in reaching the target. Although the director has fallen

FIGURE 11.1. NUMBER OF YOUTH TRAINED IN COMMUNITY DISASTER EDUCATION PROGRAMS.

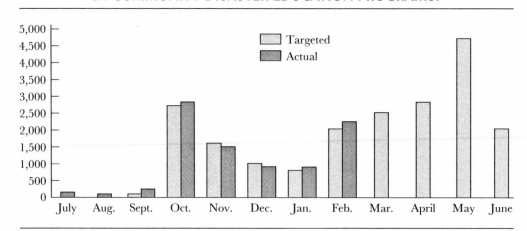

slightly short of the targets in November and December, overall she is running slightly ahead of the targets over the first eight months of the fiscal year. However, the targets for March through June appear to be quite ambitious, so it remains to be seen whether the overall target of twenty-two thousand youth trained will be met by the end of the fiscal year.

Measures for Monitoring Systems

For the most part, performance monitoring systems track measures that pertain to ongoing programs, service delivery systems, and activities at regular intervals of time. Whereas MBO systems often include a mix of continuous measures along with discrete indicators of one-time efforts (for example, the satisfactory completion of a particular project), performance monitoring systems focus exclusively on measures of recurring phenomena, such as the number of lane-miles of highway resurfaced per week or the percentage of clients placed in competitive employment each month. Whereas MBO-type performance management systems typically draw on information from performance measurement systems as well as a number of other sources, performance monitoring systems actually constitute measurement systems.

For example, the City of Phoenix (2001) uses a monitoring system to track the performance of each operating department and major program—for example, community and economic development, fire protection, housing, human services, parks and recreation, police, and public transit—on a variety of indicators on a monthly basis. Each month, the performance data are presented in the *City Manager's Executive Report*, which states the overall goal of each department, identifies the key services provided, and affords data on a variety of performance indicators, most often displayed graphically and emphasizing comparisons over time.

Figure 11.2 presents excerpts of the performance data for Phoenix's neighborhood services program, taken from the June 2001 edition of the *City Manager's Executive Report*. All of these measures are presented on a rolling twelve-month basis (with May therefore the most recent month with data available); the report also shows data from the previous year to provide more of a baseline and to facilitate comparing the current month's performance against the same month in the prior year, which is particularly relevant for measures that exhibit significant seasonal variation, such as the number of neighborhood cleanup efforts assisted.

As we might expect, many of these indicators tracked on a monthly basis are output measures, such as the number of residential infill units completed or the number of properties acquired, redeveloped, or demolished for revitalization purposes. Others focus on service quality, such as the cycle time for adjudicating or administering neighborhood preservation cases in terms of average calendar days.

FIGURE 11.2. NEIGHBORHOOD SERVICES PROGRAM:
CITY OF PHOENIX.

CITY MANAGER'S EXECUTIVE REPORT   **MAY 2001**

Neighborhood Services

Program Goal

To preserve and improve the physical, social, and economic health of Phoenix neighborhoods, support neighborhood self-reliance, and enhance the quality of life of residents through community-based problem-solving, neighborhood-oriented services, and public/private cooperation.

Key Services

Neighborhood Preservation/Code Enforcement, Housing Rehabilitation, Lead Hazard Control Program, Historic Preservation, Neighborhood Coordination, Community Development Block Grant Program, Graffiti Abatement, Neighborhood Fight Back Program, Neighborhood Economic Development, Neighborhood Initiative Area/Redevelopment Area Plan Implementation.

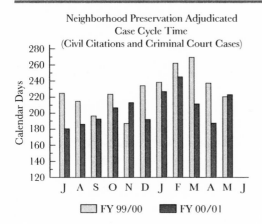

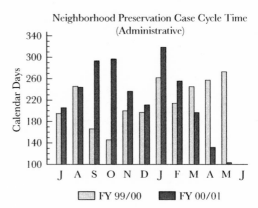

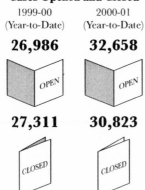

Cases Opened and Closed

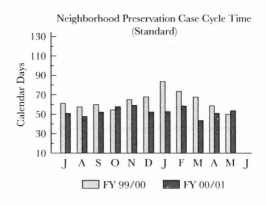

FIGURE 11.2. NEIGHBORHOOD SERVICES PROGRAM: CITY OF PHOENIX, Cont'd.

Neighborhood Services — continued

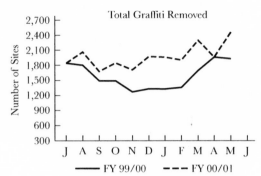

Total Graffiti Removed

FY 99/00 — — — FY 00/01

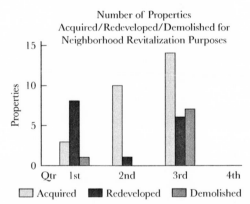

Number of Properties Acquired/Redeveloped/Demolished for Neighborhood Revitalization Purposes

Acquired ■ Redeveloped ▨ Demolished

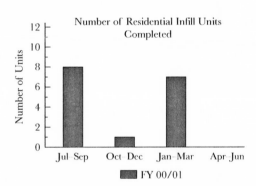

Number of Residential Infill Units Completed

■ FY 00/01

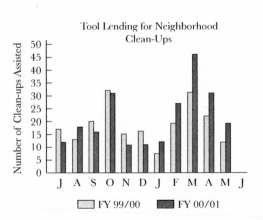

Tool Lending for Neighborhood Clean-Ups

☐ FY 99/00 ■ FY 00/01

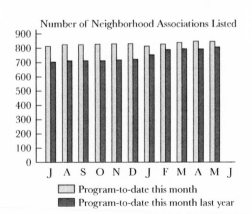

Number of Neighborhood Associations Listed

☐ Program-to-date this month
■ Program-to-date this month last year

FIGURE 11.2. NEIGHBORHOOD SERVICES PROGRAM: CITY OF PHOENIX, Cont'd.

Neighborhood Services — continued

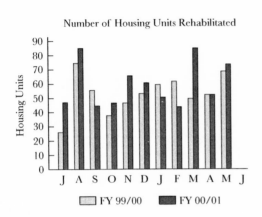

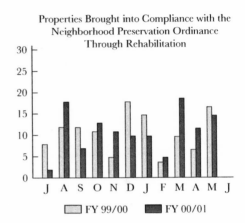

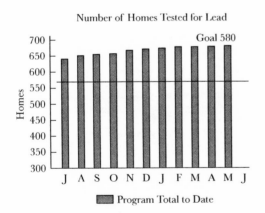

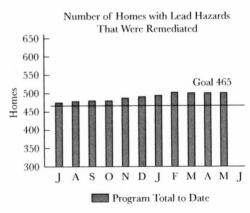

Source: City of Phoenix, 2001. Reprinted with permission.

A couple of outcome measures are also incorporated into this portion of the report. For instance, whereas the number of housing units rehabilitated is an output measure, the number of properties brought into compliance with the neighborhood preservation ordinance is an outcome indicator. Similarly, whereas the number of homes tested for lead is an output indicator, the number of homes with lead hazards that were remediated is a measure of outcome.

Performance Monitoring: The Compass

Many public agencies use performance monitoring systems proactively as management tools. The Compass system of the New Mexico State Highway and Transportation Department (NMSH&TD) constitutes a prototypical case in point. The Compass incorporates seventeen customer-focused results, and there is at least one performance measure for each result, with a total of eighty-three measures at present. Whenever possible, the measures have been chosen on the basis of available data in order to minimize the additional burden of data collection as well as to facilitate the analysis of trends back over time with archival data. However, as weaknesses in some of the indicators have become apparent, the measures have been revised to be more useful.

The seventeen results tracked by the Compass range from a stable letting schedule, adequate funding and prudent management of resources, and timely completion of projects, through smooth roads, access to divided highways, and safe transportation systems, to less traffic congestion and air pollution, increased transportation alternatives, and economic benefits to the state. Each result has an assigned "result driver," a higher-level manager who is responsible for managing that function and improving performance in that area. Each individual performance measure also has a "measurement driver," assisted in some cases by a measurement team, who is responsible for maintaining the integrity of the data.

The Compass was initiated in 1996, and for four years it constituted the department's strategic agenda. NMSH&TD has since developed a formal strategic plan; the bureaus and other operating units develop supportive action plans, all tied to Compass results and measures. However, the top management team still considers the Compass as the main driving force in the department. Thus, a group of one hundred or so departmental managers—the executive team, division directors, district engineers, and middle-management "trailblazers"—meet quarterly to review the Compass. They conduct a detailed analysis of all eighty-three performance measures to assess how well each area is performing, identify problems and emerging issues, and discuss how to improve performance in various areas. NMSH&TD officials credit their use of the performance measures monitored by the Compass with significant improvements in traffic safety and decreases in traffic congestion and deficient highways over the past five years.

Individual and Programmatic Performance Management

Performance measures are often essential to the effectiveness of performance management systems designed to direct and control the work of people in an organization and to focus their attention and efforts on higher-level goals and objectives. Governmental and nonprofit agencies use both MBO-type performance management systems and performance monitoring systems to do this. Monitoring systems are essentially measurement systems that focus on the performance of agencies, divisions, work units, or programs, whereas MBO-type systems focus on the performance of individual managers and, in some cases, individual employees. MBO systems often make use of data drawn from performance monitoring systems, but they may also use a number of other discrete one-time indicators of success that are not monitored on an ongoing basis.

Because MBO systems set up personal-level goals for individuals, managers and staff working in these systems often tend to resist including real outcome measures because the outcomes may be largely beyond their control. Because managers are generally considered to have more control over the quantity and quality of services produced, as well as over internal operating efficiency and productivity, MBO systems often emphasize measures of output, efficiency, quality, and productivity more than outcome measures. Because performance monitoring systems are less personalized, they are more likely to emphasize true effectiveness measures.

MBO systems and performance monitoring systems are both intended to impact directly on the performance of managers, employees, organizational divisions, and work units. However, for this to work in practice, the performance measures must be perceived as legitimate. This means that to some degree at least, managers and employees need to understand the measures, agree that they are appropriate, and have confidence in the reliability of the performance data that will be used to assess their performance. Thus, building ownership of the measures through participation in the process of designing them, or "selling" them in a convincing manner after the fact, is of critical importance. It is also essential that the integrity of the data be maintained so that participants in the process can know that the results are "fair."

CHAPTER TWELVE

IMPROVING QUALITY, PRODUCTIVITY, AND CUSTOMER SERVICE

T o what extent does performance measurement play a role in public and non-profit agencies' drives to improve quality, productivity, and customer service? What kinds of measures are typically used to track quality and productivity? What do these particular monitoring systems look like, and how are they different from the other kinds of measurement systems described in this book? How are such systems used to improve quality and productivity? Whereas previous chapters discuss measurement systems that are tied to other processes at higher management levels, this chapter discusses the use of performance measures at the operating level to help improve quality, productivity, and customer service.

Monitoring Productivity

As used in this book and throughout the public management literature, the term *productivity* is used at two different levels. At a macro level, productivity is almost synonymous with overall performance, a kind of composite of efficiency, effectiveness, and cost-effectiveness. At this level, a productive organization is one that is functioning effectively and efficiently to deliver public services and produce desired outcomes. At a micro level, however, productivity refers more specifically to the relationship between inputs or the factors of production and the immediate products, or outputs, produced. Thus, productivity monitoring is actually more output oriented, focusing on the amount of work completed, units of service provided, or number of clients served rather than looking at actual outcomes, which are the real impacts that are generated out in the field or in a target population as a result of services being delivered or clients being served. However, the two are directly related inasmuch as improving productivity will lead to increased outputs, which will lead in turn to greater impact, assuming a valid program logic and an effective intervention strategy.

At this level, productivity is very closely related to internal operating efficiency in that they both relate outputs to inputs. However, whereas efficiency indicators relate outputs to the overall direct cost of providing them, usually expressed as unit costs, productivity measures relate the outputs produced to the amount of specific kinds of resources needed to produce them. By far the most common type of productivity measure refers to labor productivity, but other types of productivity measures—such as those focusing on the use of equipment—are sometimes also incorporated in productivity monitoring systems. Productivity measures must also have a time dimension in order to be meaningful. In a government printing office, for example, labor productivity might be measured by the number of "images" produced per full-time equivalent (FTE) employee per week, and equipment productivity might be measured by the number of images produced per large press per hour.

Productivity analysis focuses on production processes or service delivery systems at the operating level and attempts to find ways to increase the flow of outputs per unit of inputs or resources. The most common approaches to improving productivity include setting productivity standards, training employees with better skills to work harder and smarter, streamlining methods and work processes, utilizing new technology, improving workplace design, and implementing alternative service delivery systems (Matzer, 1986; Holzer, 1992; Berman, 1998). Thus, the most common kinds of performance measures tracked by systems designed to monitor productivity and the factors that influence it include the following:

- Volume of output
- Labor productivity
- Equipment productivity
- Availability of resources, inventories
- Equipment downtime
- Cycle time, turnaround time
- Workloads or caseloads, client-staff ratios
- Pending workload, backlog of cases
- Utilization rates, flow of cases

For the purposes of real productivity analysis, these kinds of factors are often monitored with respect to an operating system or service delivery system as a whole, but they may well also be applied to component processes that make up that system.

Output-Oriented Systems

Some monitoring systems are designed primarily as output-oriented systems because the management imperative that they are developed to support is principally concerned with increasing output, often through improving productivity. For example, for several years the top priority of PennDOT was to improve the condition of the state highway system and reduce the backlog of deferred maintenance needs by making the county-level maintenance units more productive. Over time the department restructured the maintenance organizations, strengthened management capacity in the county-level units and made them more accountable to the formal chain of command, invested heavily in employee training, and used quality improvement tools to improve work processes, all aimed at making these units more productive.

Table 12.1 shows a small excerpt from a monthly activity report that PennDOT uses to track success along these lines. This part of the report covers four particular highway maintenance activities in the six counties that constitute the department's District 1. The most important measures contained in this report for June 1995 concern the actual amount of output produced by each activity—tons of manual patching material applied to fix potholes, tons of patching material applied with mechanized patching, gallons of liquid bituminous surface treatment applied, and tons of "plant mix" surface treatment completed. This report also compares the actual data on work completed against "plan," or targets that were set at the beginning of the fiscal year. It shows, for example, that for the fiscal year as a whole, Mercer and Crawford Counties applied more tons of material than targeted by their plans, whereas Venango County was able to achieve only 56 percent of its targeted output.

In addition, this activity report tracks the efficiency of these operations; for instance, the cost per ton of manual patching material applied ranges all the way from $150 per ton in Warren County to $300 in Erie County. These actual costs are contrasted with each other and assessed in the face of the statewide average cost of $198 per ton. Furthermore, the report presents data on labor productivity, measured by the number of man-hours per ton of material applied. This ranges from 4.86 hours per ton in Warren County to 9.85 in Erie County, as compared with the statewide average of 6.7 hours per ton and the standard of 7.5 hours per ton applied.

TABLE 12.1. SAMPLE PRODUCTIVITY MONITORING: PENNSYLVANIA DEPARTMENT OF TRANSPORTATION.

MORRIS HIGHWAY COUNTY MANAGEMENT SUMMARY
ACTIVITY/PRODUCTION COST REPORT
REDBOOK
FOR THE MONTH OF JUNE 1995
DISTRICT 01-0

ACT/UNTS	Description	County Name	Annual		Department Year to Date			Contract Year to Date			YTD Unit Cost	Hist Unit Cost	Average Man-Hour per Unit
			Plan	% Comp	Plan	Actual	% Comp	Plan	Actual	% Comp			
711 7121	ROADS-PAVED	CRAWFORD	851	111%	851	949	111%	0	0	0%	$205.19	$228.35	7.84
TONS	PATCHING	ERIE	3030	92%	3030	2814	92%	0	0	0%	$300.42	$325.58	9.85
	MANUAL	FOREST	535	101%	535	543	101%	0	0	0%	$159.44	$192.68	6.48
		MERCER	218	135%	218	294	135%	0	0	0%	$172.60	$237.88	6.11
		VENANGO	636	56%	636	358	56%	0	0	0%	$256.22	$236.95	9.81
		WARREN	1420	98%	1420	1404	90%	0	0	0%	$150.52	$192.90	4.86
		-TOTAL-	6690	95%	6690	6564	95%	0	0	0%	$235.24	$265.41	7.97
		ST-HIST UNIT COST: $211.46; ST-AVG UNIT COST: $198.05; ST-AVG MHRS/UNITS: 6.66; STD.MHRS/UNIT										*	7.50
711 7124	ROADS-PAVED	CRAWFORD	5133	106%	2633	2505	95%	2500	2945	117%	$69.65	$64.37	1.06
TONS	PATCHING-MEC	ERIE	2600	98%	2600	2565	98%	0	0	0%	$75.67	$78.87	1.21
		FOREST	2320	95%	2320	2207	95%	0	0	0%	$50.69	$64.38	.56
		MERCER	2780	107%	2780	2993	107%	0	0	0%	$82.24	$90.12	1.71
		VENANGO	170	100%	0	0	0%	170	170	100%	$.00	$.00	.00
		-TOTAL-	13003	102%	10533	10269	99%	2670	3115	116%	$70.77	$74.65	1.18
		ST-HIST UNIT COST: $51.86; ST-AVG UNIT COST: $54.16; ST-AVG MHRS/UNITS: .01; STD.MHRS/UNIT										*	1.10
711 7124	ROADS-PAVED	CRAWFORD	449695	98%	449695	443828	98%	0	0	0%	$1.42	$1.26	.01
GALS	SURF TREAT	ERIE	300500	99%	300500	300447	99%	0	0	0%	$1.51	$1.55	.01
	LIQ BIT	FOREST	12672	104%	12672	13286	104%	0	0	0%	$1.29	$1.59	.01
		MERCER	351000	100%	351000	352377	100%	0	0	0%	$1.34	$1.26	.01
		VENANGO	300285	100%	300285	300410	100%	0	0	0%	$1.12	$1.09	.01
		WARREN	174748	92%	174748	161351	92%	0	0	0%	$1.26	$1.60	.01
		-TOTAL-	1500900	98%	1588900	1571699	98%	0	0	0%	$1.34	$1.20	.01
		ST-HIST UNIT COST: $34.70; ST-AVG UNIT COST: $130.04; ST-AVG MHRS/UNITS: .01; STD.MHRS/UNIT										*	.01
711 7125	SURFACE	FOREST	600	99%	600	595	99%	0	0	0%	$41.33	$54.09	.67
TONS	TREATMENT 1"	MERCER	4200	107%	4200	513	107%	0	0	0%	$45.23	$96.35	.55
	PLANT MIX	VENANGO	8675	100%	0	0	0%	8675	8675	100%	$.00	$.00	.00
		WARREN	715	99%	715	714	99%	0	0	0%	$121.31	$47.75	.32
		-TOTAL-	14190	102%	5515	5825	105%	8675	8675	100%	$54.37	$65.15	.53
		ST-HIST UNIT COST: $34.70; ST-AVG UNIT COST: $36.04; ST-AVG MHRS/UNITS: .30; STD.MHRS/UNIT:										*	.01

Source: Pennsylvania Department of Transportation, June 1995. Reprinted with permission.

Standard Hours

Sometimes it is possible to measure both the numerator and denominator of productivity indicators with the same scale. For example, although the varied outputs of a government printing office can be summarized in terms of images produced, they can also be measured in another common metric, the number of "billable hours" produced during a given time period. Each job coming into the plant is assessed in terms of volume of work and degree of difficulty, and from that is derived the number of billable hours, the number of hours the job *should* require given the work standards in place. Productivity can then be measured as the ratio of billable hours produced by the plant in a week to the number of production hours worked that week (after subtracting out setup time, time spent in training, time spent in cleanup, and so on). If this ratio is less than one for any particular week, that signifies that the plant did not produce as many billable hours as it was expected to produce given the productivity standards in place.

As we saw earlier, PennDOT has established standards regarding the number of production hours allowed per unit of output produced by each one of its programmed highway maintenance activities. For instance, the standard is 7.5 hours per ton of patching material applied manually to the roads, as compared with only 1.1 hours per ton of mechanized patching completed. Beyond looking at any one activity, these standards can be used to aggregate maintenance crew productivity over a number of maintenance functions. First, the amount of each kind of output produced (for example, tons of patching material applied, gallons of seal coating, miles of guardrails replaced) can be converted to a common metric—task-hours completed—representing the number of hours that would be allowed for each of these activities based on the standards. Second, because PennDOT keeps track of the production hours actually worked (the total hours worked by maintenance crews minus check-in time, travel time to work sites, and so on), the total task-hours completed can be divided by production hours to obtain a generic measure of labor productivity.

Monitoring Service Quality

As the quality revolution has swept through government over the past fifteen years, it has made an indelible mark on the public management landscape (Carr and Littman, 1990; Berman and West, 1995; Hyde, 1997). Now more than ever, managers of public programs are challenged to improve the quality of the services they deliver as well as increase customer satisfaction with those services. From a performance measurement perspective this means they must track indicators of the quality of inputs and especially of the outputs produced and, as will be seen later in the chapter, customer satisfaction. Typically, the dimensions of quality that are considered as being the most important in the quest for improving customer service include the following:

- Timeliness, total time required, waiting time
- Accuracy, thoroughness, reliability, fairness
- Accessibility, hours of service, convenience
- Decor, cleanliness, and condition of facilities
- Personal safety and security
- Courtesy, politeness, professionalism

Interesting to note is that these and other dimensions of service *quality* can usually be measured with *quantitative* indicators, usually by defining what constitutes acceptable quality standards and then tracking the number or percentage of cases in which those standards are achieved or in which performance falls short of the standards. Looking at decentralized operations for renewing drivers' licenses, for example, managers might want to monitor the (1) percentage of customers who have to wait in line for more than twenty minutes before being served, (2) the average time required for a customer to complete the license renewal process, and (3) the percentage of renewals that are processed correctly the first time.

Quality and Productivity

Indicators of service quality and productivity indicators are often viewed as complementary performance measures and incorporated in the same reporting systems. As discussed in Chapter Six, for example, public transit systems monitor labor productivity in terms of the number of vehicle-miles operated per employee, per bus operator, and per maintenance employee; equipment productivity is measured by the number of miles and hours of service operated per vehicle in the active fleet. Service quality is measured in terms of schedule reliability, the percentage of passenger trips requiring transfers, the number of service interruptions due to mechanical breakdowns, and the number of collision accidents per 100,000 vehicle-miles operated.

A state central office supply agency, for example, is a large warehousing operation that fills orders from its customers, line agencies of the state government and perhaps local governmental units and school districts. Its mission is to meet the needs of these customers quickly, effectively, and efficiently. As shown in Table 12.2, before it was reorganized into a contract operation, the central supply function operated by the Georgia Department of Administrative Services (DOAS) monitored on a monthly basis the number of orders received, orders closed, shipments made,

TABLE 12.2. WORK FLOW: CENTRAL OFFICE SUPPLY, GEORGIA DEPARTMENT OF ADMINISTRATIVE SERVICES.

WORKLOAD AND PRODUCTIVITY

	Jul 1998	Aug 1998	Sep 1998	Oct 1998	Nov 1998	Dec 1998	Jan 1999	Feb 1999
Orders Received	2,873	3,308	2,757	2,924	2,929	2,760	2,835	3,131
Orders Closed	2,475	2,804	2,643	3,511	2,275	2,790	2,714	2,787
Shipments	2,695	3,083	2,638	3,896	2,838	2,700	2,896	2,244
Line Items Shipped—TOTAL	17,643	19,091	17,613	22,443	18,085	18,342	18,660	19,653
Average Lines Shipped/day	801.95	909.10	838.71	1068.71	1004.72	873.43	982.11	982.65
Total Lines Pending	2,987	1,573	833	1,773	2,993	1,346	1,408	1,392
Work Days Pending	3.72	1.73	0.99	1.66	2.98	1.54	1.43	1.42

QUALITY

	Jul 1998	%	Aug 1998	%	Sep 1998	%	Oct 1998	%	Nov 1998	%	Dec 1998	%	Jan 1999	%	Feb 1999	%
Elapsed Days																
1–3 days	2,117	85.54	2,323	82.85	2,321	87.82	2,319	66.05	1,543	67.82	1,724	61.79	2,094	77.16	1,973	70.79
4–5 days	235	9.49	292	10.41	246	9.31	795	22.64	518	22.77	299	10.72	387	14.26	592	21.24
6–10 days	64	2.59	60	2.14	27	1.02	323	9.20	187	6.22	302	10.82	18	66.00	40	1.44
11 days and over	59	2.38	129	4.60	49	1.85	74	2.11	27	1.19	465	16.67	115	7.92	63	2.26
Shipments Required to Close Order																
1 Shipment	2,364	95.52	2,704	96.43	2,549	96.44	3,401	96.87	2,109	92.70	2,119	75.95	2,520	92.85	2,574	92.36
Backorders	111	4.48	100	3.57	94	3.56	110	3.13	166	7.30	671	24.05	164	7.15	94	3.37

and total line items shipped. Overall productivity was measured as the number of line items shipped per day, and managers tracked the backlog of line items pending and work days pending as well.

The principal measure of service quality here concerned the number of days elapsed between receiving the order and shipping it out. The DOAS's target was to ship 90 percent of all orders within three days of receipt and to ship all orders within ten days of receipt; clearly performance fell short of that target each month contained in the table, particularly October through December. The other quality indicator shown in Table 12.2 concerns complete shipments. The DOAS's target was to fill 95 percent of all orders completely in one shipment, without having to resort to back-ordering some items and sending them late to customers in a second shipment. Central supply achieved this standard during several of the months shown in the table, but fell short of it in November through February.

Rework

In the past, managers often thought that quality improvement was antithetical to maintaining or increasing productivity. They felt that if they were forced to focus too much on achieving high-quality service, operations would slow down and productivity would necessarily suffer. More recently, though, advocates of the quality movement have pressed the argument that improving quality actually leads to greater productivity in the long run, largely by eliminating *rework*, or cases that have to be processed over again because they were done incorrectly the first time.

In the case of the central office supply, an additional quality criterion concerned accuracy, measured by the percentage of orders shipped that contained all the correct items, so that customers did not have to report mistakes and then wait for the agency to ship the correct items. Clearly, shipping more lines per employee per day will speed up the time in which customers receive the materials they order, but what about the effect of the accuracy measure on productivity? In the short run, taking greater pains to ensure that the right items are included in the shipment could conceivably slow down the operation somewhat and reduce the number of lines shipped per employee, but in the long run it will reduce the number of items that have to be returned and replaced with the correct ones—which constitutes rework—and thereby improve overall productivity in the long run.

Thus, rework indicators are often monitored by public and nonprofit agencies as links between quality and productivity. Agencies are increasingly using such measures as the number of cases processed incorrectly, the percentage of transactions that must be done over again, and the number of "rejects" or defective products that have to be replaced. A highway department, for instance, might set ambitious targets for the number of miles of highway resurfaced per crew-day, but if it does not also insist on high-quality work, such targets may lead to fast but deficient applications that do not last very long. To guard against this, the department may also monitor the number of months between repeat treatments as an indicator of rework required.

Disaggregated Measures

As indicated earlier, quality and productivity measures are often monitored in the aggregate but also broken down into the constituent elements of an operating system. Tracking such measures for individual work units or individual field offices delivering services, for example, provides much more detailed information regarding the strengths and weaknesses, or the locus of problems, within an overall operating system. Thus, a public transit system might well monitor schedule reliability or on-time performance on each individual bus route; a state transportation department might compare labor productivity among districts, county-level maintenance units, and even individual maintenance crews within those county units.

Performance measurement systems that focus on quality and productivity at the operating level often break service delivery down into specific work processes. In the case of the office supply agency, for instance, overall productivity was measured by the average number of line items shipped from the warehouse per day. However, as shown in Table 12.3, this work is actually accomplished through three parallel processes: a "flow thru" process, a "thru put" process, and a metered mail process. Here labor productivity was measured more specifically in terms of the number of line items shipped per production hour worked by designated "pickers" and "shippers," excluding administrative and support staff. A different standard had been set for each of these three processes, and actual performance was measured against the standards. For the time period in question, the data show that productivity in the "thru put" and metered mail processes mostly met or exceeded their respective standards each month, but that in the "flow thru" process actual productivity fell below the standard October through December.

Quality and Productivity Improvement

As suggested by the examples we've looked at, quality and productivity measures are often monitored at fairly detailed levels. Whereas performance measures designed to track success in achieving an agency's strategic goals or to monitor the overall performance of a major program may be more "global" and are observed at a macro level, perhaps on an annual basis, quality and productivity measures often tend to be analyzed at a more micro level. What has become the conventional quality improvement process (which in practice usually focuses on improving

TABLE 12.3. LABOR PRODUCTIVITY: CENTRAL OFFICE SUPPLY, GEORGIA DEPARTMENT OF ADMINISTRATIVE SERVICES.

MEASURES AND STANDARDS

	Jul 1998	Aug 1998	Sep 1998	Oct 1998	Nov 1998	Dec 1998
Production Hours: Flow Thru						
Lines Processed	9,526	11,518	11,325	13,999	9,778	11,110
Lines/Production Hr.	27.24	27.25	28.31	26.20	25.48	26.67
Standard	27.00	27.00	27.00	27.00	27.00	27.00
Production Hours: Thru Put						
Lines Processed	10,974	11,733	11,790	12,048	7,411	7,583
Lines/Production Hr.	22.58	23.79	25.27	23.61	22.72	23.21
Standard	22.00	22.00	22.00	22.00	22.00	22.00
Production Hours: Meter						
Cartons Processed	4,007	4,628	4,382	5,484	4,337	4,650
Ctns/Production Hr.	66.78	66.11	65.40	56.29	65.71	65.49
Standard	65.00	65.00	65.00	65.00	65.00	65.00

productivity as well as service quality) typically focuses on identifying customers and suppliers and analyzing work processes to improve service. This may be done by outside consultants or by groups of employees using a variety of approaches, including brainstorming, the nominal group technique, check sheets, histograms, flowcharts, run charts, scatter plots, and fishbone (cause-and-effect) diagrams to identify problems and develop solutions to improve the operation (Lefevre, 1992; Cohen and Brand, 1993; Milakovich, 1995). This work is necessarily carried out in some detail. Thus, public agencies often define quality and productivity indicators in detail, focusing on the operating level, and observe them quite frequently.

For example, the U.S. Social Security Administration (SSA) contracts with a state agency in each state to adjudicate claims for disability benefits; if the claim is found to be eligible, the claimant then begins to receive the benefits. The work of determining eligibility itself is a serious and onerous responsibility, and the workload is heavy. The Georgia Disability Adjudication Section of the Georgia Department of Human Resources, for instance, receives nearly one hundred thousand new claims each year. It has on the order of three hundred FTE employees and an annual budget of approximately $30 million to determine for each case whether the claim should be approved or denied. In managing the adjudication program, the SSA has established at least three standards:

1. Cases should be closed within seventy working days of receipt of the claim.
2. The initial accuracy rate should be maintained at 95 percent or higher.
3. The pending workload should be kept within ten weeks.

Looking at the Southeast Region, Table 12.4 shows the kind of performance indicators tracked on a *weekly* basis to monitor this operation in each state. First, the number of new claims received during the week by each state is compared against the number of claims received in the same week of the prior year, to take seasonal variation into account. Then, claims received year to date (YTD) are compared against the previous year. Second, the number of cases cleared by each state is tracked in the same way. On a regional basis these agencies cleared more cases than they received during the week, thus reducing the backlog somewhat. On a YTD basis, the cases cleared have increased by 27 percent, while receipts have increased by only 14 percent.

Regionwide there were 123,102 cases pending at the end of this particular week, and over 20 percent of them had been in process for more than seventy days; in Georgia almost 30 percent of the pending cases had not been cleared within seventy days, thus falling short of the standard set by SSA. The Georgia agency also had slightly more than ten work weeks of caseload pending; all the other states had less of a backlog. For the region as a whole, these agencies were on track to close almost 270 cases per FTE, but that varied from a high of 292 in North Carolina to a low of 249 in Georgia. With respect to accuracy, several states were achieving the standard of exceeding the 95 percent initial accuracy rate, but Florida, Kentucky, Mississippi, and South Carolina all fell below this standard. Finally, the cumulative cost per case closed was $252 in the Southeast Region—ranging from $213 in Florida to $310 in Georgia—but for the most part the region still compared favorably with the national average of $304. Overall, then, the Georgia agency compares favorably in terms of quality but rather poorly in terms of productivity and operating efficiency. Although these kinds of short-term, very specific measures may not be particularly helpful for purposes of strategic planning or policymaking, they are indispensable to the SSA for monitoring both the quality and productivity of this ongoing case adjudication process.

Monitoring Customer Satisfaction

Most public agencies that emphasize quality improvement are also concerned at the same time with customer service and customer satisfaction with the services they provide. Thus, they are often interested in regularly soliciting customer feedback.

TABLE 12.4. DISABILITY DETERMINATION PERFORMANCE TRACKING REPORT: REPORT WEEK 21, FEBRUARY 18, 1999.

	Claims				Dispositions			
	Claims Received 2/18	FY 98 Receipts (Week 21)	FY 99 YTD Receipts	Receipts % Change YTD 98–99	Cases Cleared 2/18	FY 98 Dispositions (Week 21)	FY 99 YTD Dispositions	Dispositions % Change YTD 98–99
Alabama	1,118	1,235	32,243	21%	934	1,263	34,102	49%
Florida	3,319	2,352	71,527	16%	3,578	2,676	68,999	23%
Georgia	1,673	1,488	39,350	3%	2,162	1,790	38,284	15%
Kentucky	1,526	1,522	33,614	16%	1,124	1,584	35,408	30%
Mississippi	1,157	1,114	28,202	17%	1,373	1,423	29,073	41%
North Carolina	1,564	1,417	36,149	9%	1,816	1,812	37,745	21%
South Carolina	812	792	20,498	6%	1,098	849	22,009	35%
Tennessee	1,566	1,545	35,275	19%	1,556	1,220	37,011	21%
Region	12,746	11,482	297,104	14%	13,657	12,635	302,901	27%

	Workload and Productivity				Quality and Efficiency	
	Cases Pending	% Over 70 Days	Work Weeks Pending	Dispositions per FTE Work Year	Initial Accuracy 3-Month Rolling Quarter	Cumulative Cost per Case
Alabama	14,603	24.8%	8.8	267.1	98.7%	$272
Florida	28,716	20.9%	8.4	272.0	92.4%	$213
Georgia	22,549	29.4%	10.2	249.9	95.8%	$310
Kentucky	15,028	19.5%	8.2	269.9	91.2%	$251
Mississippi	11,492	22.9%	7.7	287.4	94.2%	$247
North Carolina	9,987	11.7%	4.9	292.9	96.0%	$236
South Carolina	8,405	17.0%	7.3	271.8	93.2%	$247
Tennessee	12,284	12.4%	6.9	254.5	96.2%	$262
Region	123,102	21.1%	7.9	269.8	94.6%	$252
Nation					94.0%	$304

Although that customer feedback might well focus for the most part on the same performance criteria addressed by the quality indicators, obtaining satisfaction measures directly from customers themselves provides feedback from a different source that might or might not be consistent with the results generated with the programmatic data. In general, agencies solicit or receive direct input and feedback from customers through the following mechanisms: advisory groups, customer councils, focus group sessions, complaint systems, customer surveys, and response cards.

The latter three of these channels are good means of accumulating data on a regular, ongoing basis so as to facilitate monitoring performance indicators over time. Although complaint systems principally record negative feedback from customers and therefore cannot be expected to provide a balanced picture of customer attitudes, they can be useful in tracking the extent to which customer dissatisfaction and perceived problems change over time. Surveys can be conducted on a systematic basis by public and nonprofit organizations to solicit unbiased customer feedback, and if they are replicated regularly, they will also allow managers to track trends in customer satisfaction over time. Ongoing use of response cards, which actually constitute very brief surveys focusing attention on specific instances of service delivery, can also indicate trends over time (Hayes, 1997; Hatry, Marcotte, Van Houten, and Weiss, 1998).

Customer Surveys: Girl Scout Council of Northwest Georgia

Broad-based customer or client surveys have become a favored method of soliciting feedback on services offered by public and nonprofit agencies. A good example of this is provided by the Girl Scout Council of Northwest Georgia, one of three hundred local chapters of the Girl Scouts of the USA; this council covers the metropolitan Atlanta areas and twenty additional counties. It provides a range of programming to girls at four levels (Brownies, Junior Girl Scouts, Cadettes, and Senior Girl Scouts) aimed at producing seven generalized outcomes. The first four of these are national goals, namely, developing individual potential, relating to others, developing values, and contributing to society; the remaining three have been added by the local council, namely, safe activities, productive activities, and structured activities outside of school hours.

To assess the extent to which the program produces the expected outcomes, the council conducts annual surveys of each of three groups that include girls at each of the four levels, leaders who staff the program, and parents. The sample sizes employed are large enough to generate 95 percent confidence intervals of only plus-or-minus 5 percentage points in the final results. Drawing from a logic model of the program, the short-answer questions contained in the three parallel survey instruments are keyed directly to attitudes and behaviors that represent accomplishment of the seven goals.

For each level of girl scouting, then, the survey responses to various items are combined to compute indexes for each of the seven goals. Furthermore, they are combined across the three surveyed populations—girls, leaders, and parents—as weighted specifically for each goal. The results from this survey for 2002 are summarized in the following list (Girl Scout Council of Northwest Georgia, 2002), basically in terms of the percentage of favorable responses, suggesting that particular goals are being met for the different levels of girl scouts in the program. This example is instructive because it is methodologically rigorous and sophisticated, breaks the results down by clientele groups, and uses customer feedback to track overall program effectiveness in producing desired outcomes.

Girls' Age Level	Program Outcomes	Met Criteria (%)
Brownie	Developing Individual Potential	81
	Relating to Others	87
	Developing Values	92
	Contributing to Society	83
	Safe Activities Outside of School Hours	94
	Productive Activities Outside of School Hours	87
	Structured Activities Outside of School Hours	72
Junior	Developing Individual Potential	83
	Relating to Others	88
	Developing Values	90
	Contributing to Society	83
	Safe Activities Outside of School Hours	93
	Productive Activities Outside of School Hours	85
	Structured Activities Outside of School Hours	74
Cadette	Developing Individual Potential	79
	Relating to Others	80
	Developing Values	85
	Contributing to Society	72
	Safe Activities Outside of School Hours	88
	Productive Activities Outside of School Hours	78
	Structured Activities Outside of School Hours	75
Senior	Developing Individual Potential	82
	Relating to Others	85

Developing Values	91
Contributing to Society	77
Safe Activities Outside of School Hours	89
Productive Activities Outside of School Hours	80
Structured Activities Outside of School Hours	72

Quality-Importance Matrixes

Some public and nonprofit agencies are beginning to solicit feedback from customers and clients regarding the importance of the services they provide as well as their quality or effectiveness. The results can yield a customer-based perspective on the strategic context of the agency. For example, nearly seven thousand Pennsylvania residents rated PennDOT services. Figure 12.1 shows a quality-importance matrix in which those ratings are cross-plotted against the average importance level assigned to each service by the respondents. This survey asked respondents to rate the quality of these services with the kind of grades typically used in schools, in which A = Excellent, B = Good, C = Fair, D = Poor, and F = Failing. This kind of

FIGURE 12.1. QUALITY-IMPORTANCE MATRIX: PENNDOT SERVICES.

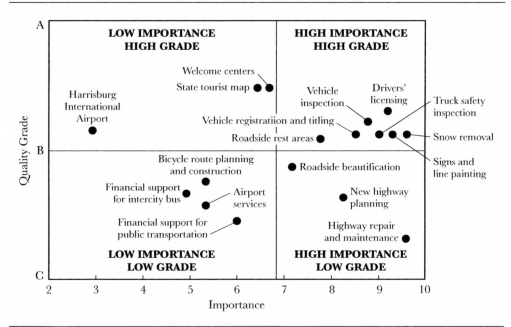

Source: Adapted from Diagnostics Plus and Pennsylvania State University, 1997, p. 12. Reprinted with permission of Pennsylvania Department of Transportation.

plot can be particularly revealing in that some services, though highly rated, may not be seen as particularly important, and services that are perceived as being much more important may receive lower ratings. In this example, although PennDOT customers see the department as doing a good job with respect to such services as driver licensing, truck safety inspections, and snow removal, all rated as being very important, they rated other very important services, such as highway construction and highway repair and maintenance, as still needing improvement.

Customer Service

As part of their overall quality improvement processes, public and nonprofit agencies often focus on improving customer service per se. Thus, in addition to monitoring customer feedback on overall program effectiveness, measurement systems also track feedback from customers about how they were *treated* by service delivery processes. Such indicators focus on detailed, individual parts of the process, and collectively they can paint a composite picture of the customers' perceptions of the quality of service they received.

For example, as we discussed in Chapter Four, state child support enforcement offices work to ensure adequate financial support for children from broken families by locating absentee parents, establishing paternity when necessary, obligating support payments through the courts system, collecting support payments from absentee parents on a regular basis, and disbursing the payments to custodial parents. In Georgia, the Office of Child Support Enforcement carries out this program through 107 local field offices, which work with both custodial and absentee parents. The office periodically conducts operational audits of the local offices to make sure that they are complying with prescribed procedures regarding program delivery, general administration, financial management, public outreach, and security, as well as customer service in terms of responding to complaints, resolving problems, and providing access to information.

To complement this "hard" data on customer service, the Office of Child Support Enforcement also conducts periodic surveys of its principal customers, including both custodial and absentee parents who have made visits to a local office or contacted one by telephone. The survey solicits reaction to several statements concerning various components of customer service, including visits to the office, service provided in the office, service provided over the telephone, use of the customer hotline, and the office itself. Customers are asked to rate the importance of each item as well as its actual performance. The indicators can be tracked separately for each individual local office. Thus, these data facilitate tracking measures of customer service locally or on a statewide basis over time; they can also be used to compare the quality of service as perceived by the customer across the 107 local offices.

Monitoring the "Nuts and Bolts"

This chapter has attempted to present the kinds of performance measures used most frequently to monitor productivity and service quality in public and nonprofit agencies and to illustrate how they are used. Rather than linking to overall program goals, policy objectives, or substantive strategic initiatives, quality and productivity measures tend to focus more on the "nuts and bolts" of service delivery systems and ongoing operations. As compared with performance measurement systems that are intended to support strategic management processes, or budgeting systems that work with annual data, for example, systems designed to monitor quality and productivity tend to focus on more detailed indicators of performance at the operating level, and often very frequently, perhaps on a monthly, weekly, or even daily basis. Assuming that the measures are designed deliberately for this purpose and that the performance data are interpreted appropriately, such monitoring systems can indeed help managers improve quality, productivity, and customer service in public and nonprofit programs.

CHAPTER THIRTEEN

USING COMPARATIVE MEASURES TO BENCHMARK PERFORMANCE

What is benchmarking, and how do public agencies and programs use it to compare their performance against that of others? What are the uses of statistical benchmarking, and how is it done? What are the pitfalls inherent in interagency or interprogram comparisons, and how can they be avoided? This chapter discusses the benchmarking of performance measures in the public and nonprofit sectors, challenges in designing and implementing such systems, and strategies for using them effectively.

Public Sector Benchmarking

Chapter Six makes the point that performance data need to be compared to something in order to provide useful information; it discusses four bases of comparisons: (1) current performance against past performance, (2) actual performance against standards or targets, (3) performance among subunits within an agency or program, and (4) an agency's or program's performance against that of other similar agencies or programs. Probably the most frequent type of comparison involves tracking trends over time, but with the general movement toward results-oriented management in the public and nonprofit sectors, comparisons of actual performance against targets and standards are becoming more common. In addition, particularly in decentralized service delivery systems, more detailed performance reports also break performance data down by subunits such as organizational divisions, field offices, or grantees in an intergovernmental program.

One of the most exciting developments in the move toward managing for results is the growing interest in using external comparisons to gauge the performance of one agency or program against other counterpart agencies or programs, such as other local jurisdictions or similar agencies in other states. The term *benchmarking* is used increasingly now to refer to such comparisons among agencies or programs. Although public managers long resisted external comparisons on the grounds that their programs and operating contexts were unique and that therefore such comparisons would be misleading, increased pressures for accountability, the drive for improved performance, and more sensitive approaches to implementing such systems have led to greater interest in the potential of benchmarking.

There are really a couple of different varieties of benchmarking in the public sector. One is corporate-style benchmarking, which focuses directly on so-called best practices. In this approach, the organization usually focuses on a particular service delivery process, such as recruitment of employers in a welfare-to-work program or case management in a crisis stabilization unit, and attempts to learn about the practices of agencies that are high performing in that area—the "benchmarking partners"—and adapt them for itself. Although public and nonprofit managers have always tried to "borrow" effective practices and approaches from cutting-edge agencies in their particular service industries through consultation, site visits, and information exchanges, corporate-style benchmarking, emphasizing the best-practices approach, has become more carefully structured in recent years to capitalize more fully on the potential of this particular form of benchmarking (Keehley, Medlin, MacBride, and Longmire, 1997).

Another form of activity—as exemplified by the Oregon Benchmarks, Florida Benchmarks, Minnesota Milestones, and Texas Tomorrow programs—has been called benchmarking, but the term is a misnomer. As discussed in Chapter Eight, these and similar efforts in other states, as well as local government versions (such as Life in Jacksonville and Sustainable Seattle), are macro-level strategic planning initiatives created to develop a vision of the future and chart progress in moving toward that future. However, although numerous performance measures are monitored by these programs and compared against targets that have been set for the "out years," they are rarely compared directly to similar measures for other comparable jurisdictions. Thus, these efforts do not really constitute the kind of external benchmarking discussed here.

There is another form of benchmarking, though, that is perhaps most relevant to the subject of this book; it might be best termed *statistical benchmarking*. This involves collecting data for the same set of performance measures for a number of similar organizations or programs in order to "peg" the performance of a particular agency in relation to comparable programs. Although this approach can lead to follow-up searches for best practices on the part of the high performers, statistical benchmarking per se is a more surface-level approach that simply provides comparative data. However, by virtue of focusing on the overall agency or program, rather than on one specific process, and by allowing one agency to compare its performance against a number of counterparts, statistical benchmarking is also a more comprehensive approach that is useful for interpreting performance in a larger context.

Before we move on, it is also useful to point out that benchmarking in general can be carried out at multiple levels. For instance, Georgia's Office of Child Support Enforcement delivers services through 107 local offices, and it regularly collects comparable performance data from each of these offices. From the perspective of the central office, these comparisons among subunits really constitute a form of internal benchmarking. From the viewpoint of an individual local office, however, these same comparative performance measures afford an opportunity for external benchmarking. Similarly, the DHHS monitors the performance of all fifty state programs to which it makes grants on a set of common performance measures and uses these data to help manage the program and make budget allocations. Although this constitutes internal benchmarking from the federal perspective, it also affords an opportunity for each state agency to engage in some external benchmarking. Thus, the term *benchmarking* most often connotes external comparisons, whereas the less frequently used *internal benchmarking* refers to the comparison of performance measures among subunits within programs or agencies.

Statistical Benchmarking

Statistical benchmarking, then, is the collection and comparison of performance data across a set of similar agencies or programs. It comes about in two different ways. Sometimes groups of organizations or programs voluntarily agree to initiate a program of collecting and sharing a common set of performance indicators on a regular basis. In many states, for example, public hospitals benchmark their performance in terms of patient satisfaction and other criteria against other hospitals using common measures that are collected through the auspices of a statewide association. Similarly, a number of municipal governments in a state may initiate a cooperative agreement to implement a common set of performance indicators on the same cycle and share the data among themselves.

In other cases, the collection or reporting of common performance measures is mandated or even carried out from outside the agencies in question. As discussed in Chapter Five, for instance, federal agencies maintain large databases on crime rates, health statistics, environmental quality, transportation systems, and other information. Typically, these data are reported by or for states and local governments and contain elements that lend themselves to comparing performance across these jurisdictions. In addition, state and federal agencies that manage grants programs often impose reporting requirements on the public and nonprofit organizations receiving these grants. The data generated by these systems tend to be designed principally for program management purposes, but they are also often used, or are available for use, in benchmarking some grantees against others.

Statistical benchmarking can serve several purposes for public and nonprofit organizations. First, it allows an agency to gauge its performance against other similar organizations—both to see the range of performance within the parameters of its particular public service industry and where it fits in that range and to see how its performance stacks up against counterpart programs elsewhere. Second, by comparing its performance data against counterpart agencies or industry leaders, an organization can develop a framework for establishing challenging but feasible objectives, performance targets, or service delivery standards for the near or middle future. Third, by identifying apparent "star performers" among counterpart programs, an agency can seek out leading-edge practices, adapt strategies, and generally learn lessons from peer organizations to improve its own performance.

Whether initiated by a number of counterpart agencies or mandated by some higher level of authority, the benchmarking process usually proceeds through the following four major steps:

1. *Identifying the measures to be used—that is, what is to be measured and what those measures will be.* Most often organizations will emphasize measures of effectiveness, cost-effectiveness, and efficiency, but they may also include measures of productivity, service quality, and customer satisfaction. Note that because the purpose of benchmarking is to make comparisons across other agencies or programs, the measures will almost always be defined as *standardized* measures in terms of percentages, rates, ratios, or averages rather than raw numbers.
2. *Developing precise definitions of the operational indicators to be used by all participants, along with clear guidelines for implementing them and uniform procedures for collecting and processing the data and computing the measures.* Note that it might be advantageous to collect raw data from the participating agencies and then compute the measures centrally in order to flag suspicious-looking numbers and ensure consistency in how the measures are computed.
3. *Collecting and reporting the data on a periodic, often annual, basis.* Although not a necessity, it can be helpful to conduct spot checks or data audits to verify reliability and ensure consistency of data collection procedures among participants.

4. *Using the comparative data to assess the performance of a particular agency or program, set targets for particular entities or more general standards for the field at large, or identify star performers and industry leaders and investigate leading-edge practices, as appropriate.*

As an example, Figure 13.1 shows the percentage of highway bridges that were rated as being substandard or deficient in 1998 for eleven states in the southeastern U.S. The data are based on physical inspections of all the bridges on all state and local government-owned highway systems. These inspections are conducted annually by state transportation departments using the federal bridge rating system, which specifies detailed procedures for carrying out the inspections and criteria for assigning various rating categories. These data are reported annually to the Federal Highway Administration along with many other measures pertaining to pavement condition, excessive volume-to-capacity ratios, and highway accidents. Clearly, South Carolina and Georgia appear to be high performers on this indicator, with far fewer substandard or deficient bridges than Mississippi, Louisiana, and North Carolina at the other end of the spectrum, and it might be worthwhile to investigate whether their superior standing in this regard is due at least in part to leading-edge practices that might be transferable to these other states.

FIGURE 13.1. PERCENTAGE OF STATE HIGHWAY BRIDGES RATED AS SUBSTANDARD, 1998.

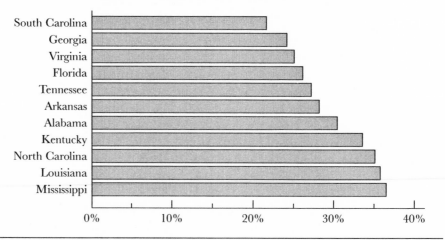

Source: Federal Highway Administration, 1999.

Problems and Challenges in Benchmarking

The benchmarking process as outlined in the preceding list is quite straightforward, but like performance measurement itself, the process is not always as simple as it looks. In addition to concerns about how the comparative data will be used and whether a program might be penalized somehow for relatively poor performance, there are also a number of more methodological issues that create special challenges for would-be benchmarkers. These include questions regarding the availability of common data elements, problems with data reliability, and variation in programs and their operating environments.

Availability of Data

Agencies engaged in benchmarking efforts often attempt to rely on readily available data, which tend to come from such traditional sources as agency records. These data lend themselves primarily to measures of resources, outputs, and efficiency, but often not to measures of real outcomes or customer satisfaction. Although it is certainly understandable to want to limit the expenditure of additional time and resources in what is an already demanding data collection effort, doing so will constrain the usefulness of the comparative data. As discussed in Chapter Three, measures of outcomes and customer satisfaction tend to be more ambitious, often involving new procedures that require going out "into the field" for data collection; they are expensive and time consuming to implement. The most obvious example would be customer surveys designed to determine whether certain outcome conditions have improved or the extent to which respondents are satisfied with the services they have received.

When an individual agency decides to initiate or strengthen its performance measurement system, it need concern itself only with committing time and resources to collect data for its own needs. For successful benchmarking, however, two or more agencies must decide that these additional data collection efforts are worth the cost, and this agreement is not always easily reached. Sometimes, therefore, benchmarking partners will begin on a more limited basis, sharing data that are relatively easy to generate and then perhaps moving to flesh out the system with more demanding data as the partners become convinced that the comparative performance measures are beneficial.

In other cases, a higher-level authority may at some point require agencies, particularly grant recipients, to implement new data systems to provide comparison data. PennDOT, for instance, had for several years required local public transit agencies in the state to report a number of operating, financial, and ridership statistics on a uniform basis, and it had published an annual report that tracked trends in the field and allowed each agency to benchmark its performance against that of other comparable systems. However, these reports did not include measures of customer satisfaction. Various local transit systems were conducting passenger surveys on a sporadic basis as part of their planning updates, but they did not yield any uniform measures. PennDOT therefore more recently mandated that all these local systems conduct periodic passenger surveys containing a core section soliciting feedback on five critical elements of performance. The data in Table 13.1 reflect the results of the first round of these surveys. They indicate a substantial amount of variation in customer satisfaction among these transit systems and suggest that a search for best practices on the part of the stronger performers might identify some worthwhile lessons for the others.

Reliability of Comparative Data

As discussed in Chapter Five, data reliability is a critical issue in performance measurement. In looking at changes in performance over time, evaluating actual performance against targets, or comparing performance across organizational units or clientele groups, for example, managers want to be assured that differences they

TABLE 13.1. PERCENTAGE OF TRANSIT PATRONS SATISFIED WITH SYSTEM PERFORMANCE, 1998.

Transit System	Service Area	On-Time Performance	Safety	Driver Courtesy	Cleanliness	Fares
LANTA	Allentown/Bethlehem	91%	86%	81%	81%	55%
AMTRAN	Altoona	93	97	94	90	88
EMTA	Erie	65	84	78	67	64
CAT	Harrisburg	64	75	75	71	46
CCTA	Johnstown	94	—	88	90	95
RRTA	Lancaster	65	83	82	72	76
BARTA	Reading	69	82	82	63	70
COLTS	Scranton	94	96	94	80	91
CATA	State College	79	87	91	93	57
LCTA	Wilkes-Barre	85	95	92	85	82
WBT	Williamsport	84	91	92	90	89
YCTA	York	66	87	85	74	88

see are real and not simply artifacts of sloppy data collection. With benchmarking this concern is further heightened because comparisons among agencies or programs are valid only to the extent that all participants employ consistent data collection procedures. Suppose, for example, that a number of municipalities want to compare their cost per mile of road maintained, but some are using data on lane-miles of local road to compute this ratio while others using centerline-miles. If this inconsistency is compounded by variation in the extent to which the cost figures incorporate overhead costs, then the resulting measures are likely to be "all over the place," and comparisons among these jurisdictions will be comparing apples to oranges.

Because these data are usually self-reported by the individual agencies or programs, ensuring consistency can be very challenging. Where possible it is far preferable to use the same instrument to collect data from different jurisdictions or programs. For instance, rather than relying on grades earned by students in various school systems around the country, the National Assessment of Educational Progress generates state comparisons of student achievement in science, math, and reading based on standardized tests administered to samples of fourth graders and eighth graders in schools in each state.

Even when benchmarking participants use standardized instruments, it is critical for them to follow uniform procedures in collecting the data—for instance, using the same sampling procedures, enforcing the same time limits in administering standardized tests, or counting things the same way in an observational survey. Obviously, the more that different agencies use uniform accounting standards and management information systems, the more likely they are to provide comparable performance measures. When participants do not employ standardized instruments for collecting primary data—for example, when the constituent data elements already reside in existing information systems—it is all the more important for there to be unambiguous definitions of the data elements to be used and clear guidelines for including some categories or cases and excluding others in tallying up counts. In such circumstances it may be worthwhile to provide for a system of reviews, at least of a sample, by outside professional "data auditors" to ensure data reliability.

Variation in Operating Conditions

One of the most critical problems in benchmarking performance measures across different agencies or programs is that these entities often function in very different operating environments. Some may feel that they are being subjected to unfair comparisons because they operate in more difficult conditions than others. For example, some human service programs work with more difficult clientele, some juvenile justice departments work in communities that are less supportive, and some welfare-to-work programs operate in local labor markets that are much weaker than elsewhere. Such differences in operating context can generate highly distorted comparisons of program performance. As the purpose of benchmarking is not to penalize weak performers or to make some programs appear inferior to others, it is important to take difference in operating conditions into account in interpreting benchmarking data.

Strategies to Improve Comparative Measures

Remedies to account for such contextual differences that can distort comparative performance measures include descriptive interpretation of explanatory variables and the use of peer groups, recalibrated measures, and adjusted performance measures.

Explanatory Variables

As discussed in Chapter Three, it is important to identify critical environmental variables—external factors beyond a program's control that can influence its performance—in developing logic models. If benchmarking partners are notably different in terms of critical environmental variables, these may need to be taken into account as explanatory factors in interpreting comparative performance data. For example, the incidence and prevalence of STDs are significantly greater in areas with high poverty rates. Thus, comparing incidence and prevalence rates to assess the effectiveness of various state and local STD prevention programs can be very misleading. Prevention programs in poverty-stricken urban areas in the Midwest, for instance, may in fact be quite effective in relative terms in containing the spread of these diseases even though the residual rates of syphilis and gonorrhea are still substantially higher there than in more affluent areas. One response to this difficulty is simply to include comment fields in the report formats presenting these data and to provide an explanatory comment to the effect that the incidence and prevalence rates in certain of the areas observed would be expected to be greater due to their higher poverty rates.

Peer Groups

A second approach is also very straightforward: limit comparative performance measures to relatively few agencies or programs that are fairly similar in terms of operating conditions. Rather than including all possible counterpart agencies, which may vary widely in terms of important environmental factors, it may be preferable to construct a "peer group" consisting of relatively few programs that are more comparable in terms of operating contexts. For example, an analysis designed to assess the current performance and future prospects of a particular local public transit system might benchmark that system against a few other systems operating in similar service areas in terms of demographics, population density, and land use patterns.

Figure 13.2 shows crime rate data for twenty-nine large cities participating in the Comparative Performance Measurement Consortium, which was created in conjunction with the International City/County Management Association for the purpose of benchmarking service delivery. One of the participating jurisdictions, the City of Atlanta, Georgia, was interested in using these data to compare the performance of its police department against other similar cities. As shown in Figure 13.2, there is a fairly pronounced statistical relationship between total crime rates and the percentage of the population living below the poverty level; those cities with higher poverty rates also tend to have higher crime rates. The City of Atlanta (near the upper right corner of the scatter plot) has the highest crime rate among all these jurisdictions, and it also has the highest poverty rate; because both these factors might also be expected to influence police department performance in responding to reported crimes, the six other cities with the next highest poverty

FIGURE 13.2. PART 1 CRIMES PER 1,000 CAPITA BY PERCENTAGE OF THE POPULATION BELOW THE POVERTY LEVEL.

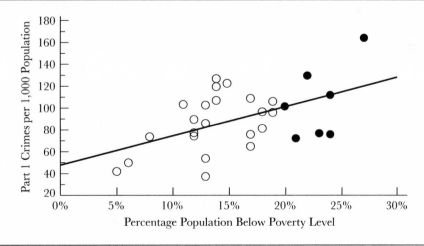

Source: Urban Institute and International City/County Management Association, 1997.

rates (represented with black markers) were selected as benchmark cities for Atlanta. Selected comparative indicators of police performance are shown in Table 13.2 for these seven cities. The data suggest that relative to these other jurisdictions, the City of Atlanta performs favorably for the most part in terms of the number of arrests made per police officer, the percentage of Part 1 crimes that are cleared, the number of crimes cleared per officer, and the overall expense per crime cleared.

Recalibrated Measures

Sometimes performance indicators can be recalibrated to take into account the environmental variable of concern. For instance, in comparing crime rates against other cities, City of Atlanta officials wanted to take into account the number of visitors and persons commuting into and out of the city for work. They felt that because Atlanta has more people who live elsewhere but work inside the city, and because it is a large convention center with more overnight guests staying in hotels, crime rates based only on the *resident* population would put Atlanta in a negative light in such comparisons. Thus, the average daytime population was estimated for each of these cities by adding in the number of people living elsewhere in the respective metropolitan area who report commuting into the central city to work, subtracting the number of central city residents who report working somewhere outside that city, and adding in the estimated number of daily hotel guests in each city.

TABLE 13.2. COMPARATIVE POLICE PERFORMANCE.

City	FTE Sworn Officers per 1,000 Population	Arrests per Sworn Officer	Percentage Part 1 Crimes Cleared	Crimes Cleared per Officer	Expense per Crime Cleared
Atlanta	3.6	42.7	25.5%	11.6	$5,671
Baltimore	4.2	22.6	18.9%	5.8	$10,336
Cincinnati	2.6	38.8	31.9%	9.2	$8,644
Houston	2.6	19.5	19.4%	5.3	$14,670
San Antonio	1.7	33.2	15.2%	6.9	$11,066
Shreveport	2.4	28.5	17.2%	7.9	$6,231
Tucson	1.6	68.4	16.4%	10.4	$8,169

Source: Figures computed from data reported in Urban Institute and International City/County Management Association, 1997.

The number of reported crimes per 1,000 residents and the number of crimes per 1,000 estimated daytime population are shown for each of the seven cities in Figure 13.3. Although Atlanta has by far the highest number of Part 1 crimes per 1,000 residents, when the indicator is recalibrated on the basis of estimated daytime population, it is in line with Baltimore, Shreveport, and Tucson, thus changing somewhat the impression of Atlanta as a city with an inordinately high crime rate relative to other areas with high percentages of people living below the poverty level. Organizations cannot often use the environmental variables that impact performance measures to recalibrate the original indicators, but when they can, it is a direct approach to addressing the impact of such variables.

Adjusted Performance Measures

Currently there is substantial interest in statistically adjusting performance measures to account for the influence of one or more environmental or explanatory variables. For example, public hospitals may want to adjust comparative data on measures of inpatient length of stay and mortality rates to take into account differences in the severity of illnesses their patients are treated for. Some hospital administrators may fear that otherwise their facilities will appear to be inferior in terms of both efficiency and the quality of care provided when the real reason for their longer average stays and higher mortality rates is that they are caring for patients with more serious illnesses. Similarly, local schools whose performance is

FIGURE 13.3. CRIMES PER 1,000 RESIDENTS AND ESTIMATED DAYTIME POPULATION.

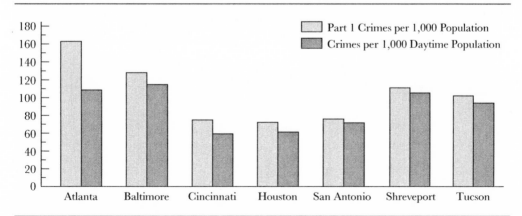

Source: Figures computed based on data reported in Urban Institute and International City/County Management Association, 1997.

being compared on standardized achievement tests may want to adjust the data by some measure of the socioeconomic status of the communities they serve in order to be evaluated on a "level playing field."

Briefly, to create adjusted performance measures, regression models are developed to predict values of the performance indicator in question as a function of the environmental variable or variables. These predicted values represent what the performance level of each case would look like if performance were solely determined by those explanatory factors. Residual values are then computed as the difference between the observed and predicted values of the performance indicator to represent the direction and extent to which actual performance deviates from what it would be expected to look like based on the explanatory variable(s) alone. These residual values are then considered to constitute adjusted performance measures that represent each unit's performance relative to industry averages adjusted for the environmental variable(s).

For example, Figure 13.4 shows the unit cost of surface treatment for a number of county highway maintenance operations, plotted against an index of the cost of materials required to do this work. Generally, those counties with lower unit costs appear to be more efficient in performing this work, whereas those with higher unit costs appear to be less efficient. However, local prices for the necessary materials vary widely from county to county, as represented by the material cost index, and they have a direct bearing on the cost per mile of surface treatment. The regression line shown in Figure 13.4 summarizes the expected unit cost

FIGURE 13.4. COUNTY HIGHWAY MAINTENANCE COST PER MILE OF SURFACE TREATMENT.

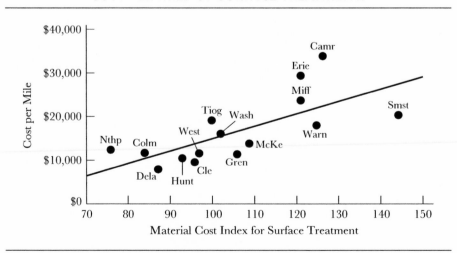

for each county based on the materials cost index. Therefore, counties that fall above the regression line are incurring higher costs than would be expected, whereas those below the line appear to be performing surface treatment work more efficiently than would be expected given the cost structure.

Table 13.3 shows the predicted cost per mile for each county based on the regression model (with an R^2 of .51), along with the actual unit cost and the material cost index value on which the predicted value is based. Then an adjusted cost per mile is computed as the residual, the difference between the actual and predicted unit costs. Adjusted cost measures less than one (negative numbers) indicate counties that appear to be more efficient than would be expected by taking the material cost index into account. These adjusted performance measures provide a different interpretation of which counties exhibit more or less operating efficiency. For example, with a cost of $20,571 per mile resurfaced, Somerset County would appear to be one of the least efficient counties. But when the inordinately high cost of materials in that county is taken into account, Somerset County is shown to be quite efficient, spending $7,148 *less* per mile than would be expected given the cost of materials in that area.

Potentially, adjusted performance measures offer a means of providing "fair" comparisons by "subtracting out" the influence of contextual factors beyond

TABLE 13.3. ADJUSTED PERFORMANCE MEASURES: COST PER MILE OF SURFACE TREATMENT.

County	Actual Cost per Mile	Material Cost Index	Predicted Cost per Mile	Adjusted Cost per Mile
Erie	$29,254	121	$21,049	$8,205
Warren	$18,030	125	$22,209	−$4,179
Clearfield	$9,566	96	$13,798	−$4,233
Cameron	$33,843	126	$22,499	$11,344
McKean	$13,841	109	$17,569	−$3,728
Mifflin	$23,736	121	$21,049	$2,688
Columbia	$11,619	84	$10,318	$1,301
Tioga	$19,224	100	$14,958	$4,266
Northumberland	$12,248	76	$7,998	$4,250
Delaware	$8,116	87	$11,188	−$3,072
Huntingdon	$10,468	93	$12,928	−$2,460
Somerset	$20,571	144	$27,719	−$7,148
Greene	$11,478	106	$16,699	−$5,220
Washington	$16,106	102	$15,539	$567
Westmoreland	$11,508	97	$14,088	−$2,581

management's control that might have substantial bearing on comparative program results. However, the usefulness of the adjusted performance measures depends heavily on the validity of the contextual factors employed. If these variables are inappropriate, incomplete, or in fact not causally related, the adjusted measures may indeed yield more distorted data rather than a fair basis for comparison.

The Prospects for Benchmarking

The benchmarking of performance measures is starting to catch on with public managers in this country and elsewhere, and the idea of comparing measures against other agencies or programs in order to help gauge performance, and possibly help improve it, would seem to be a commonsense one. Identifying other organizations or programs as potential benchmarking partners should not be too difficult for most state and local agencies, as they often have counterparts in other governmental jurisdictions. The same is true for many nonprofit agencies at the state and local level. However, as discussed earlier in this chapter, issues concerning data reliability and differences in programs or operating conditions create methodological challenges in developing useful benchmarking systems.

Furthermore, in terms of political and managerial contexts, the prospect of statistical benchmarking carries both problems and opportunities. Obviously, comparing the performance of individual agencies or programs on a set of common measures is a sensitive issue simply because some may "look bad" in comparison with others whether or not the indicators have been adjusted for contextual factors. Yet the comparative data may be useful in a number of ways, not the least of which is to provide an incentive for less efficient and effective programs to improve their performance. Indeed, just participating in efforts to define and report common measurements on a uniform basis may spur some agencies to upgrade their own measurement systems and use them more productively. Thus, the prospects for increased benchmarking will depend on the extent to which its usefulness outweighs the costs. This in turn will depend largely on the extent to which benchmarking can be used as an opportunity for improving performance through incentives and sharing information about leading-edge practices rather than as a basis for penalizing poorly performing programs.

Recommended Readings on Benchmarking

Adamaschek, B. *Intermunicipal Comparative Performance Measurement: Innovation Through Competition.* Gutersloh, Germany: Bertelsmann Foundation Publishers, 1998.

Ammons, D. N., Coe, C., and Lombardo, M. "Performance-Comparison Projects in Local Government: Participants' Perspectives." *Public Administration Review,* 2001, *61*(1), 100–111.

Hatry, H. P. (ed.). "Mini-Symposium of Intergovernmental Comparative Performance Data." *Public Administration Review*, 1999, *59*(2), 101–134.

Keehley, P., Medlin, S., MacBride, S., and Longmire, L. *Benchmarking for Best Practices in the Public Sector.* San Francisco: Jossey-Bass, 1997.

Morley, E., Bryant, S. P., and Hatry, H. P. *Comparative Performance Measurement.* Washington, D.C.: Urban Institute Press, 2001.

Stiefel, L., Rubenstein, R., and Schwartz, A. E. "Using Adjusted Performance Measures for Evaluating Resource Use." *Public Budgeting and Finance*, 1999, *19*(3), 67–87.

Urban Institute and International City/County Management Association. *Comparative Performance Measurement: FY 1995 Data Report.* Washington, D.C.: Urban Institute Press and International City/County Management Association, 1997.

PART FOUR

THE PROCESS SIDE
OF PERFORMANCE
MEASUREMENT

Implementing a performance measurement system in a public or nonprofit agency involves the process of managing organizational change. This means that in addition to the more technical issues inherent in defining and evaluating performance measures, managerial challenges are also likely to arise in trying to implement them effectively. Managers need to recognize that resources are required to develop, implement, and maintain measurement systems, and they should view this as an investment, with the objective of maximizing the rate of return in terms of generating useful information.

Part Four consists of a single chapter, Chapter Fourteen, which identifies critical elements of successful approaches to developing and implementing measurement systems, emphasizing the importance of strong leadership and stakeholder involvement as well as the need to manage the overall developmental effort as a deliberate process using a project management approach. The chapter concludes by presenting thirty strategies for the successful implementation of measurement systems; these strategies are intended to respond to such issues as resource requirements, lack of utilization, lack of stakeholder buy-in, internal resistance, goal displacement and "gaming the system," and potential system abuse. Building these strategies into the process of designing and implementing performance measures in your public or nonprofit agency can help you substantially in installing a worthwhile, cost-effective measurement system.

CHAPTER FOURTEEN

IMPLEMENTING EFFECTIVE MEASUREMENT SYSTEMS

W hat is the best way to manage the process of designing and implementing a performance measurement system? Who should be involved in this process? How can you overcome the resistance that often builds up against such systems and build support for them instead? What are the most frequent problems that plague efforts to implement measurement systems, and how can you avoid or surmount them? This chapter discusses organization and management issues involved in designing and implementing performance measurement systems and suggests strategies for success in developing systems that are useful and cost-effective.

Managing the Process

Performance measurement systems can make a difference in government. Good performance measures, particularly outcome measures, signal what the real priorities are, and they motivate people to work harder and smarter to accomplish organizational objectives. Measurement systems provide managers and decision makers with information regarding performance that they use to manage agencies and programs more effectively, redirecting resources and making adjustments in operations and service delivery systems to produce better results. And the performance data generated by measurement systems provide information to elected officials that can be useful in setting goals and priorities, making macro-level budget decisions, and holding public agencies and managers accountable.

In the nonprofit sector as well, outcome measures can help agencies improve services and overall program effectiveness, increase accountability, guide managers in allocating resources, and help funding organizations make better decisions. At an operational level, performance measures provide feedback to staff, focus board members on policy and programmatic issues, identify needs for training and technical assistance, pinpoint service units and participant groups that need attention, compare alternative service delivery strategies, identify potential partners for collaboration, recruit volunteers, attract customers, set targets for future performance, and improve an agency's public image (Plantz, Greenway, and Hendricks, 1997).

As observed by a principal authority in the field (Wholey, 1999), effective performance-based management requires three essential elements:

1. Developing a reasonable level of agreement among key stakeholders regarding agency mission, goals, and strategies
2. Implementing performance measurement systems of sufficient quality
3. Using performance information to improve program effectiveness, strengthen accountability, and support decision making

But success does not come easily. It is a grand understatement to say that designing and implementing a performance measurement system in a public or nonprofit agency is a very challenging process. Obviously, the technical aspects of identifying appropriate performance criteria, defining valid and reliable indicators that are resistant to goal displacement and "gaming," deciding on useful comparisons and reporting formats, and developing workable software support present many challenges from a methodological perspective, and these are largely the focus of this book. However, installing a system in a real, live organization and building commitment to it, using it effectively on an ongoing basis, and embedding it in other management and decision-making processes present an even more daunting challenge.

Many governmental agencies and nonprofit organizations have set out to design a performance monitoring system but aborted the effort before it was completed, or they completed the design but failed to move on to the implementation stage; still others have gone through the motions of installing a system but to no good avail. Sometimes a promising measurement system is implemented in an agency but fails to really take hold or be used in any meaningful way; then it may be maintained in a halfhearted way or be abandoned at some point. Still others are installed and maintained, but they never make a significant contribution to improved management, decision making, or performance.

Why do these things happen? There are numerous reasons. In some cases the measurement system as designed simply does not meet the needs of the managers it is intended to serve. Or implementing the system and maintaining it on an ongoing basis may consume too much time and resources, and the information the system provides is not viewed as being worth the effort. There may also be considerable resistance from within the organization to a new system, and the resulting lack of support and cooperation may stifle its effective implementation. Sometimes such systems wither before they really get off the ground for lack of "champions" who can build support for them and persistently guide the organization through the process of system design and implementation.

Elements of Success

Installing a performance measurement system and embedding it in management processes involve bringing about organizational change, and this can be difficult. Even technically sound systems may face substantial problems in effective implementation, as already mentioned. Obviously, successful design and implementation will not occur automatically, but several factors can elevate the probability of success significantly. A review of best practices among both public agencies and private firms conducted by the National Performance Review (1997) drew the following conclusions about the ingredients of successful performance measurement programs:

- Leadership is critical in designing and deploying effective performance measurement and management systems. Clear, consistent, and visible involvement by senior executives and managers is a necessary part of successful performance measurement and management systems.
- A conceptual framework is needed for the performance measurement and management system. Every organization needs a clear and cohesive performance measurement framework that is understood by all levels of the organization and that supports objectives and the collection of results.
- Effective internal and external communication is the key to successful performance measurement. Effective communication with employees, process owners, customers, and stakeholders is vital to the successful development and deployment of performance measurement and management systems.
- Accountability for results must be clearly assigned and well understood. High-performance organizations make sure that all managers and employees understand what they are responsible for in achieving organizational goals.

- Performance measurement systems must provide intelligence for decision makers, not just compile data. Measures should be limited to those that relate to strategic goals and objectives and that yield timely, relevant, and concise information that decision makers at all levels can use to assess progress in achieving goals.
- Compensation, rewards, and recognition should be linked to performance measurements. Such a linkage sends a clear and unambiguous message to the organization as to what is important.
- Performance measurement systems should be positive, not punitive. The most successful measurement systems are not "gotcha" systems, but rather are learning systems that help identify what works and what does not so as to continue with and improve on what is working and repair or replace what is not working.
- Results and progress toward program commitments should be openly shared with employees, customers, and stakeholders.

In working to build these elements of success into a performance measurement program, public and nonprofit managers should (1) ensure strong leadership and support for the effort by involving a variety of stakeholders in developing the system, (2) follow a deliberate process in designing and implementing it, and (3) use project management tools to keep the process on track and produce a suitable measurement system.

Leadership and Stakeholder Involvement

In a small agency, a performance measurement system could conceivably be designed and implemented by a single individual, but this approach is not likely to produce a workable system in most cases. A wide variety of stakeholders usually have an interest in, and may well be affected by, a performance measurement system, as shown in the list that follows.

Stakeholders in the Performance Measurement Process

Governmental Agencies	*Nonprofit Organizations*
Agency or program managers and staff	Agency or program managers and staff
Employees	Employees
Labor unions	Volunteers
Contractors, grantees, and suppliers	Contractors, grantees, and suppliers
Elected officials	Governing board members

Clients and customers	Clients and customers
Advocacy groups	Advocacy groups
Other governmental units	Local chapters
Citizens and community organizations	Community organizations and the public
Funding organizations	Funding organizations
Management analysts and data specialists	Management analysts and data specialists

Including at least some of these stakeholders in the design and implementation process will have two big advantages. First, they will raise issues and make suggestions that would not otherwise surface, and ultimately this will result in a better system. Second, because they have had a chance to participate in the process, voice their concerns, and help shape a system that serves their needs or at least is sensitive to issues that are important to them, they will be more likely to support the system that emerges. Thus, although it may be somewhat more cumbersome, involving a variety of stakeholders in the process is likely to produce a more effective system and build *ownership* for that system along the way.

In a public or nonprofit organization of any size and complexity, therefore, it usually makes sense at the outset to form a working group to guide the process of designing and implementing a performance measurement system. Normally, this group should be chaired by the top manager—the chief executive officer, agency head, division manager, or program director—of the organizational unit or program for which the system is being designed, or another line or staff manager whom that individual delegates. Although the makeup of this working group, task force, or steering committee may vary, at a minimum it needs to include managers or staff from whatever agencies, subunits, or programs are to be covered by the performance measurement system. In the case of agencies or programs where service delivery is highly decentralized, it is advisable to include managers from field offices or local chapters in addition to those from the central office or headquarters. As Swiss (1991, p. 337) notes, a measurement system should be "designed to bring the most usable information to bear on the most pressing problems facing managers. Only the managers of each agency can say what their most pressing problems are and what kinds of information would be most useful in attacking them." In addition, public agencies might well be advised to include an elected official or staff representative from the appropriate legislative body on the steering group; nonprofit agencies should include members of their governing boards in such a group.

The following are some other internal stakeholders who might be included in this steering group:

- A representative of the central executive office (for example, the city manager's office, the secretary or commissioner's office)
- Representatives from central office administrative or support units, such as the budget office, the personnel department, or a quality/productivity center
- A "systems person" who is knowledgeable about information processing and the agency's existing systems
- A representative from the labor union if the employees are unionized

Obviously, the steering committee also needs to have a resident measurement expert on board. In a large organization this might be someone from a staff unit such as an office of planning and evaluation or a management analysis group. If such technical support is not available internally, this critical measurement expertise can be provided by an outside consultant, preferably one who is familiar with the agency or the program area in question.

In addition, it may be very helpful to include external stakeholders in the steering group. With respect to programs that operate through the intergovernmental system, for example, representatives from either sponsoring or grantee agencies, or other agencies cooperating in program delivery, might make significant contributions. Private firms working as contractors in delivery services should perhaps also be included. Furthermore, it may be helpful to invite consumer groups or advocacy groups to participate on the steering committee to represent the customer's perspective or the "field at large."

Finally, if it is anticipated that the performance measurement issues may be particularly difficult to work through or that the deliberations may be fairly contentious, it may be advisable to engage the services of a professionally trained facilitator to lead at least some of the group's meetings.

Whatever the makeup of the steering committee, however, its role should be to guide the process of developing the measurement system through to a final design and then to oversee its implementation. As is true of any such group process, the members need to be both open minded and committed to seeing it through to the successful implementation of an effective system.

Deliberate Process

A recommended process for designing and implementing a performance measurement system was discussed in Chapter Two and is presented here again. Although the steps and the sequence suggested here can be modified and tailored to fit the needs of a particular agency or program, all the tasks listed, with the exception of the optional pilot, are essential in order to achieve the goal of implementing and utilizing an effective measurement system on an ongoing basis. Thus, very early on in its deliberations, the steering group should adopt, and perhaps further elaborate, an overall process for designing and implementing a performance measurement system like the one shown here.

Process for Designing and Implementing Performance Measurement Systems

1. Secure management commitment.
2. Organize the system development process.
3. Clarify purpose and system parameters.
4. Identify outcomes and other performance criteria.
5. Define, evaluate, and select indicators.
6. Develop data collection procedures.

     Provide for quality assurance.

7. Specify system design.

     Identify reporting frequencies and channels.

     Determine analytical and reporting formats.

     Develop software applications.

     Assign responsibilities for maintaining the system.

8. Conduct a pilot and revise if necessary (optional).
9. Implement full-scale system.
10. Use, evaluate, and modify the system as appropriate.

Developing such systems can be an arduous undertaking, and it is easy to get bogged down in the details of "data" and specific indicators and to lose sight of what the effort is really about. Thus, having agreed on the overall design and implementation process can help members of the steering group keep the big picture in mind and track their own progress along the way. It will also help them think ahead to next steps—to anticipate issues that might arise and prepare to deal with them beforehand. Along these lines, one of the most important steps in this process is the third one, clarifying the purpose and scope of the measurement system to be developed.

Clearly identifying the purpose of a particular system—as, for example, the tracking of the agency's progress in implementing strategic initiatives, as opposed to, say, the monitoring of the effectiveness of a particular program or the measuring of workforce productivity on an ongoing basis—establishes a clear target that can then be used to discipline the process as the committee moves through it. In other words, for the steering group to work through the process very *deliberately* and thus accomplish its objective more efficiently and effectively, it would do well to ask continually whether undertaking certain steps or approaching individual tasks in a particular way will advance its objective of developing a measurement system to serve this specific, clearly established purpose.

Project Management

A clearly identified purpose will also help the steering committee manage the design and implementation process as a *project*, using standard project management tools for scheduling work, assigning responsibilities, and tracking progress. Although in certain cases it may be possible to get a system up and running in fairly short order, more often it will take a year or two to design and implement a new system, and more complex systems may well require three or four years to move into full-scale operation, especially if a pilot is to be conducted. This is a complicated process, and over the course of that period, the steering group (or some subgroup or other entity) will have to develop several products, including the following:

- A clear statement of scope and purpose of the measurement system
- A description of the performance criteria to be captured by the system
- Definitions of each measure to be incorporated in the system and documentation of constituent elements, data sources, and computations
- Documentation of data collection procedures
- A plan for ensuring the quality and integrity of the data
- A plan for reporting particular results to specified audiences at certain frequencies
- Prototype analytical and reporting formats
- Software programs and hardware configurations to support the system
- Identification of responsibilities for data collection and input, data processing, report preparation, system maintenance, and utilization
- A plan for full-scale implementation of the measurement system

The committee will also conduct and evaluate the pilot, if one is deemed necessary, and be responsible for at least early-stage evaluation and possible modification of the full-scale system once it is being used. It usually helps to sketch a rough schedule of the overall process out over a year or multiyear period, stating approximate due dates when each of these products, or deliverables, will be completed. Even though the schedule may change substantially along the way, thinking it through will give the steering group a clearer idea of what the process will involve and, one hopes, help them establish realistic expectations about what will be accomplished by when.

Managing the project also entails fleshing out the scope of work by defining specific tasks and subtasks to be completed. The steering group might elaborate the entire scope of work at the outset, partly in the interest of developing a more realistic schedule; alternatively it may just flesh out the tasks one step at a time, projecting a rough schedule on the basis of only a general idea of what will be involved at each step. Detailing the project plan sooner rather than later, though, is advantageous in that it will help clarify what resources, what expertise, what levels of effort, and what other commitments will be necessary in order to design and implement the system, again developing a more realistic set of expectations about what is involved in this process.

The project management approach also calls for assigning responsibilities for leading and supporting each step in the process. It may be that the steering group decides to conduct all the work by "committee as a whole," but it might well decide on a division of labor whereby various individuals or subgroups take lead responsibility for different tasks. In addition, some individual or work unit may be assigned responsibility for staffing the project and doing the bulk of the detailed work between committee meetings. Furthermore, the steering group may decide to work through subcommittees or to involve additional stakeholders in various parts of the process along the way. Typically, the number of participants grows as the project moves forward and particular kinds of expertise are called for at different points along the way, and a number of working groups may "spin off" the core steering committee in order to get the work done more efficiently and effectively. A further advantage of involving more participants along the way is that they may serve as "envoys" back to the organizational units or outside groups they represent and thus help build support for the system.

Finally, project management calls for monitoring activities and tracking progress in the design and implementation process along the way. This is usually accomplished by getting reports from working groups or subcommittees and comparing progress against the established schedule. It also means evaluating the process and deliverables produced, noting problems, and making adjustments as appropriate. The overall approach here should be somewhat pragmatic, especially when members of the steering group have little experience in developing such systems, and no one should be surprised to have to make adjustments in the scope of work, schedule, and assignments as the group moves through the process. Nevertheless, managing the overall effort as a project from beginning to end will help the steering committee keep the process on track and work in a more deliberate manner to install an effective measurement system.

Strategies for Success

Structuring the design and implementation effort with committee oversight, using a deliberate process, and using project management tools—together these constitute a rational approach to installing an effective measurement system, but by no means does this approach guarantee success. Implementing any new management system is an exercise in managing change, and a performance measurement system is no different. This places the challenge of designing and implementing a measurement system outside a technical sphere and in the realm of managing people, the culture, organizations, and relationships. Indeed, recent research finds that even though decisions by public organizations to adopt measurement systems tend to be based on technical and analytical criteria, the ways in which systems are implemented are influenced more strongly by political and cultural factors (De Lancer Julnes and Holzer, 2001).

Clearly both technical and managerial issues are important in designing and implementing performance measurement systems. Proponents and observers of performance measurement in government have noted a number of problems in implementing such systems and proposed strategies to overcome them (Swiss, 1991; Kravchuck and Schack, 1996; Hatry, 1999, 2002; Kassoff, 2001; Wholey, 2002). Others have summarized lessons learned by nonprofit agencies in developing measurement systems and made suggestions for ensuring success in implementing such systems in the nonprofit sector (Plantz, Greenway, and Hendricks, 1997; Sawhill and Williamson, 2001).

Although the process of developing performance measurement systems is similar for both public and nonprofit organizations, such efforts may be even more challenging for nonprofit managers, on account of several factors:

Many nonprofit agencies rely heavily on the work of volunteers to deliver services, who may be particularly leery of attempts to evaluate their performance.

Local chapters often have a high degree of autonomy, and it may be more difficult to implement uniform reporting procedures for roll-up or comparison purposes.

Nonprofit agencies are often funded by a variety of sources and are often highly dependent on a changing mix of grants for funding, creating a more fluid flow of services that may be more difficult to track with ongoing monitoring systems.

Many nonprofit agencies have relatively limited managerial and analytical resources to support performance measurement systems.

At the same time, though, because most nonprofit agencies are governed by boards of directors that are more closely focused on the work of their particular agencies than is the case with legislatures and individual public agencies, they may have an advantage in terms of ensuring alignment of the expectations of the managerial and governing bodies regarding performance as well as building meaningful commitments to actually use the measurement system.

Despite these differences between public and nonprofit agencies, for the most part both face similar kinds of issues in developing a measurement system, including problems concerning the information produced, the time and effort required to implement and support the system, the lack of subsequent use of the measurement system by managers and decision makers, the lack of stakeholder support for it, internal resistance to it, undesirable consequences that might arise from putting certain measures in place, and possible abuses of such a system. Thus, this concluding section presents thirty strategies that address these problems and help ensure the successful design and implementation of performance measurement systems in both public and nonprofit agencies.

Usefulness of the Information Produced

Performance measurement systems will be used only if they provide worthwhile information to managers and decision makers, but many systems do not provide relevant and useful information. Sometimes they are simply not well conceived in terms of focusing on the kinds of results that are of concern to managers. If, for example, the measures are not consistent with an agency's strategic agenda, they are unlikely to "ring true" to managers. In other cases, measures are selected on the basis of what data are readily available, but this approach rarely provides decision makers with a well-rounded picture of program performance. To ensure that measurement systems do provide relevant information that will help manage agencies and programs more effectively, those who commission measurement systems as well as those who take the lead in designing them should be sure to

1. *Clarify mission, strategy, goals and objectives, and program structure as a prelude to measurement.* Use this strategic framework to focus the scope of the performance measurement system on what is truly important to the organization and its stakeholders.

2. *Develop logic models to identify the linkages between programmatic activity and outputs and outcomes, and use this framework to define appropriate measures.* As presented in Chapter Three, these logic models help you sort out the myriad of variables involved in a program and identify what the important results really are.

3. *Be results driven rather than data driven in the search for relevant measures.* Do not include measures simply because the data are already available. Use need and usefulness rather than data availability as the principle criteria for selecting measures.

4. *Work toward "omnidirectional alignment" across various management processes.* Work to ensure that programmatic and lower-level goals and objectives are consistent with strategic objectives, that budget priorities are consistent with strategic objectives, and that individual and organizational unit objectives derive ultimately from higher-level goals and objectives. Then develop performance measures that are directly tied to these objectives.

5. *Periodically review the measures and revise them as appropriate.* Performance measurement systems are intended to monitor trends over time, which is why it is important to maintain consistency in the measures over the long run. However, this should not be taken to mean that the measures are cast in stone. Over time, the relevance of some measures may diminish substantially, and needs for other indicators may emerge. In addition, the reliability of some indicators may erode over time and require adjustment or replacement. It therefore makes sense to review both the quality and the usefulness of the measures and make changes as needed.

Resource Requirements

Performance measurement systems may require too much time and effort, especially when they require original data collection instruments, new data collection procedures, or substantial data input from the field. Measurement systems are not free, and they should be viewed as an investment of real resources that will generate worthwhile payoff. Obviously, the objective is to develop a system that is itself cost-effective, but at the beginning of the development process, system planners often underestimate the time, effort, and expenditures required, which then turn out to be much greater than expected. This leads to frustration and can result in systems whose benefit is not worth the cost. To avoid this situation, system planners should

6. *Be realistic in estimating how long it will take to design and implement a particular measurement system in the first place.* The design and implementation process itself involves a substantial amount of work, and creating realistic expectations at the outset about what it will require can help avoid disillusionment with the value of performance measurement overall.

7. *Develop a clear understanding of the full cost of supporting and maintaining a measurement system, and keep it reasonable in relation to the information produced.* Conversely, you should try to ascertain your resource constraints at the outset and then work

to maximize the information payoff from available resources. This approach creates fair expectations regarding what investments are necessary and is more likely to result in a system whose benefits exceed its costs.

8. *Use existing or readily available data whenever appropriate, and avoid costly new data collection efforts unless they are essential.* Although you want to avoid being data driven, very often the desirable measures can be provided by existing data systems. Some additional, potentially expensive data collection procedures may need to be instituted but only when it is clear that they add real value to the measurement system.

Lack of Utilization

Even when they are relevant, performance measures can be ignored. They will not be used automatically. Although in some cases this is due to a lack of interest, or outright resistance, on the part of managers, it may also result from poor system design. Managers often feel overwhelmed, for instance, by systems that include too many measures and seem to be unnecessarily complex. Another problem is that some systems track appropriate measures but do a poor job of presenting the performance data in ways that are understandable, interesting, and convincing. More generally, some systems simply are not designed to serve the purpose for which they were intended. The following guidelines are aimed at maximizing the useful content of performance data:

9. *Be clear about why you are developing performance measures and how you will use them.* Tailor the measures, reporting frequencies, and presentation formats to the intended use so as to encourage utilization.

10. *Focus on a relatively small number of important measures of success.* Managers often feel inundated by large numbers of measures and by detailed reports and thus will often disregard them. There is no "magic number" of measures to include, however, and sometimes you will need additional measures to provide a more balanced portrait of performance or to balance other measures in the effort to avoid problems of goal displacement. Everything else being equal, though, it is preferable to have fewer measures rather than too many.

11. *Keep measures and presentations as simple and straightforward as possible.* The "KISS principle" (Keep It Simple, Stupid) applies here because so many higher-level managers who are the intended audiences for the performance data will not have the time or the inclination to wade through complex charts, tables, and graphs.

12. *Emphasize comparisons in the reporting system.* Showing trends over time, gauging actual performance against targets, breaking the data down across operating units, comparing results against other counterpart agencies or programs, breaking

results out by client groups, or some combination of these is what makes the performance data compelling. Make sure that the comparisons you provide are the most relevant ones, given the intended users.

13. *Develop multiple sets of measures, if necessary, for different audiences.* The data might be rolled up from operating units through major divisions to the organization as a whole, providing different levels of detail for different levels of management. Alternatively, different performance measures can be reported to managers with different responsibilities or to different external stakeholders.

14. *Identify "results owners," the individuals or organizational units that have responsibility for maintaining or improving performance on key output and outcomes measures.* Holding particular people accountable for improving performance on specific measures encourages them to pay attention to the system.

15. *Informally monitor the usefulness and cost-effectiveness of the measurement system itself and make adjustments accordingly.* Again, the system design is not cast in stone, and getting feedback from managers and other intended users helps you identify how the measurement system might be improved to better serve their needs.

Lack of Stakeholder Buy-In

As discussed earlier in this chapter, a wide variety of stakeholders have interests in performance measurement systems, and the perceived legitimacy of a system depends in large part on the extent to which these stakeholders buy into it. If stakeholders fail to buy into a measurement system because they don't think the measures are meaningful, the data are reliable, or the results are being used appropriately, it will lose credibility. The system will then be less than effective in influencing efforts to improve performance or in demonstrating accountability. Thus, in developing a measurement system, the agency should

16. *Build ownership by involving stakeholders in identifying performance criteria, measures, targets, and data collection systems.* This can be done by including some internal stakeholders, and even some external stakeholders, on the steering group developing the system and on subcommittees or other working groups it establishes. The steering committee can solicit input and feedback from other stakeholder groups as well.

17. *Consider clients and customers throughout the process and involve them when practical.* In addition to ensuring that the resulting system will include measures that are responsive to customer needs and concerns, this will also develop buy-in from these important stakeholders.

18. *Generate leadership to develop buy-in for the measures, and demonstrate executive commitment to using them.* One of the best ways to develop buy-in on the part of inter-

nal stakeholders, and sometimes external stakeholders as well, is to show that the agency's top managers are committed to the measurement system and that they are personally involved in developing and then using it.

Internal Resistance

Managers and employees may resist the implementation of performance measures because they feel threatened by them. Employees often view performance monitoring systems as "speed-up" systems intended to force them to work harder or allow the organization to reduce the workforce. Middle-level managers may see such systems as attempts to put increased pressure on them to produce added results and hold them accountable for standards beyond their control. Even higher-level managers may resist the implementation of measurement systems if they perceive them as efforts to force them to give up authority to those above and below them. Because the success of measurement systems depends on the cooperation of managers at all levels, and sometimes of rank-and-file employees as well, in feeding data to the system and working to register improvement on the measures, avoiding or overcoming this kind of internal resistance is critical. Thus, executives wanting to install measurement systems should

19. *Be sure to communicate to managers and employees how and why measures are being used.* Take every opportunity to educate internal stakeholders about the purpose of a new system and to explain what kinds of measures will be monitored and how they will be used to improve the performance of agency programs; doing so will serve to reduce "fear of the unknown" and help build credibility for the new system and a higher level of comfort with it in the organization.

20. *Provide early reassurance that the system will not produce across-the-board actions such as budget cuts, layoffs, or furloughs.* This is often a very real fear among managers and employees, and alleviating it early on will help preempt opposition and gain greater acceptance of any new management system. If reductions in force do in fact result from productivity gains, they can probably be accomplished through attrition rather than firing.

21. *Consider implementing the system in layers, or by division or program, to work out problems and demonstrate success.* In addition to allowing time to "work out the bugs" before going full scale, implementing the system incrementally—and perhaps beginning in parts of the organization that are most likely to readily accept it—can also be an opportunity to show not only that the performance measures really can be useful but also that they are not harmful to the workforce.

22. *Make sure that program managers and staff see performance data first and have a chance to check and correct them, if necessary, before sending reports up to the executive level.*

Asking program managers to verify the data first not only strengthens the accuracy and integrity of the reporting system but also helps reinforce their role as "process owners" rather than self-perceived victims of it.

23. *Include fields in the reporting formats for explanatory comments along with the quantitative data.* The use of such comment fields gives higher-level managers a much fuller understanding of why performance is going up or down while also giving program managers and staff a safeguard—that is, allowing them the opportunity to shape realistic expectations and point out factors beyond their control that might be negatively affecting performance.

24. *Delegate increased authority and flexibility to both program managers and staff administrators in exchange for holding them accountable for results.* This is a critical mechanism for allowing monitoring systems to translate into positive action: holding managers responsible for bottom-line results while giving them wider discretion in how they manage to achieve those results. The added flexibility can also help managers accept a system that they may view as putting more pressure on them to perform.

25. *To the extent possible, tie the performance appraisal system, incentive system, and recognition program to the measurement system.* Tying these rewards systems to the performance measures puts more "muscle" in the monitoring system by giving managers and employees added incentive to work harder and smarter in order to perform well on the measures. By "putting its money where its mouth is" in tying rewards directly to measures, top management can build additional credibility for the system and positively reinforce improved performance.

Goal Displacement and Gaming

Performance measurement systems can encourage undesirable behavior. As discussed in Chapter Five, unbalanced sets of measures can focus undue attention on some performance criteria to the detriment of others, producing undesirable consequences. When managers and employees strive to perform well on less than optimal measures, while ignoring other more important goals because they are not reflected in the measures, goal displacement occurs and overall performance suffers. In other instances, performance standards or incentives are poorly specified in ways that also allow certain entities to "game the system" in order to "look good" on the measures while not really achieving the true goals. Thus, in designing performance measurement systems, it is important to

26. *Anticipate possible problems of goal displacement and gaming the system and avoid them by balancing measures.* The most systematic approach here is to probe the likely

impact of measures by asking the following question: If people perform to the extreme on this particular measure, what adverse impacts, if any, are likely to arise? Usually the antidote to goal displacement and gaming the system is to define additional measures that will counterbalance whatever potential adverse impacts are identified in this way. Along these lines, managers would do well to heed the adage, Measure the wrong things, and that's what you will be held accountable for.

27. *Install quality assurance procedures to ensure the integrity of the data, and impose sanctions to minimize cheating.* Problems with the reliability of data can arise for a variety of reasons, ranging from sloppy reporting to willful cheating. Installing quality assurance procedures, perhaps tracing the "data trail" in a quality audit on a very small sample basis, is usually sufficient to "keep the system honest" in most cases, particularly when everyone knows there is a policy in place to impose serious sanctions when anyone is found to have falsified data or otherwise tried to "cook the books."

System Abuse

Performance measurement systems can also be abused. Data indicating suboptimal performance, for example, can be used to penalize managers and staff unfairly, and performance data in general can be used either to reward or penalize certain managers and employees on a selective basis. Or, less blatantly, authoritarian-style managers can use performance measures and the added power they provide over employees to micromanage their units even more closely in ways that are unpleasant for the employees and counterproductive overall. In order to avoid such problems, higher-level managers should

28. *Be wary of misinterpretation and misuse of measures.* Higher-level managers should not only review the performance data that are reported up to their levels and then take action accordingly, but also monitor in informal ways how the measurement system is being used at lower levels in the organization. If they become aware that some managers are making inappropriate use of the measures or manipulating the system to abuse employees, they need to inform the abusers that behavior of that kind will no longer be tolerated.

29. *Use measurement systems constructively, not punitively, at least until it is clear that sanctions are needed.* Top managers need to model this constructive use of performance measures to their subordinates and others down through the chain of command, relying on positive reinforcement to provide effective inducements to improve performance; they must also insist that their subordinates use the system to work with their employees in the same manner. When the data show that performance is

subpar, the most productive response is to engage managers in an assessment of the source of the problem and approaches to remedying it, rather than punishing people because they failed to achieve their goals.

30. *Above all, recognize and use the measures as* indicators *only.* Although measures can be invaluable in enabling managers and others to track the performance of agencies and programs, they cannot tell the whole story by themselves. Rather, they are intended to serve as one additional source of information on performance; the data they generate are purely descriptive in nature and provide only a surface-level view of how well or poorly programs are actually doing. Thus, managers should learn to use performance data effectively and interpret the results within the fuller context of what they already know or can find out about a program's performance, but they should not let measures themselves dictate actions.

A Final Comment

Performance measurement is essential to managing for results in government and nonprofit organizations. Although measurement can aid greatly in the quest to maintain and improve performance, however, it is by no means a panacea. Performance measures can provide managers and policymakers with valid, reliable, and timely information on how well or how poorly a given program is performing, but then it is up to those managers and policymakers to respond deliberately and effectively to improve performance.

Clearly, the time for performance measurement in the public and nonprofit sectors has arrived, and agencies are installing new measurement systems and fine-tuning existing systems on an ongoing basis. Yet a substantial amount of skepticism remains about both the feasibility and the utility of measurement systems, and numerous fallacies and misperceptions about the efficacy of performance measurement still prevail in the field (Ammons, 2002; Hatry, 2002). Nevertheless, tracking the results produced by public and nonprofit programs and using the information produced to attempt to improve performance as well as provide accountability to higher-level authorities is a commonsense approach to management that is based on simple but irrefutable logic.

Although many public and nonprofit agencies have developed and implemented performance measurement systems in recent years solely in response to mandates from elected chief executives, legislative bodies, and governing boards, many of these systems have proved to be beneficial to the agencies themselves, and many public and nonprofit managers have become converts. We can expect to see efforts continue to proliferate along these lines, and that should be good news for those who are interested in promoting results-oriented management approaches. However, it must always be understood that performance measurement is a necessary but insufficient condition for results-oriented management or results-oriented government. For measurement to be useful, it must be effectively linked to other management and decision-making processes, as discussed in Chapter One of this book.

Thus, public and nonprofit managers at all levels, in cooperation with elected officials and governing bodies, must build and use effective measurement systems as components that are carefully integrated into processes for strategic planning and management, operational planning, budgeting, performance management, quality and productivity improvement, and other purposes. Without strong linkages to such vital management and decision-making processes, performance measurement systems may generate information that is "nice to know," but they will not lead to better decisions, improved performance, or more effective accountability and control.

This book has dealt with a number of components of the measurement process from a technical design perspective, and this concluding chapter has discussed issues concerning the implementation of measurement systems from an organizational and managerial perspective, all with an eye to helping you install the most effective system you can. Yet you need to understand that difficulties abound in this area, that real challenges are likely to persist, and that the perfect measurement system doesn't exist. Although you obviously should work to implement the best measurement system possible and address the kinds of problems discussed in this chapter, you will also need to make the necessary pragmatic trade-offs regarding system quality and usefulness versus cost and level of effort in order to install a workable, affordable, and effective measurement system. Although this may not produce the perfect system, it will clearly be preferable to the alternatives of not having a workable system or having no system at all.

REFERENCES

Altman, S. "Performance Monitoring Systems for Public Managers." *Public Administration Review*, 1979, *39*(1), 31–35.

American Society for Public Administration. *Resolution Encouraging the Use of Performance Measurement and Reporting by Government Organizations*. Washington, D.C.: American Society for Public Administration, 1992.

Ammons, D. N. (ed.). *Accountability for Performance: Measurement and Monitoring in Local Government*. Washington, D.C.: International City/County Management Association, 1995a.

Ammons, D. N. "Overcoming the Inadequacies of Performance Measurement in Local Government: The Case of Libraries and Leisure Services." *Public Administration Review*, 1995b, *55*(1), 37–47.

Ammons, D. N. "Benchmarking as a Performance Management Tool: Experiences Among Municipalities in North Carolina." *Journal of Public Budgeting, Accounting & Financial Management*, 2000, *12*, 106–124.

Ammons, D. N. *Municipal Benchmarks: Assessing Local Performance and Establishing Community Standards*. Thousand Oaks, Calif.: Sage, 2001.

Ammons, D. N. "Performance Measurement and Managerial Thinking." *Public Performance & Management Review*, 2002, *25*(4), 344–347.

Anthony, R. N., and Young, D. W. "Measurement of Output." In *Management Control in Nonprofit Organizations*. Boston: Irwin/McGraw-Hill, 1999.

Aristiqueta, M. P. *Managing for Results in State Government*. Westport, Conn.: Quorum/Greenwood, 1999.

Behn, R. D. "The Big Questions of Public Management." *Public Administration Review*, 1995, *55*(4), 313–324.

Behn, R. D., and Kant, P. A. "Strategies for Avoiding the Pitfalls of Performance Contracting." *Public Productivity & Management Review*, 1999, *22*(4), 470–490.

Berman, E. M. *Productivity in Public and Nonprofit Organizations: Strategies and Techniques.* Thousand Oaks, Calif.: Sage, 1998.

Berman, E. M., and Wang, X. "Performance Measurement in U.S. Counties: Capacity for Reform." *Public Administration Review,* 2000, *60*(5), 409–420.

Berman, E. M., and West, J. P. "Municipal Commitment to Total Quality Management: A Survey of Recent Progress." *Public Administration Review,* 1995, *55*(1), 57–66.

Berman, E. M., and West, J. P. "Productivity Enhancement Efforts in Public and Nonprofit Organizations." *Public Productivity & Management Review,* 1998, *22*(2), 207–219.

Berry, F. S., and Wechsler, B. "State Agencies' Experience with Strategic Planning—Findings from a National Survey." *Public Administration Review,* 1995, *55*(2), 159–168.

Bouckaert, G. "Measurement and Meaningful Management." *Public Productivity & Management Review,* 1993, *17*(1), 31–44.

Broom, C. A. "Performance-Based Government Models: Building a Track Record." *Public Budgeting and Finance,* 1995, *15*(4), 3–17.

Broom, C. A., Harris, J., Jackson, M., and Marshall, M. *Performance Measurement Concepts and Techniques.* Washington, D.C.: Center for Accountability and Performance of the American Society for Public Administration, 1998.

Brown, R. E., Myring, M. J., and Gard, C. G. "Activity-Based Costing in Government: Possibilities and Pitfalls." *Public Budgeting and Finance,* 1999, *19*(2), 3–21.

Brown, R. E., and Pyers, J. B. "Putting the Teeth into the Efficiency and Effectiveness of Public Services." *Public Administration Review,* 1988, *48*(3), 735–743.

Bruder, K. A. "Public Sector Benchmarking: A Practical Approach." *Public Management,* 1994, *76*(9), S9-S14.

Bryson, J. M. *Strategic Planning for Public and Nonprofit Organizations: A Guide to Strengthening and Sustaining Organizational Achievement.* (2nd ed.) San Francisco: Jossey-Bass, 1995.

Bugler, D. T., and Henry, G. T. *An Evaluation of Georgia's HOPE Scholarship Program: Impact on College Attendance and Performance.* Atlanta: Council for School Performance, 1998.

Carr, D. K., and Littman, I. D. *Excellence in Government: Total Quality Management in the 1990s.* Arlington, Va.: Coopers & Lybrand, 1990.

City of Phoenix. *City Manager's Executive Report: June, 2001.* Phoenix, Ariz.: City of Phoenix, 2001.

Coe, C. "Local Government Benchmarking: Lessons from Two Major Multigovernment Efforts." *Public Administration Review,* 1999, *59*(2), 110–123.

Cohen, S., and Brand, R. *Total Quality Management in Government: A Practical Guide for the Real World.* San Francisco: Jossey-Bass, 1993.

Cope, G. H. "Local Government Budgeting and Productivity: Friends or Foes?" *Public Productivity Review,* 1987, *41,* 45–47.

Davenport, T. H. "Managing in the New World of Process." *Public Productivity & Management Review,* 1994, *18,* 133–147.

De Lancer Julnes, P., and Holzer, M. "Promoting the Utilization of Performance Measures in Public Organizations: An Empirical Study of Factors Affecting Adoption and Implementation." *Public Administration Review,* 2001, *61*(6), 693–708.

De Woolfson, B. H. "Public Sector MBO and PPB: Cross Fertilization in Management Systems." *Public Administration Review,* 1975, *35,* 387–395.

Diagnostics Plus and Pennsylvania State University. *QUIK 97: Quality Use Importance Knowledge.* State College, Pa.: Diagnostics Plus and Pennsylvania State University, 1997.

Downs, G. W., and Larkey, P. D. *The Search for Government Efficiency: From Hubris to Helplessness.* New York: Random House, 1986.

Eadie, D. C. "Building the Capacity for Strategic Management." In J. L. Perry (ed.), *Handbook of Public Administration.* San Francisco: Jossey-Bass, 1989.

Epstein, P. D. *Using Performance Measurement in Local Government.* New York: Van Nostrand Reinhold, 1984.

Epstein, P. D. "Get Ready: The Time for Performance Measurement Is Finally Coming!" *Public Administration Review,* 1992, *52*(5), 513–519.

Epstein, P. D., and Campbell, W. "GASB SEA Research Case Study: City of Austin." In *State and Local Government Case Studies on Use and Effects of Using Performance Measures for Budgeting, Management, and Reporting,* 2000. Available online: www.accounting.rutgers.edu/raw/seagov/pmg/acsestudy/casesmain.html.

Faigin, B., Dion, J., and Tanham, R. *The National Highway Traffic Safety Administration Case Study: Strategic Planning and Performance Measurement.* Washington, D.C.: American Society for Public Administration, n.d.

Federal Highway Administration. *1999 Highway Statistics.* Washington, D.C.: Federal Highway Administration, 1999.

Fukuhara, R. S. "Productivity Improvement in Cities." *The Municipal Year Book: 1977.* Washington, D.C.: International City Management Association, 1977, pp. 193–200.

Girl Scout Council of Northwest Georgia. *2002 Outcomes Study Report.* Atlanta: Girl Scout Council of Northwest Georgia, 2002.

Glaser, M. "Tailoring Performance Measurement to Fit the Organization: From Generic to Germane." *Public Productivity & Management Review,* 1991, *14*(3), 303–319.

Governmental Accounting Standards Board. *Resolution on Service Efforts and Accomplishments Reporting.* Norwalk, Conn.: Governmental Accounting Standards Board, 1989.

Governmental Accounting Standards Board and National Academy of Public Administration. *Report on Survey of State and Local Government Use and Reporting of Performance Measures.* Washington, D.C.: Governmental Accounting Standards Board, 1997.

Grant, D. L. *Monitoring Ongoing Programs.* San Francisco: Jossey-Bass, 1978.

Grizzle, G. A. "Performance Measures for Budget Justification: Developing a Selection Strategy." *Public Productivity Review,* 1985, *8*(4), 328–343.

Halachmi, A., and Bouckaert, G. *Organizational Performance and Measurement in the Public Sector: Toward Service, Effort, and Accomplishments Reporting.* Westport, Conn.: Quorum Books, 1996.

Harkreader, S. A., and Henry, G. T. "Using Performance Measurement Systems for Assessing the Merit and Worth of Reforms." *American Journal of Evaluation,* 2000, *21*(2), 151–170.

Harris, J. (ed.). "Special Issue on Service Efforts and Accomplishments (SEA) Reporting." *International Journal of Public Administration,* 1995, *18*(2 & 3), 253–608.

Hartgen, D. T., and Presutti, E. L. *Resources Versus Results: Comparative Performance of State Highway Systems: 1984–1996.* Charlotte: Center for Interdisciplinary Transportation Studies, University of North Carolina, 1998.

Hatry, H. P. "The Status of Productivity Measurement in the Public Sector." *Public Administration Review,* 1978, *38*(1), 28–33.

Hatry, H. P. *Performance Measurement: Getting Results.* Washington, D.C.: Urban Institute Press, 1999.

Hatry, H. P. "Performance Measurement: Fashions and Fallacies." *Public Performance & Management Review,* 2002, *25*(4), 352–358.

Hatry, H. P., and Fisk, D. *Improving Productivity and Productivity Measurement in Local Government.* Washington, D.C.: Urban Institute Press, 1971.

Hatry, H. P., Marcotte, J. E., Van Houten, T., and Weiss, C. *Customer Surveys for Agency Managers: What Managers Need to Know.* Washington, D.C.: Urban Institute Press, 1998.

Hatry, H. P., Van Houten, T., Plantz, M. C., and Greenway, M. T. *Measuring Program Outcomes: A Practical Approach.* Alexandria, Va.: United Way of America, 1996.

Hatry, H. P., and others. *How Effective Are Your Community Services?* Washington, D.C.: Urban Institute Press, 1977.

Hayes, B. E. *Measuring Customer Satisfaction: Survey Design, Use, and Statistical Analysis Methods.* Milwaukee, Wis.: ASQ Quality Press, 1997.

Hendricks, M. "Outcome Measurement in the Nonprofit Sector: Recent Developments, Incentives, and Challenges." In K. E. Newcomer and others (eds.), *Meeting the Challenges of Performance Oriented Government.* Washington, D.C.: Center for Accountability and Performance of the American Society for Public Administration, 2002.

Henry, G. T., and McMillan, J. H. "Performance Data: Three Comparison Methods." *Evaluation Review,* 1993, *17*(6), 643–652.

Holzer, M. (ed.). *Public Productivity Handbook.* New York: Dekker, 1992.

Holzer, M., and Callahan, K. *Government at Work: Best Practices and Model Programs.* Thousand Oaks, Calif.: Sage, 1998.

Howard, S. K. *Changing State Budgeting.* Lexington, Ky.: Council of State Governments, 1973.

Hyde, A. "Quality, Reengineering, and Performance: Managing Change in the Public Sector." *The Enduring Challenges in Public Management: Surviving and Excelling in a Changing World.* San Francisco: Jossey-Bass, 1995.

Hyde, A. "A Decade's Worth of Lessons in Continuous Improvement." *Government Executive,* July 1997, pp. 58–68.

Joyce, P. G. "Using Performance Measures for Federal Budgeting: Proposals and Prospects." *Public Budgeting and Finance,* 1993, *13*(4), 3–17.

Joyce, P. G. "Using Performance Measures for Budgeting: A New Beat, or Is It the Same Old Tune?" In K. E. Newcomer (ed.), *Using Performance Measurement to Improve Public and Nonprofit Programs.* New Directions for Evaluation, no. 75. San Francisco: Jossey-Bass, 1997.

Joyce, P. G., and Tompkins, S. S. "Using Performance Information for Budgeting: Clarifying Terms and Investigating Recent State Experience." In K. Newcomer and others (eds.), *Meeting the Challenges of Performance Oriented Government.* Washington, D.C.: Center for Accountability and Performance of the American Society for Public Administration, 2002.

Kaplan, R. S., and Norton, D. P. "The Balanced Scorecard: Measures That Drive Performance." *Harvard Business Review,* Jan./Feb. 1992.

Kaplan, R. S., and Norton, D. P. *The Balanced Scorecard: Translating Strategy into Action.* Boston: Harvard University Press, 1996.

Kassoff, H. "Implementing Performance Measurement in Transportation Agencies." *Performance Measures to Improve Transportation Systems and Agency Operations.* Washington, D.C.: National Academy Press, 2001.

Keehley, P., Medlin, S., MacBride, S., and Longmire, L. *Benchmarking for Best Practices in the Public Sector: Achieving Performance Breakthroughs in Federal, State, and Local Agencies.* San Francisco: Jossey-Bass, 1997.

Kettner, P., and Martin, L. "Performance Contracting in the Human Services: An Initial Assessment." *Administration in Social Work,* 1995, *19*(2), 47–61.

Kopczynski, P., and Lombardo, M. "Comparative Performance Measurement: Insights and Lessons Learned from a Consortium Effort." *Public Administration Review,* 1999, *59*(2), 124–134.

Koteen, J. *Strategic Management in Public and Nonprofit Organizations.* New York: Praeger, 1989.

Kravchuck, R. S., and Leighton, R. "Implementing Total Quality Management in the United States." *Public Productivity & Management Review,* 1993, *17*(1), 71–82.

Kravchuck, R. S., and Schack, R. W. "Designing Effective Performance-Measurement Systems Under the Government Performance and Results Act of 1993." *Public Administration Review*, 1996, *56*(4), 348–358.

Lee, R. D. "A Quarter Century of State Budgeting Practices." *Public Administration Review*, 1997, *57*(2), 133–140.

Lefevre, J. (ed.). *Government Quality and Productivity: Success Stories.* Milwaukee, Wis.: ASQ Quality Press, 1992.

Legislative Budget Board, State of Texas. "Budget and Performance Assessments: State Agencies and Institutions, Fiscal Years 1997–2001." *Texas Department of Economic Development.* Austin, Texas: Legislative Budget Board, State of Texas, 2001a, pp. 198–199.

Legislative Budget Board, State of Texas. ""Legislative Budget Estimates for the 2002–2003 Biennium." Articles IV–XII. *Department of Agriculture.* Austin, Texas: Legislative Budget Board, State of Texas, 2001b, pp. VI1–VI5.

Lyden, F. J., and Miller, E. G. *Public Budgeting: Program Planning and Evaluation.* Skokie, Ill.: Rand McNally, 1978.

Mallory, B. L. "Managing the Strategic Plan with Measures: The Pennsylvania Department of Transportation." Paper presented at the annual meeting of the Transportation Research Board, Washington, D.C., January 2002.

Matzer, J., Jr. (ed.). *Productivity Improvement Techniques: Creative Approaches for Local Government.* Washington, D.C.: International City Management Association, 1986.

Melkers, J. E., and Willoughby, K. G. "The State of the States: Performance-Based Budgeting Requirements in 47 out of 50." *Public Administration Review*, 1998, *58*(1), 66–73.

Melkers, J. E., and Willoughby, K. G. "Budgeters' Views of State Performance Budgeting Systems: Distinctions Across Branches." *Public Administration Review*, 2001, *61*(1), 54–64.

Milakovich, M. E. *Improving Service Quality: Achieving High Performance in the Public and Private Sectors.* Boca Raton, Fl.: St. Lucie Press, 1995.

Morrisey, G. L. *Management by Objectives and Results in the Public Sector.* Reading, Mass.: Addison-Wesley, 1976.

Mowitz, R. J. *The Design and Implementation of Pennsylvania's Planning, Programming, Budgeting System.* Harrisburg: Commonwealth of Pennsylvania, 1970.

National Academy of Public Administration. *Performance Monitoring and Reporting by Public Organizations.* Washington, D.C.: National Academy of Public Administration, 1991.

National Academy of Public Administration. *Implementing the Results Act.* Washington, D.C.: National Academy of Public Administration, 1997.

National Governors' Association. *Performance Based Governance: An Action Agenda to Redesign State Government.* Washington, D.C.: National Governors' Association, 1994.

National Performance Review. *Serving the American Public: Best Practices in Performance Measurement. Benchmarking Study Report.* Washington, D.C.: National Performance Review, 1997. Available online: www.npr.gov/library/papers/benchmark/nprbook.html.

Newcomer, K. E., and Wright, R. E. "Managing for Outcomes: Federal Uses for Performance Measurement." *Public Manager*, 1996, *25*(4), 31–36.

Nutt, P. C., and Backoff, R. W. *Strategic Management of Public and Third Sector Organizations: A Handbook for Leaders.* San Francisco: Jossey-Bass, 1992.

Oregon Progress Board. *Achieving the Oregon Shines Vision: The 1999 Benchmark Performance Report.* Salem, Oreg.: Oregon Progress Board, Mar. 1999.

Osborne, D., and Gaebler, T. *Reinventing Government: How the Entrepreneurial Spirit Is Transforming the Public Sector.* Reading, Mass.: Addison-Wesley, 1992.

O'Toole, D. E., and Stipak, B. "Budgeting and Productivity Revisited: The Local Government Picture." *Public Productivity Review*, 1988, *12*(1), 1–12.

Pennsylvania Department of Transportation. *County Management Summary*. Harrisburg, Pa.: Pennsylvania Department of Transportation, June 1995.

Pennsylvania Department of Transportation. *Moving Pennsylvania Forward: Journey to the Strategic Agenda*. Harrisburg, Pa.: Pennsylvania Department of Transportation, 2000.

Plantz, M. C., Greenway, M. T., and Hendricks, M. "Outcome Measurement: Showing Results in the Nonprofit Sector." In K. E. Newcomer (ed.), *Using Performance Measurement to Improve Public and Nonprofit Programs*. New Directions for Evaluation, no. 75. San Francisco: Jossey-Bass, 1997.

Poister, T. H. *Public Program Analysis: Applied Research Methods*. Baltimore: University Park Press, 1978.

Poister, T. H. *Performance Monitoring*. Lexington, Mass.: Heath, 1983.

Poister, T. H. *Performance Measurement in State Departments of Transportation*. Washington, D.C.: Transportation Research Board, 1997.

Poister, T. H., McDavid, J. C., and Magoun, A. H. *Applied Program Evaluation in Local Government*. San Francisco: New Lexington Press, 1979.

Poister, T. H., and McGowan, R. P. "The Use of Management Tools in Municipal Government: A National Survey." *Public Administration Review*, 1984, *44*(3), 215–223.

Poister, T. H., and Streib, G. D. "Management Tools in Municipal Government: Trends over the Past Decade." *Public Administration Review*, 1989, *49*(3), 240–248.

Poister, T. H., and Streib, G. D. "Municipal Management Tools from 1976 to 1993: An Overview and Update." *Public Productivity & Management Review*, 1994, *18*(2), 115–125.

Poister, T. H., and Streib, G. D. "MBO in Municipal Government: Variations on a Traditional Management Tool." *Public Administration Review*, 1995, *55*(1), 48–56.

Poister, T. H., and Streib, G. D. "Performance Measurement in Municipal Government: Assessing the State of the Practice." *Public Administration Review*, 1999a, *59*(4), 325–335.

Poister, T. H., and Streib, G. D. "Strategic Management in the Public Sector: Concepts, Models, and Processes." *Public Productivity & Management Review*, 1999b, *22*(3), 308–325.

Ridley, C. E., and Simon, H. A. *Measuring Municipal Activities: A Survey of Suggested Criteria for Appraising Administration*. Chicago: International City Management Association, 1943.

Rodgers, R., and Hunter, J. E. "A Foundation of Good Management Practice in Government: Management by Objectives." *Public Administration Review*, 1992, *52*(1), 27–39.

Rossi, P. H., Freeman, H. E., and Wright, S. R. *Evaluation: A Systematic Approach*. Thousand Oaks, Calif.: Sage, 1979.

Rossi, P. H., and Williams, W. *Evaluating Social Programs: Theory, Practice, and Politics*. New York: Seminar Press, 1972.

Sawhill, J. C., and Williamson, D. "Mission Impossible? Measuring Success in Nonprofit Organizations." *Nonprofit Management and Leadership*, 2001, *11*(3), 371–386.

Schick, A. *Budget Innovation in the States*. Washington, D.C.: Brookings Institution, 1971.

Schuster, J. "The Performance of Performance Indicators in the Arts." *Nonprofit Management & Leadership*, 1997, *7*(3), 253–269.

State of Virginia, Department of Mines, Minerals and Energy. Virginia Results Performance Measure Information. Richmond, Va.: Virginia Department of Planning and Budget, 2003.

State of Washington, Office of Financial Management. *2001–03 Operating Budget Instructions, Part I.* Olympia, Wash.: State of Washington, 2001. Available online: www.ofm.wa.gov/budinst01–03/budinst01–03part1/budinst01–03part1.htm#section2

Steiss, A. W. *Strategic Management and Organizational Decision Making.* Lexington, Mass.: Heath, 1985.

Steiss, A. W., and Daneke, G. A. *Performance Administration.* Lexington, Mass.: Heath, 1980.

Suchman, E. A. *Evaluative Research: Principles and Practice in Public Service and Social Action Programs.* New York: Russell Sage Foundation, 1967.

Swiss, J. E. *Public Management Systems: Monitoring and Managing Government Performance.* Englewood Cliffs, N.J.: Prentice Hall, 1991.

Syfert, P. "Customer-Based Performance Management in Charlotte." Paper presented at a conference on Managing for Results: Performance Measures in Government, Austin, Texas, 1993. Reprinted in D. N. Ammons (ed.), *Accountability for Performance: Measurement and Monitoring in Local Government.* Washington, D.C.: International City/County Management Association, 1995.

Taylor, M. E., and Sumariwalla, R. D. "Evaluating Nonprofit Effectiveness: Overcoming the Barriers." In D. R. Young and others (eds.), *Governing, Leading, and Managing Nonprofit Organizations: New Insights from Research and Practice.* San Francisco: Jossey-Bass, 1993.

Tigue, P., and Strachota, D. *The Use of Performance Measures in City and County Budgets.* Chicago: Government Finance Officers Association, 1994.

United Way of America. *Outcome Measurement Activities of National Health and Human Service Organizations.* Alexandria, Va.: United Way of America, 1998.

United Way of America. "Teen Mother Parenting Education Program Logic Model." Unpublished chart, United Way of America, 2002.

Urban Institute and International City/County Management Association. *Comparative Performance Measurement: FY 1995 Data Report.* Washington, D.C.: Urban Institute Press and International City/County Management Association, 1997.

U.S. Department of Education. *1999 Performance Report and 2001 Annual Plan.* Washington, D.C.: U.S. Department of Education, 2000.

U.S. Department of Health and Human Services. *Strategic Plan FY 2001–2006.* Washington, D.C.: Department of Health and Human Services, 2000.

Usher, C. L., and Cornia, G. "Goal Setting and Performance Assessment in Municipal Budgeting." *Public Administration Review,* 1981, *41*(2), 229–235.

Vinzant, D. H., and Vinzant, J. "Strategy and Organizational Capacity: Finding a Fit." *Public Productivity & Management Review,* 1996, *20*(2), 139–157.

Waller, J. D., and others. *Monitoring for Government Agencies.* Washington, D.C.: Urban Institute Press, 1976.

Walters, J. "The Benchmarking Craze." *Governing,* 1994, *7*(7), 33–37.

Weiss, C. H. *Evaluation Research: Methods of Assessing Program Effectiveness.* Englewood Cliffs, N.J.: Prentice Hall, 1972.

Wholey, J. S. *Evaluation: Promise and Performance.* Washington, D.C.: Urban Institute Press, 1979.

Wholey, J. S. *Evaluation and Effective Public Management.* New York: Little, Brown, 1983.

Wholey, J. S. "Performance Based Management: Responding to the Challenges." *Public Productivity & Management Review,* 1999, *22*(3), 288–307.

Wholey, J. S., "Making Results Count in Public and Nonprofit Organizations: Balancing Performance with Other Values." In K. E. Newcomer, E. T. Jennings, C. A. Broom, and A. Lomax (eds.), *Meeting the Challenges of Performance-Oriented Government.* Washington, D.C.:

Center for Accountability and Performance of the American Society for Public Administration, 2002.

Wholey, J. S., and Hatry, H. P. "The Case for Performance Monitoring." *Public Administration Review*, 1992, *52*(6), 604–610.

Wholey, J. S., and Newcomer, K. E. "Clarifying Goals, Reporting Results." In K. E. Newcomer (ed.), *Using Performance Measurement to Improve Public and Nonprofit Programs*. New Directions for Evaluation, no. 75. San Francisco: Jossey-Bass, 1997.

Williamsport Bureau of Transportation. *1999 Performance Report and Plan Update*. Williamsport, Pa.: Williamsport Bureau of Transportation, 2000.

Young, D. R. "The First Seven Years of NML: Central Issues in the Management of Nonprofit Organizations." *Nonprofit Management and Leadership*, 1997, *8*(2), 193–201.

INDEX